IDENTITY

IDENTITY

ALEXANDRA BAYER

Aya Ellen Publishing

Copyright © 2020 Alexandra Bayer

All rights reserved. No part of this book may be reproduced in any manner whatsoever without written permission except in the case of brief quotations embodied in critical articles and reviews.

The characters and events portrayed in this book are fictitious. Any similarity to real persons, living or dead, is coincidental and not intended by the author.

ISBN: 978-1-7772243-1-8

Cover editor: Aagnay Kariyal
Image of girl by Wesner Rodrigues from Pexels
Image of background by Abdel Rhaman Abu Baker from Pexels

First Printing, May 2020

To my father. You may not remember, but one Christmas many years ago I promised you the dedication of my first book.

Contents

Dedication v

Prologue 1

1
Chapter One 3

2
Chapter Two 17

3
Chapter Three 39

4
Chapter Four 69

5
Chapter Five 99

6
Chapter Six 107

7 Chapter Seven	131
8 Chapter Eight	167
9 Chapter Nine	185
10 Chapter Ten	209
11 Chapter Eleven	229
12 Chapter Twelve	247
13 Chapter Thirteen	273
14 Chapter Fourteen	285
15 Chapter Fifteen	295
16 Chapter Sixteen	301
About The Author	311

Prologue

Sometimes things change over an extended period of time, and sometimes they change all at once. I've had it both ways.

I can't entirely decide which way I prefer. When it happens over a period of time, it's comfortable. Easy. Unsurprising. But when your life is flipped upside down all at once, it's exciting. Terrifying. And it can turn out to be the best or worst thing that's ever happened to you.

I've begun to learn that change comes with everything, and maybe that's not a bad thing. Sometimes the best thing you can do for yourself is to effect a change. Sometimes someone else has to make a change for you.

Places change. People change. I've changed, hopefully for the better. It's difficult to pinpoint the exact moment when a change begins to occur, but I have a pretty good idea of this timeline.

Chapter One

I hate Wednesdays. You're halfway through the week, but still have another half to go. Already exhausted from the early mornings of Monday and Tuesday, and still have to dread those of Thursday and Friday.

I suppose it wouldn't be so bad if I was able to go somewhere I actually wanted. But no – because school lasts forever. Or at least it seems to. I've finally finished high school, and was thrust directly into university. At least this school year is somewhat nearing the end. There are only two more months of classes before exams.

God. Two months. Despite already being through six months, two still seems like a long time.

I kick through the snow as I walk across campus to my next class. It's the end of February, and the weather is so temperamental. Snow one day, rain the next, sun and clouds, cold and warm – but that's Toronto for you. I hate the winter.

I finally arrive at the class – Creative Writing – but even though I'm now in a heated room, I can't concentrate on the lecture. Which is a disappointment, because I really enjoy writing. But my mind is too caught up in thoughts of seeing Asher soon.

This is a bad thing, because Asher broke up with me.

We'd met in high school, although we didn't truly get to know each other until the end of grade eleven, and we didn't start dating until grade twelve. He'd said he loved me, and I thought I loved him too. We even made sure to pick the same university – the University of Toronto – so we could stay together once we graduated.

And it was good, for a while. The summer was full of parties and campfires and kissing, sometimes more than kissing. I was living on a perpetual high. But then the school year started.

Asher and I were in none of the same classes, so we hardly saw each other. This frightened me, because I depended on seeing Asher. The only times I got to see him were at the ends of the school days, at newspaper editing, the one thing we had in common.

Truthfully I did see him more than that, at first. We would meet up on weekends, or go out for lunch between classes. But slowly, the number of our dates began to drop, and I seemed to be the only one who cared. Asher claimed to be busy with schoolwork, and I was too, but I knew that even the engineers had the occasional free moment, and Asher certainly isn't an engineer. Still, I didn't want to push it. I guess I was scared of what would happen if I began to get on Asher's nerves.

Maybe I should have pushed it. Maybe I should've planned dates and told him weeks ahead, so he couldn't weasel out of them. Maybe that would have made a difference. But then again, maybe it wouldn't have.

It was October when he broke up with me. Right around Thanksgiving, actually. I got turkey dumped, and we went to the same school. I thought that was only supposed to apply to long-distance relationships.

He claimed that he couldn't handle the responsibilities of a girlfriend on top of all his schoolwork and extracurriculars. I was shocked, perhaps unreasonably so, since he had been making excuses to get out of dates I'd suggested lately. I couldn't believe that he really had no time for a girlfriend; it's not like I was such a burden. Even so, I let it go. Because that's what I did throughout our whole relationship. Asher always called the shots, and I followed along. He wanted to go to a party, so I went with him. He wanted to hang out with his group of friends, so I went with him.

That's part of what made the breakup so bad. Not only did I still love him, but we'd spent so much time with his friends throughout grade twelve and the summer that when I didn't have him or his friends anymore, I had no one left to hang out with. No one offered me a shoulder to cry on, and I guess I deserved it. After all, I wasn't there to offer any of my old friends a shoulder throughout our final year of high school.

Through rumours circulating around Twitter and by word-of-mouth, I discovered that it turns out a girlfriend wasn't too much for Asher. Well, perhaps 'girlfriend' is the wrong word. Maybe 'hoe' works better. I never saw her in person, and I don't know for sure if the rumours are true, but Asher certainly never denied them. I don't know if it was going on when we were still together or if it started directly after our break up, but it bothers me either way. I don't know if it's a good thing that Asher made something up to try and make the break up amicable, or if he just didn't respect me enough to tell me the truth.

I think he and the mystery hoe are done now, anyway, which gives me some hope that our relationship can be salvaged. Because despite everything, I still have feelings for him.

I'm brought back to the present when I notice all the other students around me get to their feet and sling their backpacks over their shoulders. I've been in something of a trance throughout the class, so immersed in thoughts of Asher, probably aided by my sleepiness. I quickly pack up as everyone leaves the room, and follow them out.

Next stop: the newspaper editing room.

When I walk in Asher is already there, talking to – well, really, *flirting with* – Savannah, another editor. I roll my eyes. Asher's always been a huge flirt, even when we were dating. I take the moment to study him.

He has ashy blond hair, and a strand of it flips in front of his eyes as he talks. I clench my fists as my fingers itch to push it back, as I'd used to. His blue eyes never really focus on Savannah, even though he seems to be telling her a story. Instead, they flit around the room. At one point he catches my eye and smirks.

Ugh. I avert my eyes and push my long brown hair forward to cover my face as I feel it start to burn.

God, I *hate* blushing.

I find my usual seat and inch the chair back quietly, which is quite the task, considering how old, creaky, and scratchy they can be.

Even despite being caught staring, I'm still half-hoping that he'll sit near me. Just about everyone here has their usual seat, but not Asher. He plays musical chairs, almost every day switching seats.

I sneak a peek back at him, and see that he seems to have forgotten about me completely. He's taken the desk next to Savannah today, and I let out a silent sigh, not knowing whether it's relieved or disappointed.

I finish my assigned work fairly quickly but linger in my seat, hoping to talk to Asher before I leave. When everyone else goes, finished their editing, and it's only me, Asher and Savannah in the room, I finally give up. I slowly pack up my things, peeking at Asher from the corner of my eyes, then walk out the door, watching each foot as it steps.

Well. At least I didn't embarrass myself today.

Outside the door, I see a few leftover copies of this week's paper. I pick one up as I pass. Even though I spend so much time working on the paper, I hardly ever actually read the final result.

I flip through it as I amble toward the parking lot. Now that I'm free from school for the day, the snow doesn't seem quite as cold or wet. I smile as I see a couple of the articles that I'd edited. I raise an eyebrow as I see a celebrity gossip section. Um, what? Since when did our newspaper cater to fangirls?

I skim it. I see a few familiar names pop out at me – Lani Core, the singer; Mister Right, the band; and Aviva Jersey, the actress – but I don't bother actually reading the articles. I've never really been interested in the celebrity lifestyle. I mean sure, fifteen minutes of fame might be interesting, but I would definitely not want to be followed around by fans and hounded by paparazzi 24/7.

I end up in the parking lot, and I toss the paper in a recycling bin as I pass by. I fish my keys out of my bag and climb into my car, cranking up the heat. I lean back against my seat and close my eyes for a moment, simply unwinding.

I love my car. It's old and ugly, but it works, and best of all, it's *mine*. Back in August I'd searched the web and picked the cheapest car that still worked properly. As soon as I took it for a test drive, I was convinced that it was the one for me. It had still taken a good chunk out of my bank account, but in my opinion, it was worth it. After all, I need to get between school and home, and I hate taking the subway. It's cramped, dirty, hot, and smelly.

I start up the car and navigate my way out of the parking lot. It's not a far drive to get home. My family has a modest house in Toronto, but it's always been big enough for the four of us.

I had to eat lunch early today, before my two-hour Creative Writing class and newspaper editing, so I'm starving by this point. It's only about five, but I can smell something cooking as soon as I walk in the door.

I throw out a greeting as I wander toward the kitchen to see where the smell is wafting from. My mom is stirring a bubbling red sauce on the stovetop, and I can see some noodles boiling on the burner next to it. It's almost finished, so I take the few minutes to unload my backpack in my room upstairs and set out my homework for the night.

As I make my way down the stairs, my brother bumps into me as he rushes past from his bedroom. I grunt out a complaint but he pays me no attention as he continues toward the kitchen. I roll my eyes. Connor is the poster boy for the 'teenage boys and their never-ending appetites' stereotype.

I make my way to the main floor at a more reasonable pace, and am just beginning to scoop my spaghetti when I hear the front door open, and my father arrives home.

My dad is a quiet man, at home, at least. He's a car salesman during the day, and it's like a switch just flips in him. His voice becomes huge and booms across the lot so that every potential buyer can hear him as he raves about each and every vehicle. I think that by the time he gets home, he's so tired, both vocally and mentally, that his portion of the conversation is minimal.

After some soft greetings, he joins the rest of us at the table. Connor is already digging in, but I wait until everyone is seated before I begin to eat. My mom asks about our days, and since Connor is still stuffing his face, I have to answer to break the silence. I tell her about my Anthropology tutorial from the morning, and gloss over the Creative Writing class, since I can remember about three words of that lecture.

Connor has already finished his bowl of pasta, and as he gets up to scoop a second helping, Mom asks him again about his day. Connor is still in high school – grade eleven – but he doesn't mention any of his classes when he speaks. He talks about hockey practice and his lunch date with Marina, his third girl of the week. Connor has never been fully focused on his classes, although my parents encourage him to be. He's also completely girl-crazy, but can't seem to settle on any one. As long as he doesn't treat any of them badly, Mom just seems to accept this. I can't really gauge Dad's opinion on it, since he just chews thoughtfully throughout the conversation.

After dinner I excuse myself to go do some of my schoolwork. The one thing I like less about university than high school is the amount of homework and readings. I enjoy university's classes and lack of restrictions more, but free time is sometimes hard to come by.

Tonight I can't focus on the work. It may have something to do with the fact that every time I try to read a page, my eyes stray and I end up thinking about Asher and Savannah.

Suddenly I can't bear to be cooped up for another second. I abruptly stand, pushing my chair out from my desk against the wall. My room seems too small and confining, and I ache to get out.

I know I need to burn off this excess energy in order to actually pay attention to my work, so I head downstairs and grab my car keys.

Near the beginning of the school year, I bought a membership to a tiny gym between the university and my house. The university gives students free membership to some gyms on campus, but I'm ridiculously paranoid of seeing someone I know there, and I wanted somewhere to go on weekends that doesn't remind me of my piles of homework. This gym's not in the best shape, and the parking lot is a crazy distance from the entrance, but it has all the necessary equipment, and I am on a university budget. There also aren't usually many people there when I go. I'm a night owl, and I can't convince myself to work out any time other than when the sky is dark.

When I finally get inside – I consider the walk from the parking lot my warmup, since it's so far – there's only one other girl there. She's using an elliptical trainer, which is what I usually like to use. Unfortunately, there are only two, and they're side-by-side. I groan internally, but I'm really not in the weights mood, so I settle onto the elliptical beside the girl.

Her hair is red and cut into a bob, the back just reaching the nape of her neck while the front rests just above her shoulders. Up close I can see that she's very pretty – and very in-shape. Her workout bra and leggings make me feel frumpy in comparison, in my T-shirt and sweats. She must sense my gaze, because her head turns and she focuses on me. She flashes me a smile with perfectly straight white teeth before looking forward again.

Great. Second time caught staring in one day.

The only thing I can do is start my workout, so I pop in my earbuds and press the necessary buttons to begin. As I get into the rhythm, I gradually feel my self-consciousness dissipate. All of a sudden, I feel a tap on my arm. I turn, eyes wide, and see the pretty girl looking at me, arm still half reaching out. I see her mouth move, and I shake my head as I take my earbuds out.

"Sorry, what?" I ask, trying to manage my continuous movement on the machine while I talk to her. I feel like I'm about to topple over, so I let my legs relax and slow my pace.

She grins at me again. She's completely stopped, but is still standing on her elliptical trainer. I can see beads of sweat on her forehead, but she wipes them away before she speaks again.

"Sorry to interrupt," she says, still smiling, "but I was hoping you would know if there's an AC setting around here somewhere?" She gestures at the empty walls.

I smirk. "I don't even think there's AC in here." Luckily, I do know the solution. One of the first times I was here, I saw another member pull out a huge fan from a storage room. I step off my elliptical, explaining this to her as I walk toward the rusty, unwieldy door against the back wall. After several tugs, it creaks open, and I see the fan.

Suddenly I smell perfume, and flinch when she speaks from behind me. I should really pay more attention to my surroundings.

"Here, I'll give you a hand." Together we drag the fan across the room to directly in front of our ellipticals.

Once it's plugged in and switched on, we stand there, regaining our breath. The girl is staring at the fan gratefully, and I notice that she's several inches taller than me, which is unsurprising, since I'm only 5'3". I used to wear heels to disguise this, but my feet began to complain too much, so I gave up. My gym shoes definitely have no heel, and neither do hers, so I'd estimate her to be around 5'7".

She turns back to me suddenly, face regretful, and says, "Oh, I forgot!" She sticks out her hand toward me. "I'm Brynn."

I take her hand. "I'm Naya."

She shows off her pearly whites again. "Nice to meet you."

Her good mood is beginning to rub off on me. I'm not usually grumpy or anything, but I don't always get along with the perpetually peppy cheerleader type either. Brynn's not bubbly, exactly, but she seems genuinely happy, which is something I struggle with at the gym.

I smile back at her, and she seems to take this as encouragement. "Have you been coming here long?" she asks, and something in her face looks as though she's actually interested in the answer, not just making small talk.

I shrug, responding with, "Kind of."

We walk back to our elliptical trainers, and I see her bite her lip, not looking entirely satisfied with my answer, so I elaborate.

"I bought my membership at the beginning of the school year – I go to U of T, and it's nearby, which is convenient – but I haven't actually used it much," I admit sheepishly. "I don't always have the motivation."

She looks at me knowingly now, as we step back onto the machines. "I have the same problem."

I glance down at her toned midsection before meeting her eyes again. "Really?"

My incredulity must show in my voice, because she laughs. "Really. I just happen to have outside motivation too." At my questioning glance, she explains, "My boyfriend. And... other things. It helps me to keep on track."

Makes sense, I guess. "Yeah, my boyfriend and I broke up in October, so... I guess my only encouragement comes from me."

Her eyebrows pucker as she frowns, then her eyes light up. "Okay, this might sound weird, but... want to be gym buddies? For as long as I'm in Toronto, at least."

It doesn't sound weird to me. It sounds very welcome, considering the number of friends I have left. If Brynn is willing to make this commitment with a girl she just met, I'd be happy to agree. Then the Toronto comment hits me.

"How long are you going to be in Toronto?" I ask, a bit warily.

She grimaces. "Currently undecided."

I don't want to push her – I mean, I've just met her – but I do need to know an approximate length. I cautiously ask, "Are you on vacation?"

Her eyes flicker with amusement, but she responds seriously. "No, it's more of a work thing."

Okay. So if it's work, that should be longer than a vacation at least. I wonder what her work is – she looks about my age, barely out of high school – but I don't want to scare her away with too many questions. I smile as I say, "Then I'd love to."

She grins and we exchange cell numbers before starting up our individual workouts again. I leave my earbuds out this time, and it's a good thing, because she makes comments or inserts questions to me at random times. They're not annoying, though; instead, I find that I'm enjoying the conversation. It's helping to keep my mind off the torture I'm putting my body through, and it turns out that she's funny. I'm almost sad when my workout ends – almost. She cheerily waves good-bye at me as we arrange to meet back here tomorrow, same time as tonight.

When I get outside, I'm relieved to feel the cold air. Even with the fan inside, I'd still been overheating. By the time I get to my car in the distant parking lot though, my relief has become a vague memory and my fingers are freezing as I insert the cold metal of the key into my car. Thank god for car heating.

When I get home, the house is quiet. I sneak upstairs and sit at my desk again. I find that I can finally settle into my work now. I finish it in an hour and a half and check my phone, relaxing into the brainless activity. I decide to look up Brynn on social media. I frown as I realize it'll be harder since I never got her last name, but there can't be too many Brynns with her distinctive red hair online. Brynn's not a very common name, is it?

Turns out it is. Or maybe my parameters are just too large, since I don't know where she's from, either, since she said she's just in Toronto for work. Either way, I can't find her on Facebook, Twitter, or Instagram. I finally give up, deciding to ask her about it tomorrow instead of wasting precious sleep tonight.

I perform my regular night-time routine of brushing my teeth, wiping off makeup and washing my face, before curling up under my warm blankets in bed. Today has felt very long. Brynn feels like today, but my awkward moment with Asher at newspaper feels like at least a day ago, if not more.

Well, good. At least if I embarrass myself further tomorrow, it won't feel like two days in a row. I sleepily laugh at my convoluted logic, and my mind further disintegrates as I'm pulled into sleep.

Chapter Two

I wake up a little bit happier than yesterday. Maybe it's because I'm one day closer to the weekend, or maybe it's because it seems like there's potential for friendship with Brynn, but I'm glad for it either way. I'll need as much positivity as possible to get through my classes today.

They go as well as I expect. Not riveting, but not terribly boring either. I still have a slight smile playing on my face as I walk to newspaper editing.

Asher's not at newspaper when I walk in. He's not there halfway through either, when I finally give up on looking for him. Then a stray thought catches my attention, and I stiffly scan the room for Savannah.

Crap. She's not here either.

I really don't want to think about the possibilities, so I force myself to work even harder on my editing. Even without going into deep analysis, my good mood has disappeared. I push my chair out harder than usual once I've finished, and walk quickly out of the room, head down.

Well, at least I have my new gym buddy. I grimace, but the thought does cheer me a minute amount.

I know that the only thing awaiting me at home is my schoolwork, so I take some time to myself in my car, putting on the radio and scrolling through social media on my phone. The photos of all my old friends going on exciting new adventures just serve to depress me though, so I click my phone off and cross my arms, staring at nothing out the window until I muster up enough motivation to start my car and drive home.

The night is nearly an exact repeat of last night, but tonight after dinner I force myself to do some homework before I head to the gym. I run downstairs when I've deemed that I've done a sufficient amount, and shout a quick good-bye to my family as I slam the door behind me.

Wow. Apparently the gym is the highlight of my day, and I don't even like working out. How depressing.

When I arrive, though, my mood has lifted incrementally. I feel stupid – I mean, maybe Brynn will have forgotten about our plans. Maybe something came up. Hell, I hardly know the girl – but when I walk in and see her, I know that my worries are unfounded. I smile.

She returns it, greeting me in a way that puts all my concerns to ease. She's on the same elliptical trainer as last night, so I return to the same one I'd been on. She's a bit quieter today than she had been yesterday, and I didn't even bring my earbuds tonight in anticipation of her chatter, so I feel the need to start the conversation.

"I tried to find you on social media last night." Ugh. Way to sound like a stalker, Naya.

Her eyes flick to me, and the humour in them alleviates my worries about my intentions being misconstrued. Even so, she takes a few seconds longer than expected to formulate her response. Finally, she says simply, "I don't do social media."

That surprises a snort out of me. She giggles a bit too, somewhat awkwardly.

"How do you just not *do* social media, in this day and age?" I ask, genuinely curious. It's almost enough to distract me from the automatic acceleration of my elliptical.

She chews her lip, looking straight ahead, seeming to give the question serious thought. I continue to stare at her until she answers.

"I find that, when I have the time to destress and unwind... I don't want to waste it on my phone," she replies, somewhat haltingly.

Damn. I've spent less than two hours with her, and I can already tell she's a better person than me.

"You have some willpower," I comment, and she laughs.

"Trust me," she says, turning her head toward me, "I'm usually so busy that aside from the gym, all I use my free time for is napping."

I laugh with her, slightly winded, and manage to get out, "That's some job you have."

This seems to sober her, and she nods. "That it is."

I'm afraid that my mention of her job has ruined the mood,

but it appears that my inept intro has done the trick. She's back in the same talkative mood as yesterday, and I'm back to being more of a listener. Thank god, too, since my elliptical trainer seems to have a mind of its own and is trying to kill me with excessive exercise.

Even though it's difficult to finish my workout, it's slightly less difficult than it has been in the past. I could chalk that up to finally increasing my stamina a bit, but I think the real reason has more to do with Brynn. She's much more interesting and distracting than simply listening to music as I usually do, and I find that I'm genuinely enjoying the interaction. The truth is that I haven't had many people to talk to lately, at least in a personal, friendly manner. All of my conversations have either been with family or acquaintances at university, discussing school matters. Even newspaper editing, which used to be my safe zone, seems to have been slowly removing me from the inner circle. Speaking with Brynn, even if it is at the same time as my workout, sheds me of a few layers of stress I've been carrying around.

When my elliptical finally slows to a stop and I can talk without sounding like a fish out of water, I reluctantly excuse myself. As much as I'd like to continue talking with Brynn, I still do have stacks of homework waiting for me. Brynn wishes me good luck on my voyage through the parking lot, and I accept it.

Despite her well wishes and my fervent desire for warmth, snow is falling as I make my way to the parking lot. I consider breaking into a run, but my legs are too tired to carry me that quickly and I fear I'll fall on my face if I attempt it.

My bad luck continues as I reach traffic on my way home. There's been a car crash, probably due to black ice, and all the vehicles are crawling home to avoid the same fate. When at last I reach my dark house, it's later than I'd wanted to continue doing schoolwork. But seeing as how schoolwork waits for no mere mortal to finish it before piling up, I recognize that I must complete it if I ever plan on being ready for exams.

When I've determined that I can officially do no more, I perform my night time routine and crawl into bed, exhausted and once again back to a negative mood. I'm about to turn my phone off when I see that I have a text waiting, probably received when I was in the bathroom. Curiously I click on it and see that it's from Brynn.

So I've been looking into social media... I never realized there were so many to choose from!

I smirk, my bad mood vanishing in an instant. I type back quickly.

Yeah, that's how people make money nowadays. Creating new social media.

Her reply is almost instant.

If I were to sign up for one, which would u recommend?

Although my tiredness insists that I wrap up the conversation, my rational brain tells me to encourage this friendship. I consider the questions carefully, attempting to determine which social medium I enjoy the most and which would be best for a beginner.

Probably Instagram, I send.

That's the one with all the pics, right?

So you do know something about social media! I accuse, laughing softly to myself.

My bf doesn't have the same reservations as I do about free time...

I smile as I reply. *Fair enough. I probably check insta the most, but there are a few more that are also rlly popular...*

We continue the conversation, eventually expanding from the topic of social media to life in general.

I don't know what convinced Brynn to befriend me, but I'm very happy that she did. Unfortunately, I do have school tomorrow, which I belatedly remember after midnight. Brynn apologizes for keeping me up, but I insist that I really needed the talk. This seems to ease some of her concern, and we sign off with promises of seeing each other at the gym tomorrow.

This friendship has potential to be the healthiest one I've had in a while. Brynn has such an easy way about her that to me, at least, it feels like I've known her for much longer than two days. And if we keep meeting up at the gym, my body will soon be thanking me as well as my loneliness.

Tomorrow is Friday, which means the last day of school before the weekend. I haven't had Friday plans in a while, so even just going to the gym is better than nothing. With the weekend in sight and thoughts of my new friend, I drift off to sleep slightly happier than the past few nights.

Unfortunately, my happiness evaporates when my alarm blares the next morning and, as I stand, every muscle in my body complains.

Ow. I'd been slightly sore yesterday, but this is a whole new level. Well, that's what I get for not going to the gym regularly. Even as I attempt to walk the stiffness off and know deep down that I won't be able to go to the gym again tonight, I deny it.

Maybe after my classes, my muscles will feel better. Maybe I just need to wake up. Didn't I hear somewhere that it takes at least fifteen minutes after you get out of bed to be fully awake?

With that in mind, I limp to the bathroom and get ready for school.

The soreness remains as I slowly approach my classes. A few people give me odd looks, and I temporarily close my eyes in exasperation. I must be limping, despite my best efforts. My class before lunch is English, and when I finally reach my seat and carefully sink into it, I see that I'm one of the last to arrive. Oh well. Hopefully that just means I won't have to spend as much time in the classroom.

The lecture drags on, but at least my muscles don't hurt as much when I'm sitting down. When the professor dismisses us and everyone gets up to leave, I find that the pain has alleviated a little bit. Enough that I *know* I'm no longer limping as I walk across campus to the lot where I parked my car this morning. Still not enough for me to be able to go to the gym tonight, though. I sit down in my car but leave the key in my backpack for the moment. Reluctantly, I pull out my phone instead and bring up my conversation with Brynn from last night. I send her one quick text explaining my situation. Only after I send it do I realize that this means I no longer have Friday night plans. Well, there goes today's bright spot.

She responds quickly and understandingly. I sigh and dig out my car key and am about to start driving when my phone vibrates again. I check it and see an unread message from Brynn.

We could do something else tn, if you want?

I type back in the affirmative so quickly I'm almost sure she can sense my desperation. I don't care, though. Someone actually wants to spend time with me outside of the regularly allotted spots. *Brynn* wants to spend time with me, someone who probably has a dozen other friends she could call up to hang out with. Then again, probably not if she's only here temporarily for work.

That thought brings me down a bit. She could be gone at any time. *She* doesn't even know when she'll be gone.

Well, at least I have now. May as well live in the moment. Even if I just happened to be the first person she met in Toronto, she's still choosing to associate with me.

My thoughts are interrupted by the familiar vibration of my phone.

Okay cool, where do you want to go?

If she doesn't yet know Toronto, that means I have an advantage. I can pick a location where I can hopefully avoid any potential awkwardness between us and still have fun.

How about the mall? I send back. It should be a large enough place to provide plenty of distractions while not being so overwhelming that we can't still have a good, relaxed time.

She accepts, and I give her the address and general location. We plan to meet earlier than we would for the gym, around five o'clock. It's the soonest I can get there after my English tutorial and newspaper editing this afternoon. I text my mom, telling her my evening plans and assuring her that I'll pick up something to eat at the mall. Then I finally drive away from campus to pick up something for lunch.

Lunch is something Asher and I used to do together every day in September, then almost every day in October up until our breakup. It's now one of the loneliest parts of my day. In lectures, my mind is too occupied to focus on other people, and most of the time at newspaper I force myself to focus on my work. High school was easier because everyone ate at the same time and in the same place, so no one was truly isolated unless they chose it. Since lectures run at entirely different times in university, and the chances of running into someone you know at random on campus are minimal due to the sheer size of the place, unless you plan to eat lunch with someone, you'll be on your own.

So I'm alone. It gives me some time to unwind and start homework, at least. I wouldn't be able to do that if I had company. I also get to choose food that I like, a bonus not always available when eating with others.

I pick up a chicken salad with fries, because healthy only goes so far. I manage to complete a decently sized chunk of homework assigned in English this morning as I eat, which should allow me more time with Brynn tonight.

My afternoon class – my English tutorial, which elaborates on the topics introduced this morning – drags by as I anticipate my mall date. Newspaper editing feels almost slower, although it actually has the potential to be faster. The tutorial has a set time of one hour, whereas with newspaper, you can leave as soon as you've finished the pieces assigned to you to edit. That makes it almost worse, as I feverishly make my way through the freshly-printed papers with a red pen to catch any final errors, because I know that the faster I work the sooner I can leave, but I still have to do a quality job.

I finish by four p.m., which actually is earlier than usual, thankfully, and swiftly walk out. It's only as I reach my car that I realize I didn't even look to see if Asher was there. Oh well. I'm out of the room now, and I'm certainly not going back to check. The sun shines down on me, and some of the snow has devolved into slush. I hope that the bright sky is a good omen for tonight, or life in general, though that may be pushing things too far.

My loneliness from lunch has disappeared, although there's still no one around me. I find that I'm even smiling slightly as I unlock my car and climb in. Maybe it wasn't smart to finish up newspaper early, because I'm not scheduled to meet Brynn until five, which means I have some time to kill now. Well, I'm certainly not staying here for another empty half hour. I'll just take a circuitous route on my way there.

The drive is nice, or at least as nice as driving in Toronto can be. Traffic on the main roads is crazy, so I go through some more residential areas, cranking up the music and singing along. I make sure my windows are all the way rolled up, both to keep out cold air and because nobody wants to hear me singing full-blast. It feels good though, no matter how it may sound.

Even with my wandering, I still arrive at the mall ten minutes early. I text Brynn, letting her know, and walk inside to avoid the cold.

Around Christmas, the mall was all decked out with huge wreaths, silver, gold, and red garlands, and a miniature North Pole in the centre of all the shops with a Santa Claus who took pictures with children. Nearly everything was taken down by New Year's, but I can still see a few stray garlands up high as I continue further inside. They'll probably just leave them up until next year if they're not down by now.

My phone buzzes. It's Brynn.

Just got here! Where should I meet you?

I look around. I'm between a candle store and a children's clothing store, neither of which I'm interested in entering. I see an interactive map of the mall down the hall, so I approach it and text Brynn to meet me there.

I'm studying the map, curious to see if there've been any new stores constructed here since my last visit two years ago. Aside from the occasional pair of new shoes or jackets, I haven't needed to buy much lately. Besides, it's not like I'm growing anymore.

In my periphery I see a familiar flash of bronze. I turn, and I was right: it was Brynn's distinctive hair. I greet her happily, if somewhat shyly, and she returns the hello with double my confidence. Her everyday clothes appear to be just as trendy as her workout clothes, and just as complimentary to her body. She's wearing dark reddish-brown leather pants with a flowy white tank top and several silver necklaces underneath her winter coat, which she takes off as she speaks.

"Okay, this is my first time here," she admits, raising one perfectly arched, full eyebrow. It's a shade somewhere between blonde and brown, and for the first time, I wonder if red is her natural hair colour.

I laugh. "I haven't been here in at least two years, so I'll probably be just as lost as you are."

We study the map together, deciding to do some shopping before eating. Brynn suggests a fashionable clothing store fairly close to our current location. I've heard of the brand before, although I don't own anything made by them. But hey, if it's somewhere Brynn would shop, I may as well try it, seeing as how not a single outfit I own contains the simple elegance and subtle sexiness of Brynn's.

The store is nice, large and well-lit. The sheer amount of clothes almost overwhelms me, but Brynn beelines to a certain section and I mutely follow. She seems to have some sort of clothing radar, because the pieces she arrives at and begins to examine seem to fit right into her style. I pick at some of them too, but they seem too *much* for me. Too sexy, or too fancy, or too gothic. Brynn picks off a few shirts and dresses and heads to the change room. I trail behind her, still trying to take in all the other items.

I sit in a pleather armchair outside the change stalls as I wait, too intimidated to shop the clothes on my own. I don't have to wait long, though – Brynn changes very quickly. She steps out in one of the dresses, a soft green maxi with a brown belt at the waist. My jaw drops. I have nothing against people who like maxi dresses, but I've never seen anyone actually look *good* in one. Brynn defies my previous observations. The dress complements her height; it's loose at the top then tucked in at her waist, then flows out again over her hips.

"What do you think?" she asks, spinning in a circle. The movement causes the skirt to flare out, filling up with air, then settle down again when she stops and faces me expectantly.

"Buy it," I say immediately. She chews her lip, examining herself critically in the full-length mirror.

"I don't know..." she wavers. "I mean, I like it, but does the bottom fall right?"

I can't let her leave without this dress, though. "Brynn, if you don't buy this dress, I'll buy it for you."

She eyes me with amusement. "I guess I'm buying this dress then."

I grin, and she laughs before spinning around again and returning to the dressing room. Every item she comes out in after has a similar effect to the first dress. There doesn't seem to be a single piece that Brynn can't wear and still look attractive. She's picky, though, and only chooses to buy one shirt and one dress other than the first one.

When she comes out for the last time, dressed in the clothes she came in, she guides me by the elbow back into the racks. "Now it's your turn."

"I don't really know if anything here suits me..." I say, but she doesn't seem to hear. Instead, she gives me a quick once-over.

"Is that your usual style?" she asks. I look down at what I'm wearing. Slouchy off-the-shoulder indigo sweater and dark grey skinny jeans with my usual black sneakers. I nod.

"Do you like your outfit?" I look up sharply, but her face is completely innocent of malicious intent and her voice was merely curious, so I take the question into consideration.

"For the most part... but I could use some more variety," I carefully say after several seconds.

She nods thoughtfully, and I can see her scanning the surrounding racks. Although it takes a bit longer than it took when she was picking for herself, she eventually manages to put together a pile of clothes which she then unceremoniously dumps into my arms. She shoos me toward the change rooms, and I end up in the same stall she'd recently vacated.

Once in, I finally take a look at the pieces she's chosen. There are a number of shirts, with a few pairs of pants and dresses thrown into the mix. I try on the dresses first, since I never wear dresses and am eager to clear some of the clothes out of the stall so I don't feel so crowded. As I slip it over my head, I'm surprised to feel it settle perfectly and comfortably over me. Brynn really has an eye for size.

I step out and avoid Brynn's eyes, afraid to see her reaction. Instead I turn to the full-length mirror – and gasp.

I've been told that I'm pretty, and I think I have a decent figure. Not as good as Brynn's, but then, not many have bodies that good, aside from supermodels. But I've never really seen the prettiness that others have claimed was there. I mean, I love my hair. It's a rich dark brown, and long. I've been growing it out since I made the tragic mistake of cutting it to a bob when I was a kid. My bob didn't look nearly as good as Brynn's. And I think I have nice eyes. They're somewhere between green and hazel, and are topped with thick eyelashes. But my olive-toned skin somehow still manages to be too pale to match my dark hair, and my nose gives my face something of a 'cute' appearance, according to my grandmother; in my opinion it makes me look childish, much younger than my nineteen years.

In this dress, though, I can look at myself and actually see someone pretty. Someone mature and sophisticated, and who definitely looks her age.

The dress is white and simple, yet still has that subtly sexy look that Brynn seems so good at picking out. It has a loose back and high neckline, but hugs my hips and thighs until it ends just above my knees. The colour is so bright that the contrast makes my hair look even darker, and my skin more tanned.

I'm rendered speechless. Usually it takes me forever to pick out clothes that I actually like, and even with spending all that time I've never once found an item like this. Maybe I need to be more open to different types of clothes.

Finally I turn to face Brynn. She's smiling, and her face is hopeful. "What do you think?"

I just nod, a few times too many so that I probably look like a bobblehead.

She grins. "Yay! Okay, next item."

I follow her directions and return to the change room. It's nearly painful to remove the dress, but I'm excited to see the other clothes Brynn chose for me now. No longer does the change room seem crowded; in fact, I almost consider asking Brynn to choose more, before deciding to finish trying on everything in here first.

Brynn's good taste shines through in every piece that I try on, although I don't end up buying everything. I do choose an amount sufficient enough that it's a good thing I hadn't asked her to choose more, or I wouldn't have been able to afford it.

When I look at the price tag on the first white dress I'd tried on though, my face falls. There's no way I can reasonably factor this into my clothes budget. It's simply too much to spend on any one piece of clothing. I'm slowly adding it to the discard rack of clothes when I hear Brynn's sharp voice.

"What are you doing?"

I look over at her, arm still outstretched to put the dress with the other rejected clothes. I smile sadly and shrug. "It's too expensive."

Her face is determined. "Naya, if you don't buy this dress, I'll buy it for you," she says, in a dead-on impression of my earlier words to her.

I muster up one laugh. Unfortunately, my answer will have to be different than hers was. "Sorry. Still can't afford it." And I place it firmly on the rack and walk away.

I hear a clank behind me and turn to see Brynn pulling the dress back off the rack.

"What are you doing?" I ask warily.

She smirks. "I warned you."

Wait. Is she really planning on spending that much money on me? "Brynn, no, seriously, it's okay. It's a nice dress–" Understatement of the year. "–but I can't let you buy it."

She shakes her head, the same determined look still playing across her face. "Nope, still buying it. If it makes you feel better, I'll borrow it a few times."

I scan her from head to toe. "You're kind of way taller than me. It won't fit."

She tsks. "Details, details."

I protest all the way up to the cash register, where she slips out a shiny gold credit card and places it with a clack against the metal counter. She purchases the white dress along with the other outfits she'd tried on earlier. Brynn turns to me as the girl behind the counter tiredly rings everything through. She gives me a reassuring smile. "Trust me, Naya. I can afford it."

I feel a bit guilty, but it's not like I hadn't tried to stop her. Besides, she probably does have more money than me, considering she's working while I'm spending huge amounts of money on school. Unless she's taking classes too?

I wait until I make my purchases and we're walking out of the store, bags in hand, until I ask her.

"So are you in school?"

She shakes her head, swinging her bags rhythmically. "Nope. I wanted to take a break after high school, so I'm working for now." She checks out every store that we pass but doesn't show any inclination of going in, so we continue wandering.

I'm reminded that I don't actually know what her work entails. What is this mystery occupation that sends her, a fairly young-looking girl, on business trips of indeterminate lengths of time? Then again, I probably shouldn't be basing my estimation of her age solely off of her looks, considering how frequently my own age is underestimated.

"How old are you?" I ask, genuinely curious. I'm surprised that I hadn't asked before; for all I know, she could be several years older than me.

"Just turned nineteen in January," she answers with satisfaction.

Okay, so she is my age. "Me too! But February."

She gives me a knowing smile. "Nineteen in Toronto is a good age to be."

I laugh. "Definitely." Now I'm even more curious about her job. I've never known anyone my age to have a position important enough for their work to pay for them to travel for business. "What is your job?"

Her smile slips a bit. Whoops. I hope that's not an off-limits topic. She recovers quickly though, pasting on an exaggeratedly tired look, and says, "Oh, you know. Just doing what my boss tells me to do."

I laugh awkwardly. Um, all right then...

Brynn continues to look into every store, and at almost every person we pass. She seems very attentive to her surroundings.

Actually, I don't think I've ever seen someone pay that much attention to their surroundings.

I'm about to ask her if she's looking for someone or something in particular when I spot a familiar head. Thoughts of questioning Brynn drop completely from my mind as my eyes lock in on a figure two stores away.

Asher. With Savannah beside him.

Brynn immediately notices my shift in focus and follows my gaze. "Do you know him?" she asks confusedly, probably wondering why I'm staring so intently.

"Um, yeah," I mutter distractedly. "I'm just going to go talk to him..."

I'm already walking away when I feel a yank at my wrist and am halted dead in my tracks.

"Hold up," Brynn insists. "Who is that?"

I take a deep breath, then turn to face her. "My ex, Asher."

Her eyebrows shoot up slightly, but that's the only reaction I get from her before her next query. "Why do you need to talk to him?"

This gives me pause, since I hadn't actually planned out what I was going to say to him. Instead, I give her the simple, pathetic truth. "I want him back."

She presses her lips together, and scans around before her eyes lock on something over my shoulder. I turn around and see some benches. When I face her again, her eyes are back on my face and she looks serious. "Can we go sit down for two minutes and just discuss this before you talk to him?"

I'm about to protest, but her face is steely, and two minutes isn't really that long. Asher will likely still be there. It will probably take more time to argue with her, so I nod, half-confused and half-concerned. Hand still on my wrist, she leads me to the benches.

We sit and she doesn't even take a pause before she begins speaking. "Is he the one you broke up with in October?"

I'm surprised she remembers the month – I'd only mentioned it once, the first day I saw her at the gym – but I nod, amending, "Well, he broke up with me."

Her eyes encourage me to continue, so I do. I explain everything, from our summer together after grade twelve, to our diminishing dates at the beginning of university, to him turkey dumping me with a flimsy excuse, and the gossip about him cheating after. I leave out my lack of friends, though. I don't want my friendship with her to be because she pities me.

She releases a breath after I finish, and looking me directly in the eyes, says, "Okay, I'm going to say something, and you can take it or leave it. I'll be fine either way."

"Okay..."

She nods, looking relieved that I didn't just ignore her completely and go after Asher again, probably. "I have some 'rules of love'," she begins sheepishly, putting air quotations around the phrase. "Number one: respect."

"I'm not going to be rude when I see him," I say promptly, and maybe a bit defensively.

She shakes her head. "I don't mean you. Well, obviously you need to respect your partner too, but I'm referring to the cheating rumours, and his lying to you when you broke up."

I can feel my cheeks burn. It was one thing for me to talk about him dumping me, but it's even more embarrassing to hear beautiful, probably-never-broken-up-with-in-her-life Brynn discuss it. I look down, but Brynn continues with her speech.

"That was disrespectful. The respect for you wasn't there, and everyone deserves respect.

"Number two: desperation and jealousy. I am in no way saying that you're desperate–" I grimace, because honestly, I kind of am. "–but if you're serious about winning him back, there are better ways than interrupting him in the mall when it looks like he may be on a date." She cranes her neck around, once again locating him and Savannah.

Ouch. That hurts a bit. I mean, we're not together and haven't been in about four months, so I have no claim on him, but the fact of it doesn't make my feelings for him go away. It makes it even harder that his feelings for me have so clearly gone out the window.

Brynn turns back to me and continues. "Desperation – or anything guys may view as such – turns them off of a girl more than... well, probably just about anything else. You know that whole 'playing hard to get' thing? Obviously overusing it can be destructive to a relationship, but a little bit in the right situation can do wonders." Her eyes look distant, and I wonder what memories she's accessing. Suddenly her gaze returns to my face with razor-sharp intensity, and she picks up where she left off.

"Sometimes looking like you're having the time of your life while ignoring him will get him interested." She lifts an eyebrow and smirks, and I smile back tentatively, glad to see some humour again.

"Number three... and don't worry, I know it's been more than two minutes but I promise this is the last one... three: space. This kind of fits into what I was saying about desperation, but space is very important. Like, I'm sure there are people out there who don't ever want to be separated from their partners even for a washroom break–" I wrinkle my nose in disgust and giggle at the mental image. "–but most of us want some time with other people than our partner, or just alone time. So be prepared to give your partner space, with minimal questioning."

She laughs. "And I don't mean never ask about where they're going or what they'll be doing, but don't turn it into an interrogation.

"I've found that when you follow these guidelines, the relationship is healthier... and when your guy receives respect and space from you, he's usually more willing to return it." She's been gazing off into space again, but now she looks at me again, smiling. "And you shouldn't expect anything less than what you give."

This definitely gives me a lot to think about. And I'm kind of awed. Seriously, where did Brynn get all this wisdom?

I clear my throat to interject my first comment of the conversation. "If you know so much about love, you must be in love."

Her smile turns into a grin, and she looks down at her feet for a moment before responding. "I'm in a dedicated relationship." Oh, that's right. The boyfriend she'd mentioned at the gym the day we'd met.

I wait for her to elaborate, but when she doesn't, I propose a question. "So in your expert opinion, what should I do?" I ask teasingly.

She responds quickly. "Don't talk to him. The first thing he needs to learn is some respect for you. Honestly, I'd look for someone else. But, if you're determined to try and get him back...

then, I suppose ignoring him for a bit may pique his interest again."

Looking for someone else really isn't a bad idea, but it's not something I can picture myself doing right now. And maybe she's right. Aside from my week of silence toward Asher after our breakup, I've been doing my best to get him to notice me. Maybe the best way to recapture his attention is to pretend I no longer care.

I slowly nod, and Brynn grins again. "Yay! Okay. Let's go find somewhere else to shop now!"

I follow her over to a nearby map. I realize suddenly that I'm actually quite hungry. I check my phone – 6:17 p.m. And considering how much I spent just at that last store, it's probably better to go for dinner now. I point out the time to Brynn, and we look for the food court on the guide instead.

As we head toward the mouth-watering greasy smells drifting toward us, we pass Asher. Following Brynn's advice, I laugh perhaps a bit *too* loudly at a comment she makes on our way by him. I don't check behind to see if he noticed.

Chapter Three

We get Chinese food and manage to snag a table with two seats in the middle of the food court. I sink into it gratefully, and dig into my noodles with a plastic fork. Brynn laughs at my enthusiasm and sits across from me, handling her chopsticks expertly. We make easy conversation even after we both finish eating, until I look at the time again and realize that I really should be heading home. I may have made a dent in my homework at lunch, but I still have a sufficient amount of readings from other classes to catch up on to force me to leave now.

We dump our garbage into a nearby plastic trash bin and meander out of the food court. When we finally reach the doors near the parking lot in which I'd left my car, Brynn stops me to say good bye. She pulls me in for a hug, and I stiffen, surprised, before I return it.

"This was fun!" she says, and I'm glad she thought so, because

I certainly enjoyed myself. "I guess I'll see you at the gym tomorrow?"

My lips twitch downwards at the thought of it, but I reluctantly agree. "See, this is why it's good to have a gym buddy. Motivation."

She smirks. "Definitely good. Especially since, believe it or not," she lowers her voice conspiratorially, "I don't think all that deep-fried Chinese was actually healthy."

I snort. "Really, you don't say."

Suddenly the smile drops from her face and she looks... anxious maybe? It's hard to tell. Her eyes are focused on a spot over my shoulder, and I turn to look. I don't get to see what it is before she grips my arm, forcing my attention back to her.

"So, tomorrow. See you then." She's smiling again, but it looks forced now. I'm confused by her mood change, but I really do have to go. I say good bye and turn to push my way out the glass door.

When I'm shifting the door open, I look to the side to the focal point of Brynn's mood change. It appears to be a shop like the ones so common in airports, selling trashy novels and rag mags alongside gum and breath mints. Nothing out of the ordinary. It doesn't seem to be very busy either, and I don't see anyone inside that might invite closer examination. I wonder what Brynn saw that caused her mood shift? Whatever it was is behind me now, as I pass through the door and find my car.

On the drive home, there are a few things that jump to the front of my mind as a bit odd: the confusingly offensive shop, of course, but also Brynn's subtle refusal to tell me about her job, how she doesn't know how long she'll be in Toronto for, and how she wouldn't elaborate at all on her boyfriend. Does she have some sort of secret?

Well, if she does, it's none of my business. I've known the girl for three days, even if it does seem like longer. And besides, I have no proof of anything. Maybe I imagined the forced quality of her smile. Maybe her job is classified or something. Maybe she's just not comfortable telling me anything about her boyfriend yet.

I push everything to the back of my mind when I get home. There's no point in obsessing over things that likely have no meaning when I really do need to focus on my schoolwork.

When I open the front door though, I end up procrastinating my work even longer when the smell of garlic bread hits me. I may have just eaten, but unless I'm full to the point of vomiting, I will never turn down garlic bread.

My family is in the kitchen, eating a late dinner. I snag the last two pieces of the soft, warm bread, and join them at the table. My parents greet me – Connor is too busy eating to even look up – and my mom asks how the mall was.

Awkwardly, I avert my eyes to the garlic bread in my hands as I answer. "Good. A lot of fun, actually."

In my periphery, I can see my mom's lips turn up. I may not tell her the extent of my loneliness sometimes, but she's observant. I used to have large groups of friends over to my house on almost a weekly basis – with Asher, of course – but in the months since our breakup, I've had maybe two people over, and only to study. I think she's happy that I'm actually doing something social again.

Now my father speaks up. In his deep voice, he asks, "Who were you with?"

This is a topic I'm happy to talk about. "A girl I met at the gym a few days ago. Brynn."

My father's face softens into relief, and I suddenly realize that he'd probably thought I was with a boy. My father is fiercely protective, although he rarely expresses his concerns aloud. I've always been able to tell in the past though when he was uncomfortable, and it was usually when I told him about dates.

This time Connor speaks. I'm so shocked that he's taken a break from his meal that at first his question doesn't hit me. Then it does, and I roll my eyes.

"Is she hot?"

I stare coolly at him as I reply. "Extremely so. And also too old for you, and in a relationship. Don't you have enough girls at school?"

He smirks. "You can never have too many girls." Ew. "Do you have a picture of her?"

I realize that I don't, which is actually surprising. I usually take pictures of everything from new shoes to nature to random people on the street. I've always been afraid that my memory won't hold up in the future, considering all the cases of dementia and Alzheimer's I hear about nowadays. So I capture images to use as a sort of backup memory.

"No," I say.

Connor widens his eyes at me exaggeratedly. "Well, what does she look like?"

So I describe Brynn, from her height to her hair. When I finish, Connor looks dubious.

"A hot ginger? That's rare."

"Connor," my mother reprimands him.

I stare at him in disgust. "You're kind of a pig, you know that?"

He just shrugs and returns to his food.

By this time I've finished my garlic bread and have resigned myself to my work. I reluctantly stand, but freeze when my mom looks up sharply.

"Where are you going?" she asks accusingly.

"Um, homework," I remind her.

"Tonight is family night. You know that."

Family night is something my mom implemented not long after my breakup with Asher. Every Friday night, she forces the family to do something together. In the past, we've played board games or Twister or something else relatively mindless and relaxing.

"Mom. I have a lot of work."

"And you have the rest of the weekend to finish it."

I consider. It's true that I have two eventless days ahead of me, but I like to catch up on sleep on my days off, which takes off a good chunk of potential homework time. Still, the thought of putting my homework off even longer is tempting.

"What would we be doing tonight?" I finally ask. If it's charades again, I'm definitely just going to my room to work.

"Your pick." Her lips are pressed together, and I consider.

"Watching a movie." I mean to say it as a statement, but it comes out close to a question. We don't usually watch movies on family night, because my mom says that it doesn't provide enough opportunity for discussion. But I'm hopeful that since she seems to want me to stay with the family tonight, she'll agree to my suggestion.

Sure enough, she nods, eyebrows lowering from their earlier tense position, though her mouth stays hard. She doesn't like my choice, but she'll take it.

Connor jumps into the conversation, finally finished his food. "Okay, since Naya picked the activity, I get to pick the movie."

I frown, shaking my head vehemently. Connor goes for movies based on how hot the actresses are and how much skin they bare, which usually means there is next to no plot. "That's not fair. Mom said I get to pick what we're doing tonight. That includes what we're watching."

Connor looks at Mom pleadingly, and I know I've lost this battle. Mom always falls for his innocent act, since he's not nearly so innocent anymore. Mom may be observant, but she's also frequently ruled by emotion.

So that's how we end up watching *Death by Pom-Poms* from our TV's on-demand service. It came out five years ago, and the trailer looked terrible when we played it, which is probably why I never saw it in theatres. But Connor was convinced by the blood-soaked teenage cheerleaders running scared around the dark, empty high school. I have to admit, it is stupidly entertaining though, and it does provide a welcome distraction from my schoolwork. And the totally-fake romance between blond Brad and even-blonder Jenny, played by Callan Nyler and Aviva Jersey, serves to make me feel not as bad about my love life. If that is all a relationship can be, who would want one?

When the credits begin to roll, Connor stands up and

stretches. "It's a good thing Jenny was hot, because that movie sucked."

I agree that it was a laughably terrible movie, but there's no way I'll let Connor know. Instead, I say, "You're the one who picked it."

He yawns. "Yeah, my bad. You can choose next time."

Normally I'd be pleased by his admission, but for some reason his comments are getting to me tonight, and I feel the need to defend this actress. I don't know why. I don't know her, and I doubt she'd ever even thank me if she knew I was defending her, but I'm sick of all of Connor's careless comments.

"Aviva Jersey has been in a lot of better movies lately. Remember *The Siren's Call*? She was in that."

Connor looks at me strangely. "How do you even know that?"

I blush. God, there *has* to be a way to control that. The truth is that before I threw away the newspaper copy where I'd noticed the celebrity section, a few words from it had stood out to me, including some of the names of recent movies with Aviva Jersey. But I don't need to explain that to Connor. Instead, I say tightly, "How do you not?"

Mom jumps in. "Enough, you two. Now, do we want to play a game or something before we end family night?"

But I've had enough of Connor for the evening, and I'm quite tired. I didn't get enough sleep last night, and today was busier than usual. So I excuse myself to my room, saying that I need to go to bed sooner than usual if I want to wake up early enough for my homework and meeting Brynn at the gym. I ignore Connor's lesbian joke as I climb the stairs, and his resulting snickering. Honestly, I don't know how Connor turned out so insensitive.

Both of my parents are accepting of everyone, and I inherited their view of the world. I don't know if Connor is actually prejudiced against anyone or just likes his stupid jokes, but I don't appreciate them either way.

I go through my bedtime routine and climb into bed tiredly. I'm asleep within minutes of my head touching the pillow.

The next morning I wake a bit after ten a.m. That's pretty good – almost twelve hours of sleep. I feel much better this morning than I did last night, and after digging up some breakfast, effectively complete a fair amount of my work.

During my lunch break I decide to text Brynn to see if she can meet at the gym earlier. I'm in desperate need of a longer break from my work, and I figure the gym will provide the necessary relief to let me refocus totally on more of my work tonight.

She responds back near the end of my lunch break, when I'm slowly pushing around the few crumbs left on my plate in an attempt to convince myself I'm still eating and it's totally fine to remain away from my desk.

Yeah, that should be fine. How about 4pm?

I check the microwave clock. It's 2 o'clock now, which means I can fit in some more work before I leave. Ugh. Well, that's university life.

I text her back in agreement, then clear my placemat and load my plate into the dishwasher. Now that I have an exit in sight, it's slightly easier to return to my work.

My Latin readings never truly immerse me, but I do become so confused with my desperate Google searches that I temporarily forget about the time. When I remember to check the little digital clock on the bottom of my laptop, it's past time to leave. I leap up in relief and run to my car.

When I get to the gym, I'm weirded out by seeing it in daytime. I walk quickly on the path from the parking lot though, because it's already 4:05. I was the one who asked for an earlier meeting time; the least I can do is be here on time. Although once I've pushed the door open, with some difficulty due to a snow pileup against the outside, I can see that Brynn isn't here yet. The gym is completely empty.

Well, good. At least I can't be accused of being late, then. I deliberate over whether to start my workout or wait for Brynn so we'll be done at the same time, but when five minutes pass with me standing silently, I decide that I may as well begin. I consider pulling out the huge fan from the back closet on my own, but I dismiss the idea quickly. There's no way I'd be able to pull it out without another person's help. I get onto the elliptical trainer I usually use, resigned to feeling the heat. I didn't even bring my earbuds, prepared to talk to Brynn, so I start my workout without the benefits of a distraction.

Another ten minutes pass. I've already broken a sweat and Brynn still isn't here. Maybe she forgot? I slow down my pace enough so that I can text her.

Hey, where r u?

Her response is almost immediate. *Sry! I was held up but I'll be there rlly soon.*

Sure enough, the outside door swings open within five minutes of her text. I smile at her through my quick movements, but slow when I really take in her face.

She looks *gorgeous*. She's wearing pretty heavy makeup, but it doesn't look caked on, as I've seen on some other girls in my classes. Brynn usually wears no makeup, or maybe some mascara, as far as I've been able to tell, so this is surprising. My gaze moves to her hair, and it looks ruffled. Her clothes also look a bit off – twisted slightly to the side, or not pulled down all the way. Gorgeous, but also rushed.

She jumps up onto the elliptical beside me and starts it with deft hands. I speed up again as she does.

"So where have you been, all dressed up?" I ask teasingly.

"Um... just... I was out longer than expected."

Well, that answers officially nothing. Usually I would attribute her slow response and pauses to being out of breath, but she's definitely not, considering she only just started her workout. So, here's another thing we're not allowed to talk about. Well, I'm not going to just ignore these obvious avoidances anymore.

"Look, Brynn, if you don't want to tell me the truth, I get it. But you can trust me if you do want to talk. I'm a good secret-keeper." I give her what I hope looks like a reassuring smile.

She returns the smile, and I realize that this is the first time she's looked me full in the face since she walked into the gym. She opens her mouth to speak and I'm curious: will she actually tell me the truth about something?

"I hope you haven't been here too long. How much time is left in your workout?"

Okay. So the secrets are still in place. Well, I can't force her to tell me anything. I look down at the timer on my elliptical. "Thirty-eight minutes."

She makes a face. "Yikes. Sorry."

I shake my head. "It's fine. Honestly, I was glad just to get out of my house for a while."

She raises her eyebrows. "Is everything okay there?"

I nod. "Oh yeah. I mean, aside from my idiot brother. I just have too much homework."

She smirks, and we move onto other, more easily accessible and permitted topics. Everything seems normal again, until my workout finally finishes and I fight not to keel over. Then, she changes the subject again.

"I won't be here next week. I'm going back to the U.S. for work."

Well, that's interesting. Apparently Brynn is from the States. And she mentioned work. Maybe what I'd said was allowing her to be more open with me?

I work to keep my face carefully neutral for fear of scaring her off again. "Oh, okay. But you'll be coming back to Toronto after?"

She still has twenty minutes left in her workout, and she peddles quickly as she speaks. "Yes. It looks like I'll be here for even longer than I'd originally thought."

Well, that's good. "Where do you usually work for your job?"

Her mouth clamps shut and I sigh. Great. Even when she brings up her job, I'm not allowed to ask questions about it. I know I said that she didn't have to tell me anything if she didn't want to, but I'm kind of regretting it now. I deserve to know *some* answers, don't I?

I sigh and turn to walk away. "Good-bye, Brynn." I've already taken five steps when I hear her voice.

"Wait!" I freeze but don't turn around. "Please, Naya, can I explain something?"

An explanation is definitely what I need to hear right now, so I turn and slowly approach her again.

Her legs are moving rapidly, even faster than usual. She stares over my head and takes a large gulp of air before she begins. "I just... I've told people things before, and it didn't turn out well for me. I know it's a lot to ask, but can I... I don't know. Share a bit at a time, I guess? That might help me to feel more comfortable." Her eyes are still avoiding me.

Well, crap. Now I feel like a tool. Of course I should've realized that there was a real reason for Brynn's lack of sharing. Normal people don't just keep secrets for no reason. I say quickly, "Of course."

Brynn's eyes finally return to my face, and her face is intense, made even more so by the dark makeup. She studies me for a moment before releasing a shaky breath and murmuring, "Thank you."

I walk over to a bench on the other side of Brynn's elliptical trainer and sit down. I'm physically drained now, and it feels good to get off my feet. I'm slipping off my shoes to massage the arches of my feet when I hear Brynn say something and look up at her instead.

"I'm excited to see my boyfriend when I go home." Her face isn't overly emotional, but I can see the subtle indicators of happiness when she mentions him. Her lips curve up a bit, and the tightness in her forehead loosens.

Hmm. Her boyfriend was another off-limits topic. I'm curious to hear which pieces of information she's willing to give up now.

"What's his name?" I ask cautiously.

She doesn't hesitate this time. "Callan. We've been dating for almost three years now."

Three years. Jeez. And I'd thought my year-long relationship with Asher had been an impressive length for our age. I guess Brynn's relationship would need to be strong, though, to survive long-distance.

"Where is he, when you're in Toronto?" I ask.

She smiles sadly. "At home in L.A. That's where I normally work." She tacks the second sentence on as almost an afterthought.

Los Angeles. I've never been there, but I suppose it's as good a place as any to work. "Does Callan work too, or is he in school?"

"He works too." Her answers are coming more easily now.

"What's his job?" I hope it's not a secret, too.

She takes a gulp of water before she answers. "Same as mine."

Which means that it is, in fact, also a secret. I figure I'd better not press my luck by pushing for more job information, so I ask a question that I figure should provide lots for Brynn to say. "What's he like?"

Her face softens even more and she launches into a description of his physical and personality traits. It's sweet, and compelling, to see how much Brynn drops her guard when she talks about her boyfriend. She's usually talkative – well, about most things – but it seems as though she has endless comments to make about Callan.

Suddenly her flow of words cuts off. "What's wrong?" she asks, and I look up, surprised.

"What?"

She's looking directly at me while still continuing forward on her elliptical trainer, something that would throw me completely off-balance, but which she manages with ease. "You look sad."

So she noticed. I wasn't intentionally trying to look depressed, but Brynn's talk of Callan and their relationship was really making me miss Asher. Which is stupid, because her relationship sounds ten times better than mine and Asher's ever was. Maybe that made it worse, actually, because I could see what I was missing out on before.

"I miss Asher," I explain with a shrug.

She continues to study me and I begin to grow uncomfortable under the prolonged stare. "Do you remember my 'rules of love'?" she abruptly asks.

Surprised, I answer, "Of course." It's true. Everything she'd said at the mall yesterday really had sunk into my head. Some of it was self-explanatory, but all of it was good advice, and I really do want to remember it.

She nods with a half-smile. "Right now you have two options. You can either move on, which may or may not entail finding someone new, or you can try to get him back. And honestly, Naya, I'd recommend moving on. You really don't want to be with someone who doesn't want you too."

That really resonates with me after hearing about her relationship with Callan. I desperately want a relationship of that caliber of my own. Even so, emotions are hard to ignore. I say, so quietly that I'm not sure at first if she can hear me over the noise of her workout machine, "I still love him."

She chews her lip, finally turning back forward. "Okay. Let's make a compromise. How about for the next week, you just ignore him? That's good for you either way."

Thinking back on her 'rules of love', I recall the playing hard to get section. Ignoring him shouldn't be *too* hard for a week… and it would either catch his interest or help me to get over him. Brynn is right. It would benefit me either way.

Slowly, I nod my agreement, then voice it, since she's still facing forward, away from me.

"Okay, yay!" She looks at me slyly from the side of her eye. "Now promise me."

Laughing, I say, "I promise." The words come out easily.

She turns her whole head to me at my words. "I'm trusting you," she warns me.

I really do want to do what will be best for me in the long run, and I also don't want to disappoint Brynn. She's become a large influence in my life in a short amount of time, but I don't mind. Even if she is still keeping secrets, I know that I can trust that she wants what's best for me. Making the promise was the easy part, though. Following through on it will be harder.

But it's not as difficult as I expect. I really don't see Asher very much – only ever at newspaper, really – and it's easy enough to pretend he's not there for an hour or so a day. It's tempting to look for his reaction – to see if he notices me *not* noticing him – but I don't. I stay true to my word.

I also find that it becomes easier for me to look at other boys, in a maybe not-so-platonic way. I don't see anyone who really catches my interest, but who knows? Maybe Brynn's right. Maybe it is time for me to move on. If Asher has completely gotten over me, then I shouldn't waste my time pining over him.

I've never been a huge flirt, but I do find myself giggling more and touching my hair as I talk to a particularly good-looking guy in my Anthropology tutorial Wednesday morning. And even better, he actually seems to show interest in me. But then I find my mind wandering back to what Asher would think if he saw me right now, and I begin to wonder whether I'm flirting because I have a real interest in the guy or just to distract myself and try to make myself feel more desirable again. I don't have much time to analyze the thought before the teacher's assistant brings the class to order and we begin, thus forcing my mind to focus solely on our dead ancestors.

That night I go to the gym. I've been going every day lately, and it's hard without motivation from Brynn, since she's in L.A. this week, but it is getting physically easier now as my body begins to learn the movement of the elliptical trainer. And I really do want to make a difference in how my body looks. Brynn is so fit, and definitely slim, but not in a bony way. I don't know how long it took her to become so toned, but I've made the goal to get there eventually.

And then Asher will see how good I look and want me again, but I'll be over him. Tables turned. We'll see how he likes that.

I think that going to the gym every day, despite the extra time it takes out of my schedule, actually helps me to complete my schoolwork too. Because it gets rid of excess energy, or helps me to learn to manage my time better – or maybe both, I don't know – but it seems like I should've been doing this from the beginning of the school year. Oh well. At least I know now for the future.

Friday afternoon I receive a text from Brynn. It's the first I've heard from her since I saw her last at the gym, and I'm happy for it, but also somewhat apprehensive. Everything is fine on my end, but I hope I didn't push her too hard for information last weekend. I mean, I deserve some answers, but I don't want our already-tentative friendship to be altered. Her text is direct and to-the-point, though, so I can't get much of a read on it.

Hey, just got back. Too tired to go to the gym tn. How about tmo? Earlier than usual? I have some stuff to do in the aft.

Well, she still wants to be gym buddies. That's a good sign. I text back with an equally neutral yes, then put my phone away. Gym with Brynn takes a bit more time than gym by myself, since our conversations can delay the reason we're actually there: the workout. It's probably a good thing I won't see her until tomorrow, the beginning of the weekend, then, because I'll have more time the rest of the day to complete my schoolwork.

My week was already going pretty well, but Brynn's text lightens up the end of it. I love having weekend plans again beyond Friday family night, even if they are only going to the gym. At least I'll be seeing another person, one who actually likes me.

When I enter the gym the next day, shivering from the cold outside and reluctantly shedding my coat, Brynn is already there. The gym almost looks odd with her there again, since I'd gotten so used to seeing it completely empty. The lighting is also different, since it's earlier in the day. Brynn looks up as the door clangs shut behind me and smiles.

She looks the same, but her face is drawn. I guess the trip took a good deal out of her. She doesn't seem to be wearing any makeup at all, and I think this is the first time I've seen her entirely bare-faced. Still gorgeous, and she does look happy, which adds to her prettiness, underneath her tiredness. She greets me with enthusiasm, and I sigh silently in relief. It looks as though my worrying was for nothing. She's acting like it's only been a day since we've seen each other, not nearly a week.

I walk over to the elliptical beside her but don't get on yet. "How was your trip?" I ask.

She beams. "Fantastic. Exhausting. The usual."

She seems to be willing to be open today, so I keep asking questions. "Was it good because of the job part or the *boyfriend* part?" I ask teasingly, and so help me, she actually blushes. Maybe I just couldn't see it under her foundation before, but the unconscious response seems to humanize her. I'd been holding her to the status of a goddess, almost, but this small pinch of colour in her cheeks reminds me that she's just a girl, the same age as me. A smart one, yes, but still human.

"Both..." she says, and I raise an eyebrow, unconvinced. She giggles. "But probably more seeing Callan."

I laugh. "Knew it! What did you guys do?"

I begin my workout as she bubbles on about how she showed up early in the morning to surprise him, then gushes about how he planned a picnic lunch for them. She mentions that he picked her up from work one day, but that's the only thing she says about her job at all. And she only ever calls it 'work' or her 'job' – never anything specific or descriptive. She never mentions where the company is based, or anything about any friends who work with her.

So it seems like her secret is shackled to her job. She kept just about everything hidden before, but now the only thing she skirts around is her way of making a living.

What if it's illegal? The thought pops unbidden into my head, but I quickly push it away. Brynn is not that type of person. And maybe I don't know her that well yet, but what sort of illegitimate activity would she be suited for? And how would she have even become involved? And it's so far-fetched, anyway!

Then what? Maybe she's a spy? Far-fetched again. Maybe she works in some other secret position for the government? It's a possibility. But again, what position would she be suited for, and how could she have gotten involved?

What if she doesn't work for the government, but is on the run from the government? Or a different country's government? But then wouldn't she have an easily-explainable cover job? Her job wouldn't be a secret.

Or maybe you should mind your own business. Maybe she's just embarrassed of her job or something, a voice in my head whispers. And honestly, it's the most reasonable option of the ones I'd proposed.

I focus back on Brynn's narrative of her week, but I'm only half-listening. My focus in jolted back to her, however, when she says my name.

"Naya."

I jerk my head toward her, somewhat guiltily, wondering if she'd realized I hadn't been paying full attention to her. "Yeah?"

She looks away from me now, but her face still looks thoughtful, so I can tell she has something to say. I give her a few more moments before finally prompting, "Brynn?"

She looks back at me. "I just wanted to say thank you. For being a friend, when I was alone in the big ol' city," she says drily, "and for being understanding about my... slow sharing of information."

I duck my head. "Yeah, of course."

I can hear the smile in her voice as she continues. "You're just a lot more genuine than some of the people in L.A."

I look up at that. "I hate fake people."

Her eyes widen dramatically. "Me, too!"

I shrug. "Then dump all the fakes."

She laughs. "Trust me, I've considered it. It's just that a lot of them either work with me, or there's potential for them to work with me, so I have to be civil."

I frown. "Um, wow, that sucks. I can see why that would invite trust issues."

She smiles again, but this one looks more serious. "Oh, you have no idea."

Which of course makes me curious about her job again, but I'm done speculating on that for now. We finish up our workouts, discussing less sensitive topics. I tell her about my week ignoring Asher, and she looks both surprised and happy.

"You're actually getting over him!" I almost feel like I should be offended at her obvious joy of me getting over a guy I'd already dated, thus already indicating my apparently bad taste, but I'm too distracted by her words to worry about her tone. She's right, and she's realized it even before I have. I really am moving on from Asher. Jeez. If all it took was ignoring him for a week, I should've done it a long time ago.

Yes, I'd realized that I'd already begun to care less if he was watching. And I'd been focusing on making him jealous of me for when I reject him. But in my head they'd been just words, and I hadn't really known if my emotions backed them up. I'd hoped that the words would begin to lead my feelings in the right direction, but I hadn't really realized until this moment that it had begun to work.

My elliptical slows down, finally getting to my cooldown. Brynn's already stopped but is still standing on her machine, watching me carefully.

"You're right," I finally say, my voice low. I clear my throat. "Wow. Okay. Um, thank you."

We step off of our elliptical trainers and walk side-by-side toward the mirrors at the front of the room. We lean against them before Brynn responds.

"Hey, all I did was give some advice. You're the one who did the work. Besides, today was supposed to be *my* thank-you for *you*," she continues teasingly, "so don't upstage me."

I snort. "Oh, my bad." I reach out to give her shoulder a fake smack, and that's when several things happen, nearly all at the same time.

First, as my hand brushes against her upper shoulder, the ring on my index finger accidentally tugs at the longer section of the front of her hair, and the strands begins to move. I don't know what's happening at first – is her hair falling out? How hard is this ring pulling? – until the entire red bob falls off of her head, revealing blonde hair tethered into a bun at the nape of her neck. The red hair drops nearly silently onto the ground, finally free from my ring.

Then Brynn's face changes, suddenly turning dark and assuming a nearly hunted look. She snatches up the fiery mess from the floor, spins on her heel and stalks toward the exit.

And I realize that she'd been wearing a wig and call out for her to stop. She actually jerks back a bit, she stops so abruptly, almost as if she's a puppet attached to the strings of my words. She remains facing away from me, though, so I slowly approach her. I can see her shoulders tense as my slow steps get closer to her, and she quickly attempts to put the wig back over her real hair.

As I walk, my mind is racing. Who wears a *wig*, aside from cancer patients? It's not like she's bald – actually, her blonde hair is longer than her red wig had been. And why wear a disguise to a *gym*, of all places? Maybe she *is* on the run from someone. Or maybe she really is a spy! My earlier thoughts don't seem so far-fetched anymore.

Finally, I reach her. I stop directly behind her, forcing her to turn around again to face me. Something in the back of my mind tugs at me as I study her, blonde tendrils of hair peeking out from behind the red. She reminds me of someone. The blonde is light, almost platinum, but honey-toned. She looks different, somehow, face softer, not as bold without the bright red hair colour. I can't place the memory right now, though, when I'm still so baffled by the question of *why* she was wearing a wig in the first place.

Her face is wary as she stares back at me coldly. It frightens me a bit. This isn't the Brynn I know. It forces me to up my defences too, so my voice comes out hard when I speak.

"Why are you wearing a wig?" I half-expect her to just leave, and never come back, ignore any texts I send, and disappear off the face of the earth. But as she studies my face, her apprehensive look lessens slightly, and her tense shoulders drop.

She swallows, seemingly unconsciously, and opens and closes her mouth a few times before finally answering. "It's... complicated." She's still staring at me, a bit defiantly, daring me to question her further.

But there is no way I can just let this go. I can handle not knowing about her job, or her work buddies, or her boss, but I cannot handle her wearing a wig with no explanation. So I push on, ignoring her look.

"How complicated can it be? Everything has an explanation." She switches her focus to somewhere above my head, pressing her lips together in a silent refusal to answer.

"Brynn." I see another unconscious swallow, but then her eyes flicker back down to my face. She's not meeting my eyes, but at least she's looking at me. "Brynn, you know you can trust me. I mean, I've been complaining about all of my problems since like the first moment we met. I trust *you*. Please. Just... *trust me*." The final two words are emphatic. I'm sick of one-way trust.

She takes several more beats, but then she sighs and her eyes return to mine. "What did you see?" She sounds vulnerable, and my frustration begins to seep away.

I laugh shortly. "Um, your hair? And I don't know why you'd

try to hide it, because you look just as good blonde as you do red."

Some more air huffs out of her, but it doesn't sound frustrated – more like she's been punched in the stomach. She diverts her eyes and removes the wig, now that she knows I've already seen what's underneath. She just stands there for a few moments, letting me study her, before she brings her eyes back to me.

The same familiarity that I'd felt before niggles at me, but I don't know who she'd remind me of other than herself, in the red wig. It must be the same-but-different mind-boggler that's giving me this feeling. I don't know why Brynn's still staring at me, and it's kind of weirding me out, so I raise my eyebrows at her.

This causes her own eyebrows to quirk up. "Do you know who... Who am I?"

I look at her like she's crazy. "Well, unless you have a twin sister, you're still Brynn."

My words seem to wash over her in a wave of relief, as she slumps, all tension finally leaving her body. What does that even mean, who is she? Does she go to my school or something? Was I supposed to recognize her with her blonde hair?

She turns toward the mirror, assessing her state with critical eyes. "I won't be able to put the wig back on properly without fixing my hair. Which I can't do here." She looks concerned at this, but she stuffs the wig into her gym bag forcefully, muttering under her breath, "At least it's Toronto and not L.A."

Wait. That's a clue. But I don't have enough surrounding evidence to make this piece fit into the puzzle. So I decide to ask.

"Why? What's wrong with L.A.?"

Brynn shakes her hair out of its current messy bun and finger-combs it, trying to find its part. "Just... it's where I'm expected to be," she mumbles through the hair elastic between her teeth, still staring toward the mirror. She almost seems to be looking through the reflective wall, though.

What? Why would it matter where she would be expected to be? It's not like streets have twenty-four-hour surveillance that would transmit her location to her parents, or whoever she's attempting to hide her location from. Her wig was obviously an attempt to disguise herself from someone - maybe multiple someones - but who? And why is it better that the wig came off somewhere distant from her Los Angeles home? I have too many questions and still not enough evidence to piece together the entire picture.

Whatever it is, I'm not going to figure it out here and now. And Brynn obviously isn't going to tell me. So I have three choices, since I know she won't budge on her secret-keeping stance: accept the secret and forget about it; ignore the secret until I gather enough information to figure it out; or leave Brynn and her secrets behind.

I don't want to leave Brynn, though. Leaving her now would have a finality to it, and I know that it would end our friendship. And even if she has secrets, she's still my closest friend right now.

The first two options both involve leaving the secret alone right now, and I can decide if I want to pursue it or not later, when I have more time to think. So, with a deep breath, I make the conscious decision to forget about it, at least for the moment. And, since I do want to keep our friendship, I ask a question to try and break the tension.

"Do you want to come over to my house tomorrow?" I blurt

out. I hadn't been planning on inviting her over, but it was the first thing I could think of to say in order to make my position on our friendship clear. My gaze scans down from her face to her gym clothes, which I haven't seen before. Damn, she has a lot of gym clothes, and they're all fashionable. She looks better in her gym clothes than I do in my everyday clothes, which gives me an idea...

"Um, you could help with my wardrobe? Show me what to coordinate, get rid of clothes you don't think would look good on me..." My voice trails off, and I'm nervous to see Brynn's reaction. When I look up, though, she's smiling, and my lips quirk up too in relief.

She hesitates for a second, but then speaks in a tone *nearly* as confident as her usual voice. "Do you want to come to my place instead? I have some clothes I was just going to give away, but you can take any that you like before I do."

I smile. "More free clothes? Sure."

We slowly begin walking toward the doors leading outside, and in my periphery I see her duck her head, her long blonde strands covering her face. It makes me falter – the Brynn I knew would never hide like that. Why is she so scared to show her face?

I push one door open, standing aside to let Brynn through. She shakes her head no, motioning for me to go first. Confusedly, I do, letting the door fall back to Brynn as she follows behind me.

The sun shines down brightly – there are no snow clouds to dull the light today. I'm not used to seeing so many people walking these streets. At night time, I might see two people, if I'm lucky. Now, there are at least fifteen people, all ages, brightly coloured in their snowsuits, passing around us.

"So, what's your address?" I ask Brynn.

She's staring down at the jumble of feet passing us, and doesn't look up when she answers. "I'll text it to you."

"Oh, okay. Is it very far?"

She looks up at me this time, and begins to say, "No, only like–" when she's cut off by a girl's high-pitched shriek.

"Aviva? Oh my god, it's Aviva!"

Brynn's face is only up long enough for me to see her eyes widen, then she ducks it down again and picks up her pace. I look over at the girl who'd yelled. She seems to be about fourteen years old, with thick curly brown hair under purple earmuffs and a mouth full of braces. And she's staring right at Brynn.

No, that can't be right. Maybe there's someone named Aviva behind Brynn? I look behind us, but there's just a pair of teenaged boys who are staring suspiciously at Brynn's back. A few people behind the girl, who is now running toward us, dig out their phones, and with flashes that reflect blindingly off the snow, begin to snap pictures.

What's going on?

Brynn begins to move even faster, walking at a speed just on the verge of breaking into a run. She's long since gotten over her aversion to being in the lead, and now I'm having difficulty keeping up. It seems like the crowd around us has doubled – tripled – this is not a normal amount of people. I don't understand. What's going *on*?

We finally reach the edge of the parking lot, and Brynn grabs my hand and breaks into a full-out run, dragging me along behind her. The crowd surges after us – why are they following us? Don't they have anything better to do?

Brynn frantically searches through her bag with her free hand before landing on a key ring with a multitude of coloured and patterned keys that I can barely hear clang together over the noise of the crowd. She clicks a button and a dark car's headlights flash as it unlocks. She runs over to the driver's side, motioning for me to get into the passenger seat, and I do, yanking the door open and just barely missing scraping the paint of the vehicle next to it. I fling myself into the seat, because there are several people following *very* close behind me, and slam the door shut to block them out.

Wait. Are these tinted windows? Why does Brynn have an expensive-looking car with tinted windows?

Brynn locks the doors just before the crowd reaches us. A couple of people actually attempt to open them, and I'm appalled and, not going to lie, scared by their audacity. How does such a normal-looking crowd, just like any I'd see on the streets of Toronto, grow in size and intensity in such a short amount of time? What caused the change? Why were they chasing us?

I've lived in Toronto my entire life, and never once have I seen something like this happen. Well actually, there was a somewhat similar incident once when a huge movie was being filmed. I was maybe seven, but the filming location was fairly close to my house, and the memories are vivid. Every time an actor would leave the set, there would be a pack of fans ready to pounce. But the actors had had bodyguards to protect them, so no one got too close. When I asked my dad about it, he'd simply said, "That's the price of fame."

Is that what happened? Did the crowd think Brynn was a celebrity? I know they couldn't have thought I was a celebrity, since I've never once been told I even look like a famous person, let alone be mistaken for one. But Brynn does have the whole 'famous' look. And she is from L.A....

What was the name that girl called? I replay the scene in my head, barely noticing as Brynn finally manages to part the crowd and guns past them, veering toward the parking lot's exit.

Aviva. The girl had said Aviva. The only famous person I can think of with that name is Aviva Jersey, the lead girl in that terrible movie my family had watched last Friday... the one I'd defended to Connor.

My hands begin to shake, but I ignore them. I need to *think*. I picture the cheerleader from the movie in my head. Blonde hair. Slim figure. But she'd looked so young...

But the movie had been released five years ago.

I sneak a peek at Brynn from the corner of my eye. She looks entirely focused on driving, and I notice that we're on a road that's evidently not used often, based on the rusty soda cans rolling along the pavement, and the faded line down the centre. Where *are* we? Brynn darts a glance into her rearview mirror, and I look behind, too.

There's another car on the road. Brynn makes a sharp left at the last second, jolting me sideways and causing my seatbelt to snap tight against my chest. The car behind us follows. Brynn speeds up, to a velocity I am definitely not comfortable with on this pothole-laden road. The car behind us matches the pace.

Okay. Great. We're being followed.

I focus back on my possible realization, leaving the driving to

Brynn. I haven't been as immersed in the celebrity world as many of the people I know, but I don't understand *how* I couldn't have seen that Brynn was – is? Maybe? – Aviva Jersey.

That's what that little niggling reminder in the back of my brain was, I belatedly realize. Once the wig came off, I knew something was familiar. I just didn't place what it was...

Because it seems so far-fetched! I mean, I guessed spy before actress! It does explain her secrets, though. Why she'd never talk about her work... why it took her a while before she mentioned her boyfriend...

Oh my god. Her boyfriend, Callan. As in, Callan Nyler, Jenny the cheerleader's love interest in that movie! I feel slightly faint, but I forcibly push it aside. I need to figure everything out.

So, her job... is acting. And her body... well, I guess the press would be the 'other things' she'd mentioned that kept her motivated to work out. All the while I'd seen images of half-naked actresses and attributed their great bodies to Photoshop, thinking that I could never have a body like that, but then here was Brynn, proving that hard work could grant those types of bodies.

Oh. My. Effin'. God. Brynn is Aviva Jersey.

4

Chapter Four

Jesus. Does this mean I'm friends with a famous person?

Are we friends, though? Do I really know Brynn – Aviva – at all? I don't know if anything she told me, aside from her boyfriend's name, was actually genuine or factual. Why wouldn't she just tell me the truth? I'd certainly told her enough embarrassing details about my life for her to hold over me as leverage, if she really thought she needed it. And I'd told her, more than once, that she could trust me.

Then I remember what she'd told me about spilling too much and being burned in the past. It makes a lot more sense now, when I think of it in terms of a celebrity lifestyle in L.A. I really need to talk to her. A good old-fashioned sit-down conversation. This time, she'd better give me good explanations, or else I really don't think we can be friends anymore. I can't deal with celebrity drama without honesty.

I look over at her again. She looks tense, though when I glance behind us again I see that we've finally lost our tail. I feel like I don't know how to talk to her anymore. I choose my words carefully, making them as neutral as possible before I speak.

"Where are we going?" My tone is carefully devoid of emotion.

Brynn swivels her head to look at me for a moment. I try to keep my face unreadable too, but I've never been a good liar, so I don't know what she sees. She turns her eyes back to the road before responding.

"Um, I guess I was heading back to my apartment... if that's okay with you?" Her voice sounds fragile.

"Okay." I stare straight forward, watching the car eat up the ground in front of us. I'm not going to start anything in here, while Brynn has control of the vehicle. I see her look over at me every so often in my peripheral vision, but I never return the glance. I refuse to lose my cool until we're somewhere safer and more private.

A few minutes later I notice that the buildings surrounding us are getting bigger, shinier, newer. It looks like we're entering the more expensive part of Toronto real estate. I suppose I shouldn't be surprised, given my recent revelation.

Brynn finally pulls into an expansive parking lot outside of a huge apartment building. She flips the key in the ignition and the engine abruptly cuts off. I hadn't realized what a difference even this quiet noise made until it's gone and the silence is complete and utterly unbreakable. We sit still for a few more minutes, before Brynn inhales sharply, says, "Okay, here we are," and pushes out her door without looking at me. I follow her lead.

She walks quickly into the entrance, giving a short nod to the man at the front desk and, indicating me, says, "She's okay." He gives me a once-over, then returns her nod. Brynn presses the button to call the elevators down to us while I look around.

It's a very nice building, and, looking around, I see security posted all over the floor. The plush carpet sinks under my feet and the desk in front of the man who's still watching us looks to be made from real, old mahogany. The silver elevator doors that we're facing have no visible fingerprints covering them and shine to the point of producing reflections rivalling those of a mirror.

The elevator finally reaches our floor and the doors slide open noiselessly, revealing a man in a black suit with a patterned tie, and a grey-haired woman in a red blouse and navy blue skirt that reaches her calves. Brynn and I step into the elevator, squishing to the side in order to leave enough room between us and the other pair. She hits the button for the thirtieth floor, and I swallow. I'd been hoping to start our conversation here, on our way up, but it looks as though I'll have to wait a bit longer.

The man and woman get off on the eighteenth floor. I look over at Brynn and see that she's still staring determinedly ahead, so I resign myself to wait until we reach her room. It seems to take at least ten minutes, although I know in reality that can't be right. When the doors swoosh silently open again, Brynn breezes out, and I freeze for a half-second before once again following her.

There are only two doors on this floor, one on either side of the elevator. Christ, these rooms must be enormous. Brynn turns to the right and, sliding out a key card much more easily from her bag than the way in which she'd brought out her car keys, opens her door. She finally looks at me and motions for me to enter first, holding the door open. I obey, but am halted in my tracks in the doorway as I get my first look at the room.

It's even larger than I'd anticipated. My palms begin to sweat. I can see a sitting room directly ahead, and parts of a kitchen through a doorless entryway in the wall to the right. At the back, there's a closed white door, which I figure must be the bedroom, if I have the proportions correct in my head. There should be a lot of space back there. And the door to the left, also closed, must be the bathroom, since it should be smaller to leave space for the room next door.

Brynn doesn't do anything while I take my time looking. She just stands behind me, still propping the front door open, letting me look. When I regain my senses, I take a few steps inside. Brynn follows, closing the door behind us. I hear the lock automatically click into place. Everything looks so clean, and I don't know what to do – should I take off my shoes? I look to Brynn and see that she's kicking off her gym sneakers and leaving them on the floor by the door, so I do the same. She walks through the sitting area toward the kitchen, and I wander over to one of the white couches. There are two in the middle of the room, sitting opposite each other with a rectangular glass table between them. I sit on it gently. Yup. That's definitely real leather.

I hear glasses clanking together in the kitchen, then Brynn's voice. "Do you want a drink? I need a drink."

A drink sounds good right about now. "Sure."

She comes back with two tumblers filled with ice and a dark golden liquid. She hands it to me as she sits across from me on the other sofa, and I catch the scent. Whiskey. We drain them at the same time, and she refills them, but I don't touch the new cup yet. I don't know how to start the discussion, or what to say. I have a million jumbled things in my head, but when I try to phrase them, they slip away completely.

Minutes pass, and I watch my ice start to melt. Finally Brynn says quietly, "Please say something. You're scaring me."

Her voice sounds so vulnerable – not at all like the confident Brynn I thought I knew. I sigh. "I'm not trying to scare you. I just don't know where to start." She nods and looks down at her glass, which she also hasn't touched since the first drink. My thoughts seem easier to put in order though, now that the silence has been broken, and I ask, "What should I call you?"

The last incremental bit of hope drains from her eyes when she hears me. I hadn't realized it had been there until it left, but I suppose she'd been willing me not to realize who she really was.

She finally takes another drink of her whiskey, although a much smaller sip than the last one. "My name is Aviva. But you can call me Brynn, if you want. It is what I introduced myself as..."

I shake my head. "I'll call you by your real name." I pause as I phrase my next sentence, swirling the remaining ice in my cup. "I didn't understand, before. When you asked if I knew who you were. But I get it now." I look up at her, staring until she meets my eyes. "Aviva. As in, Aviva Jersey." The words come out as a whisper.

She flinches, but then nods.

"And your boyfriend," I continue, "is Callan Nyler."

She bites the inside of one cheek. "Yes."

I laugh harshly. "It's like a reverse Hannah Montana."

She flinches. "Well, that show did get some things right. Not a single person recognized me when I was Brynn." Her face looks wistful, and her mouth opens and closes a few times like she's about to speak. I took my sweet time before saying anything, so I figure I can give her the same liberty. I take a sip of my watered-down whisky, and when I look up, Brynn – *Aviva* – begins.

"I never wanted to be... famous." The word looks difficult for her to say, and I'm surprised.

"Why? Doesn't everyone want their fifteen minutes of fame?"

She nods, looking past me, out a window. "Sure, fifteen minutes. But when it lasts this long... with *so many* people who know who you are..." she takes another swig of her drink. "Maybe I should say I never wanted to reach this *level* of fame."

I frown. "Well, what did you expect when you started acting?" My voice comes out with more acid than I'd intended, and she blinks, her mouth tightening. I guess that I'm angrier than I'd originally thought about her lies, now that the shock has worn off.

Her voice comes out strained. "I love *acting*. Acting is my life. It's the only thing I could ever picture myself doing for the rest of my life. It's the only thing that lets me out of my body and away from *everything*. I love stepping into other characters. I love being someone else. I love..." She chews on her lip thoughtfully. "Haven't you ever had something that you loved above everything else? Something you couldn't picture your life without?" She looks at me, genuinely curious.

I think about it. I really can't think of anything that's *that* important to me. I like school well enough, but I'll be happy to leave when I'm done... and I haven't ever stuck with one sport or hobby for more than a year or so... Slowly, I shake my head.

She nods. "Yeah. The only other people I've found who really know what I mean are other actors. It's like... okay, just keep an open mind," she warns me, looking entirely serious. "It's like a soul mate, or the theory of it, at least. When you find your soul mate, you *have* to stay with them. Everyone else you've ever dated pales in comparison, and sticking with any of the people you know you're not meant to be with, for the rest of your life – well, the thought of it makes you miserable." She's looking toward the window again, but her focus is inward. "No matter how difficult it may be for you to stay with your soul mate, you know that leaving them isn't an option." Her focus transitions back to the present and she looks at me, shrugging. "Acting is like my soul mate."

I can understand the words, and the emotions behind them, but I can't completely empathize. I really haven't felt anything similar. I can definitely sympathize, though.

"Okay, so I can see why you'd get into acting, then," I say, trailing a finger around the rim of my drink, "but then I still don't see how you weren't expecting the fame."

She shakes her head emphatically. "How many famous actors can you actually name?"

I think about it. "Uh, I don't know... like thirty, maybe?" And I'm not even interested in the celebrity lifestyle. I have no idea how many famous names celeb-stalkers could rattle off.

She nods. "Even people in the business can't name every major player, let alone every single working actor. There are *so many* actors who are getting stable jobs without the fame and fan base.

That's all I ever wanted. To play interesting characters and make enough money to get by. I never expected to actually... well, make it, I guess."

I think over her words. I suppose that does make sense. "Wasn't there a way for you to keep yourself out of the spotlight?"

She grimaces. "I try. It's harder than you'd think."

"Do you not enjoy the fame at all?"

She straightens up. "No, I mean... well, yes. Just – of course there are benefits. Free stuff, lots of money, adoring fans. But then there's also a total lack of privacy, no free time, *so* much untrue gossip, and lots of hate too. Look, don't get me wrong, I like the path my life has taken. I don't mean to complain about it. I'm not – I am *so* grateful for everything I've gotten. I just want you to understand how I got to where I am, I guess.

"As many actors there are who are here for the same reason as me – love for their jobs – there are also some who do it just for the fame or money. And that was never my intention. I'd be fine with much less publicity. I love my fans, I do, but the fame was never my first choice. But I guess you just have to deal with what life throws at you." She's become much more animated. When we started out, she'd only been giving the most basic, uncomplicated answers, but now she's sharing everything. And I'm glad. It's exactly what I need if I want to remain friends, which – despite the slowly-unravelling lies – I do.

I nod slowly. "Br- Aviva. My problem isn't with the first lie you told. My issue is that you continued it after I thought I could trust you. And I didn't really know you at all. And you *knew* that, and you let me spill all my issues to you, and you never told me a thing, and–" I can't continue if I want to remain composed. I'm getting upset, and I swipe my fingers under my eyes to check for moisture; nothing's escaped so far. When I look up, I see that Aviva's eyes are bright and shiny too.

"I'm so sorry," she says. Both of us take a minute to compose ourselves, then Aviva begins again. "When I created Brynn, I was only looking for a way to escape my life for just a little bit. I didn't think about how it would affect other people." She begins to speak more rapidly. "But you have to understand, I didn't really *lie* about anything beyond my name. Everything I told you was true."

As I think about it, I realize that she never did flat-out lie about anything besides her name – at least, as far as I can tell. She'd just refused to talk about certain topics. "What about when you said you'd been burned in the past from sharing?"

She nods, eyes wide. "That was true." She pauses. "More than once, but there was one time in particular that... that really taught me to keep my secrets secret." She takes a final sip of her whisky, draining everything but the ice cubes, which rattle around the now-empty bottom. She wipes her mouth with the back of her hand, then stares at the hand studiously as she continues. "I was sixteen, and her name was Ivy."

I watch her raptly. Her face indicates that this girl had really hurt her and, actress or not, I don't think Aviva is lying about this.

"We were best friends." She smiles shakily. "I told her everything." She looks up at me. "I don't know if you've ever seen a movie called *Death by Pom-Poms*?"

I'm swallowing more of my whiskey when she asks, and I

nearly choke, but manage to keep it to a small cough. "Um, yeah, I think I caught that one," I say, trying to remain composed. I don't tell her how recently I saw it.

She nods. "That's where I met Callan, and for a while, it was also my best-known role. And it was a slutty one, if you remember." I'm about to protest but she holds up a hand, saying, "Trust me. No one knows it better than me," so I drop it.

I've finished my whiskey now too, and Aviva silently holds up the bottle again with a questioning look, but I shake my head. I'd prefer to keep my mind clear for this conversation. Aviva places the bottle back on the table, making a *clink* sound as glass meets glass.

She looks contemplative. "I didn't start dating Callan for another two years after that movie was made, but my manager didn't want to make our relationship public. Not just because it was Callan, which would already bring people's minds back to skanky Jenny, but just no relationships in general. We didn't want me to be forever typecast as the teen slut."

Here I cut in. "How could dating a guy in your real life enforce a - *promiscuous* - image? And why would that affect your future roles?" I ask incredulously, feeling slightly uncomfortable with her blasé disregard for a character she'd personified seemingly effortlessly.

She smiles sadly, and her eyes suddenly seem much older than I know her to actually be. "Hollywood breathes in hyperboles," she says simply.

Wow. I never realized how much effort actors have to put into what the press prints about them. I never realized how much the articles could affect their futures. The celebrity lifestyle may not be as simple as I'd always assumed.

"Well, I made the mistake of telling Ivy about this great new guy I was dating." Her eyes tighten on Ivy's name, but then relax again as she refers to Callan. "She not-so-subtly leaked it to the press. I mean, considering that aside from my manager and parents, she was the only one who knew, it was pretty easy to find the culprit."

She looks down at her glass. Despite the fact that it now only contains melting ice, she takes another sip, getting only water. She grabs my cup too and takes both, along with the bottle of whiskey, back to her kitchen. I remain sitting on the sofa until she returns.

"Ivy isn't an actor, but her family is loaded. Like, she didn't need the money. So I don't really know what her motivation was…" Her gaze turns introspective. It seems like today is bringing back a lot of memories for her, and I patiently wait for her to continue. "I missed out on a huge role that I was up for when the story of Callan's and my relationship came out. Especially since it was printed with photos of us together from *Death by Pom-Poms*. It just reinforced that stupid slutty image all over again, and the role I was so close to getting was a girl-empowerment thing. They told me they just didn't think I was *right* for the movie." Her eyes close as her voice becomes sharper, and I sense she's trying to keep her emotions in check.

I almost resist the urge, but I'm very curious, so I end up asking, "What was the role you didn't get?"

When she opens her eyes again, she looks calmer. "Laine, in *Untimely Events*."

I feel my eyes widen, but I try to keep my face relatively neutral. "Oh. Yeah, I can see why you'd be upset about not getting that."

Untimely Events was one of the movies that even I, as a person who rarely goes to movie theatres, saw on the big screen. It was on every magazine's countdown 'til it's out list, and I heard that it made a huge profit in the first week from the box office.

"Yeah. It took me another *year* of keeping my image clean and out of the public eye as much as I could until I got another decent booking."

I frown. "Didn't you have a lot of work three years ago? I swear I'd heard of you by then..."

She takes a quick breath. "It wasn't the success of *Untimely Events* that drew me to the project in the first place. I mean, it was already destined to be a hit, but what really got me interested was the character of Laine. She was a badass female, and like I said, the movie had a lot of empowering messages. When I talk about good roles, I mean roles that make an impact on the viewers, or leave them really feeling something. I don't care what – anger, sorrow, joy – as long as they feel *something*. Yes, I got roles, and some of them did well, but none really measured up to Laine. There aren't usually a lot of strong female lead roles up for grabs.

"But Ivy... I tried to cut her out of my life. I knew she wasn't good for me. But she had a hold over me." She smirks over 'hold', but there's no humour in her eyes. "Somehow, I just couldn't shake her off." Her voice lowers, and her next sentence is barely audible. "She was toxic."

Aviva's eyes are deepening in intensity, and I know I need to do something to lighten the mood. "Poison Ivy," I joke feebly, but it does the trick. Her eyes focus back on the present, and this time her smirk is accompanied by a spark in her eyes. Although I'm glad she seems to have shaken off Ivy for now, I can tell that there's more to the story. This wasn't Ivy's only betrayal. But I don't think Aviva is going to tell me any more about her right now, and I don't want to force her down that dark memory lane.

When she speaks again, her tone is much brighter than just a moment ago. "Ivy wasn't the first one to betray me, or the last, but she was the one who instilled trust issues into me." She smiles at me. "So, Naya, I hope you can take my incredibly long story as an apology, and reasoning for why I didn't tell you who I really was."

I smile back at her automatically. As I mentally replay her words though, I can imagine how tough it would have been to be betrayed by your best friend, and just how difficult it must be for her now, living with constant worry of having your faith in someone broken. My smile becomes more genuine as I'm flooded with a rush of compassion. Lord, I've been on an emotional rollercoaster today.

"I understand," I say, and I think I really do. She looks immensely relieved, and I almost laugh at the strength of the expression, but hold it back. "I hope you know that you can trust me now, though." I hold up two fingers in a traditional Scout's honour pose. "I swear I'll keep your secrets."

She laughs quietly at the gesture, but then her face turns serious. "I'll try." She imitates my posture, leaning forward from the couch, Scout's honour and all. "I promise." She breaks into a smile.

About this time I realize that I've taken much longer than a regular visit to the gym, and my family is probably wondering where I am. I dig my phone out of my pocket. I've been so immersed in Aviva's story that I didn't even register when it vibrated to indicate my two new text messages and one missed call. I quickly scan them before texting my mom back that I'm alive and well, and on my way home.

I stand and stretch. As comfortable as that couch was, stay in any position for long enough and you'll get stiff. "I have to go," I inform Aviva, stowing my phone back in my pocket. "But... thank you."

She looks surprised. "For what?"

"For explaining everything. For choosing to trust me."

The sides of her lips edge up. "Good bye, Naya." She stands too and strides over to the door, opening it for me.

I pause in the doorway. "Good bye, Aviva." It feels so strange to call her that after knowing her as Brynn for this long, and the name feels foreign on my lips. She smiles though, and I think she's relieved to have someone who knows her. She may be as grateful for my friendship here in Toronto as I am for hers after my past few lonely months.

When I step out of the elevator and exit through the front doors, I realize that my car is still at the gym, and I couldn't drive it anyway, due to our impromptu drinking therapy session. I'm not worried that anything will happen to it overnight, but now I have to call a taxi, which will cost money. Well, at least I have my cell phone. I use one of my very helpful apps to call and pay for a drive, and only have to stand outside for three minutes before it picks me up.

I have a lot to contemplate on the drive home, so I'm happy that the cabbie doesn't appear interested in conversing with me. The only thing I say is a thank you when I'm dropped off outside of my house, and I don't really notice when the car leaves – I just look behind me when I get to my front door and it's gone.

My silence continues through dinner with my family. I'm so busy wondering over all of today's revelations that I don't hear my mom when she asks me a question. I only become aware of my surroundings again when I register a drop in noise level and look up to see both my parents and my brother staring at me.

"What?" I ask, eyebrows raised. Mom looks a bit concerned, and Dad's gaze is simple and direct, but Connor's eyes are dancing like he thinks I'm about to get in trouble. "Sorry," I tack on, hoping to avoid a reprimand, "I was distracted."

"Yes, we noticed," Mom says dryly. "That's what I was asking about. Why are you so quiet tonight?"

Oh. I hadn't actually thought about what to say to my family. Considering Aviva only outed her true identity by necessity, and remembering my promise to keep her secrets, I don't think she'd appreciate it if I told everybody that my gym buddy Brynn is actually the famous actress Aviva Jersey. *Quick, Naya – think.*

I already told them about Brynn. And it will be easier to remember – and easier to make any lies believable – if I stick close to the truth. I nervously lick my lips. "Brynn and I had a disagreement today." I'm already scared that I'll confuse *Brynn* and *Aviva* and trip myself up. "Nothing big. We got over it."

Connor raises his eyebrows. "So I guess that means you still don't have a picture of her for me to see?"

My mother ignores him and says to me, "Is everything okay between you two now?"

I nod. "Yup. Fine. Don't worry."

After a careful examination of my face – (I really need to practice my expressions in a mirror so I know what I'm showing people) – she turns back to Connor. "Why can't you settle on a nice girl your own age?" she asks, mirroring my thoughts.

Now it's Connor's turn to ignore my mother. "Does your argument mean I can't meet her?"

I snort. "Were you planning on coming to the gym with me sometime?"

He looks at me condescendingly. "Going to the gym with my sister wouldn't exactly help my social image. I just want to meet Brynn, if she's as hot as you said. Bring her here instead."

I shake my head, nearly at a loss for words. Finally I sputter, "She has a boyfriend." I compose myself again. "And you give yourself too much credit, Connor. She's way out of your league."

He rolls his eyes. "That's hard to believe." I actually can't tell if he's joking or not.

"Right. Well." I turn to my father. "Sell many cars today, Dad?" He immediately launches into the makes and models of each car that he sold and some of the ones he didn't. Cars are the one thing he could talk about for hours, and it's very useful when I'm in dire need of a topic change or distraction.

I smile and nod along with impeccable timing learned over the years, but my mind is churning. Talking about Brynn has reminded me of the plans we'd made to go over to her apartment and view the clothes she was going to give away tomorrow. The plans had been decided in the gym, before I found out that

Brynn was Aviva. I don't know how my discovery will change the relationship between us. We seemed to leave things off on an okay note, but I don't know if that will extend past gym sessions.

We finish dinner and I escape to my room, lured by the freedom to just stay silent and contemplate as well as hooked by the need to do homework that I neglected when I went to the gym early. My responsible side wins over and files away thoughts of Aviva in the meantime, replacing them with possible essay theses.

By the time I finish writing it's nearly midnight and I think I may be developing Carpal Tunnel in my wrists from pounding away at my laptop keyboard for such an extended, concentrated stretch of time. At least I have tomorrow to sleep in again. I go through my nighttime routine, my mind finally free to wander again. Should I text Aviva to see if we're still on for tomorrow? Should I just go? Or not go? I mean, she never gave me her actual address... I saw where the building was located, but that doesn't mean I could find it again, necessarily... not to mention that I'd need a ride since I left my car at the gym.

When I reach my room again, however, my worries are assuaged by a notification that I have a text message from Brynn. Before reading it, I click on her contact information and change the name from Brynn to Aviva Jersey. Hopefully that will help me to remember which name to use. I delete 'Jersey' before I save the contact though. Our friendship is still under wraps – as far as anyone knows, the only person I know from L.A. is Brynn, a regular girl with a regular job – so it might seem just a *bit* suspicious if I had a celebrity's phone number.

I click on the text. *Hey. You still wanna come over tmo?*

Relief floods through me, alongside surprise. Even though I'd finally mentally established that Brynn wanted to be friends with me, it seemed like an entirely different affair with Aviva, because she's a celebrity. I really need to equate the two in my head. They're the same person; Brynn *is* Aviva. Brynn was always a celebrity, even if I didn't know it.

Which then gets me analysing why celebrities seem to be higher on the social scale than normal people. What is it that draws so much attention to famous people and makes virtual strangers want to be their friends? Money, sure, but it's not just that. Beauty, too, since don't they have stylists and makeup artists around them twenty-four-seven? Or maybe it's just that we're exposed to their image so much on television or in magazines, which seem so unattainable to regular people, that they then appear larger-than-life?

Whatever it is, I know that if I want us to be on an even playing field in our friendship, I need to view Aviva like anyone else. It's ridiculous that, even unconsciously, I was beginning to see her as better than me. Fame doesn't make a person better – what they do with their life establishes that.

I was so overwhelmed by emotion earlier that I never really had the chance to process what being friends with a celebrity would mean for me. I refuse to allow another person's job to make me feel inferior. I text Aviva back, struggling to retain my usual relaxed tone.

Yeah sure! Um I may need a ride tho lol...

She responds, offering to drive me. I give her my address, and then we revert to our before-bedtime small-talk that I'm accustomed to. It's odd, seeing the words and mentally hearing how

Brynn would say it, but knowing that I'm texting Aviva. It does begin to take less effort, though, to be myself, as I see that Aviva *is* the Brynn I knew. Nothing in her messages really surprises me or strikes me as different. Maybe this friendship doesn't have to be complicated. Maybe, now that Aviva's big secret has been aired, we can keep our comfortable friendship. I hope so.

The next morning my mind feels much clearer. I had some very strange dreams last night, involving giant chameleons and a mansion full of designer clothing, but I forget about them as the morning wears on. I eat breakfast in silence. I woke up relatively early, considering that I fell asleep close to one a.m., so Connor's still asleep. The quiet combined with the sun streaming in through the window calms me, or maybe my conversation with Aviva last night just helped to reaffirm our friendship in my head. Whichever it was, I don't falter before sending a quick text to Aviva telling her that I'm awake and she can come over whenever she's ready.

She gets here by ten a.m., ringing the doorbell to announce her arrival. Connor still doesn't stir. I let her in, putting down the book I'd been reading on the kitchen table.

She's wearing the wig again and I don't know what to call her, so I avoid saying either name. As she looks around the house, I suddenly wonder if I should be worried about her appraisal – our house isn't huge or glamourous, as I'm sure she's used to – but for whatever reason, the concern doesn't come.

"Nice place," she comments, and I smile. See? Nothing to worry about.

"I've just got to grab my purse," I tell her. "You can wait here."

She nods and takes a seat at the kitchen table, shrugging off her coat. She picks up the book I'd been reading and flips through it as I run up to my room, passing Connor's on the way. I sneak a peek in and see him, sprawled on his bed, face buried in the pillow, and think he'll be disappointed when he hears that Brynn came by and he didn't get to see her. I can only imagine what he'd say if he found out that Aviva Jersey was here and he was passed out in a very unbecoming position. I smirk.

When I get back downstairs, Brynn – Aviva – *she* is still sitting at the table, studiously concentrating on a paragraph somewhere midway through the novel.

"Ready to go?" I ask, and her head jerks up, making me laugh at her intense focus on the book.

She smiles and stands up, putting her jacket back on. She leads me outside to her car and we drive, music blasting from the radio and both of us singing along, to her apartment building.

When we go inside, we're both much less tense than we were yesterday. She's animatedly telling me a story and while keeping my main focus on her, I also notice the same man behind the front desk watching us. He peruses us both, studying me closely before recognition flickers over his face, before focusing elsewhere, and I realize that he must know that Brynn is Aviva. She must have had to tell somebody about her double identity, considering she's staying here for an indefinite amount of time, for safety concerns. He saw me walking in with Aviva yesterday and Brynn today, and didn't seem surprised today. I wonder exactly how many people actually know of her alter ego? Of course I hadn't expected to be the only one, but it still made me feel somewhat... special. Aviva doesn't trust many people, and Brynn was a huge secret to spill, considering she's Aviva's only way to get some anonymity.

When we step through the shining elevator doors now, the lift is empty. It gives me a chance to voice my query.

"How many people know that you are also Brynn?" Even though we're the only two in the rising cube, my voice is low – almost a whisper.

She doesn't hesitate. "Including you, six."

My eyebrows shoot up. I don't know if that number is higher or lower than I'd been expecting. "Six?"

She nods. "My parents, my boyfriend, the security at home and here, and you."

Wow. When I take into consideration who the other five are, I decide that the number definitely seems lower than I'd expected. I'd thought there would be maybe one or two other friends whom Aviva would have told. The feeling that I'm special returns, and with it, some worry. I hope that I can live up to the trust that Aviva has been somewhat forced to place in me.

I smile at her, and she returns it. "You know, Brynn is who I think I'd be if I was never famous. Whether because I never caught the acting bug," she says wryly, "or if I just never reached the level of success that I have, so far. I guess I'll never know for sure. I sometimes feel like I'm living in two separate timelines, though." She laughs, but the comment gives me pause. It's true; she'll never know with any certainty who she would have been if she didn't have to hide her true identity every time she steps outside. How her confidence, or her occupation, or even her relationships would have been affected. She could have been an entirely different person. We stand side-by-side in companionable silence while I contemplate this for the remainder of the ride up.

The elevator dings at the fiftieth floor and I'm forced to snap out of my deep thoughts. We step out and I stride up to Aviva's door confidently, and when she unlocks it, I don't hesitate this time when stepping through, even though I'm struck again by the enormity and grandeur of the space.

She leads me to the door against the back wall, which I'd expected to hold the bedroom yesterday. As she opens it, I can see I was correct. It's a huge, blindingly white room; smooth white ceiling and walls, a large modern white plastic chair in the corner that looks more for show than comfort, plush white comforter over a queen-sized bed with fluffy white pillows, and a white lamp on top of a white bedside stand. I have to blink twice just in order to separate each object from the wall behind them, the shades of white are all so similar. The only break in the brightness is a flat black television mounted directly across from the bed. Aviva ignores all this, though, instead leading me to another door – white, no surprise – which she slides open smoothly.

This room explodes with colour, providing a shocking contrast to the bedroom. I'd been expecting a closet – which, I suppose this is supposed to be – but this room is not the size of any regular old closet. It's at least the size of my bedroom, if not slightly larger, and full of racks upon racks of clothing and accessories. They seem to be categorized by event they were designed for, rather than type of clothes, so I see casual dresses alongside T-shirts and shorts, then on the other side of the room, dresses that could be worn to a prom or fancy wedding placed with studded heels and glittering jewellery. I only realize I'm gaping, mouth hanging open, when Aviva bursts out laughing. I quickly shut it with an audible *clack* of my teeth, and glower at Aviva until she reins in her giggles.

She clears her throat. "Right. Well, as you can see, I have a lot of clothes–" She has to pause to control herself again as her words begin to dissolve into more laughter. I stand, staring at her and ineffectually tapping my foot against the floor, since I took my shoes off at the front door.

She shoves me playfully, throwing me off balance and successfully stopping my tapping sock. "Oh, come on. If you'd seen your face, you'd be dying too."

I roll my eyes, but the mental image of what I must have looked like even brings me to chuckle a bit. "Yeah, okay. Just a quick question: if you were going to show me the clothes you're giving away when I still thought you were Brynn, how were you going to explain this?" I gesture to encompass the room.

She looks around. "Uh yeah, hadn't really thought that far ahead. I guess bring the clothes I'm giving away into my bedroom?"

And let me wonder about the closed door. Well, I suppose it would have posed fewer questions than if she'd shown me this enormous room when I'd still thought she was just a regular L.A. girl.

"So which clothes are the ones you're planning on giving away?" My eyes scan the room, bouncing over a dozen different designer labels.

The racks are all on wheels, and she brings two forward. "These."

Each rack is stuffed full of clothes that look barely worn, if they were ever even tried on. At first I don't grasp her meaning and think she's about to just pick a few pieces off of the racks, but when she doesn't I realize that she's giving away *everything* on the two racks.

Some air huffs out of my lungs unintentionally. "That's a *lot* that you're getting rid of."

She shrugs. "Well, I'm never going to wear it, so I figure someone should."

"But... everything is gorgeous. Why *wouldn't* you wear it?"

She sighs, tracing her fingers over the clothing hangers. "I get a lot of free stuff, and some of that is clothing. I don't usually get to choose what the clothes are that I get, either, so sometimes it's stuff that doesn't fit, or that I don't necessarily like, or that are similar to other things I already own... or that I wouldn't have anyplace to wear it to." She smirks. "I get to wear the most variety when I'm playing a character. In everyday life, I only get to wear something casual, or formal, for red carpets. I mean, I guess I could find time to go clubbing or something, but I'm usually dead on my feet by like 9 p.m. when I'm working," she explains with a self-conscious smile.

I turn away from Aviva and begin a slow circle around the racks. "I don't even know where to start," I mutter. It's like when we went shopping all over again.

And just like when we were shopping, Aviva studies the pieces and selects several that she thrusts toward me. "Try these," she says. "Bathroom's back through the living room, on the right."

I obediently follow her directions and try on piece after beautiful piece of clothing. There are a few that don't fit *just* right, or that I can't picture actually wearing outside of this room. Those I push off to the side, but the rest of the outfits are perfect. That leaves me with two dresses, three tops, a pair of shorts, and two jeans. I don't even consider taking them all – there's no way I can leave with that much, for free – so I decide to take them out to show Aviva and get her advice on which to choose.

She's flipping through a magazine on the same white couch she'd sat on yesterday, but she looks up when I exit the bathroom. "Do you like them?"

I hold up the few rejects. "These are nos." I hold up the ones I'd loved in my other hand. "But these are all good. I need your help narrowing it down."

She puts the magazine down on the glass table and stands, walking toward me. "Why do you need to narrow it down?"

I cough. "Because there are a lot? I can't take that much."

Aviva frowns. "Naya. I told you, I'm never going to wear any of them. I'm giving them away anyway, so take as many as you want."

"But–"

She grabs the ones I didn't like and places the index finger of her other hand against my lips. "Nope. If you like them, you're taking them. Besides, I have even more in L.A. to give away. It's not like you're making much of a dent, so don't worry." She turns and walks away confidently.

Well. Not very easy to argue with that. And really, why should I? Aviva's right – I have no reason to feel guilty. She can clearly afford to give these clothes away, and if she has so many other items to give anyway, why not take the ones I like?

Aviva returns with several plastic shopping bags and takes

the clothes from my hand one at a time, removing them from their hangers and folding them neatly before dropping them into a bag. When that's done, she places them at the front door.

"Thank you," I say to her.

She gives me a lopsided smile. "You're welcome." We sit back in the same positions on the white leather couches as yesterday, but we're both clearly more relaxed today. Aviva opens her mouth to say something, but then her phone begins to ring shrilly. She rolls her eyes playfully as she pulls it out and glances at the caller ID before answering with a "Hey, babe."

I raise my eyebrows at her. *Callan*, she mouths. Ah, her also-famous boyfriend. I wonder what I should do – I don't know if she'd want me to overhear her conversation with her boyfriend – so I start to stand in order to wander around, maybe flip on the TV, but Aviva waves a hand at me to sit down, shaking her head.

"Sorry, Callan, but I can't talk right now. Naya's over."

She says my name in a tone that indicates she may have mentioned me to Callan before. I wonder when she would have? Back when I only knew Brynn? Or last night, after she'd been outed as Aviva Jersey?

"I'll call you back." She pauses, and I'm happily surprised by what she's doing. She's prioritizing our time together over her phone call to her boyfriend, something that no other friend has ever done when I was there, and something I definitely never did when I was dating Asher. "Um, half an hour?" She raises an eyebrow at me, and I nod in confirmation. "Okay, talk then. Bye." She smiles as she hits the button to end the call, and taps a few other notifications on her phone before she looks up at me excitedly. "Oh! That reminds me! Social media."

Right. Brynn didn't have social media – even after our first phone call, when we'd discussed Instagram, she hadn't created an account – but Aviva almost certainly does. I hadn't thought to look her up yesterday, but now I wonder why I didn't.

She continues tapping on her phone. "Okay. What's your Twitter handle?"

We end up following each other on Twitter and Instagram, and adding each other on Snapchat. Facebook is the only one where we can't make mutual contact, although I do give her fan page a like, giggling as I show her.

It's fun and uncomplicated; exactly what I needed. Nothing was awkward, as I'd worried it would be. Instead, it seems like getting Aviva's true identity out into the air has made our friendship even easier, since she can really be herself and I don't have to wonder about all her secrets.

After we finish with social media and have flipped through the magazine on the table, I see Aviva surreptitiously checking her phone for the time and remember the call she'd promised to make to her boyfriend. I stand. "Time for me to go."

She immediately puts her phone back down, saying, "You don't have to go yet. Callan can wait–"

I cut her off. "Seriously, it's okay. I have enough homework to do when I get back, anyway."

She nods. "Okay."

She's already agreed to drive me to the gym so I can pick up my car from the parking lot. I grab my bags full of new clothing on the way out, thanking her again, and she brushes it off with a small smile. Our carefree air lasts all the way until the end of the drive, when she parks in the gym lot and stops me from leaving.

Her face is still open, but a lot more serious. "I know that yesterday we left things off assuming that we'd still be friends – which I want, I do – but I need to know if *you* still want to be friends. Because I did lie to you, which I'm sorry about, but still. And... you may not have experienced it yet, but fame comes with a lot of drama, and I'd understand if you don't want to get caught up in it all."

Her question surprises me. I hadn't realized that she'd been feeling any of the same uncertainty that I'd been feeling yesterday, and now I wonder why I *didn't* realize. If we were in the same situation but her true identity wasn't a famous actress, would I have understood that she had doubts too? Maybe, maybe not. Maybe since she is an actress, she's just really good at hiding her deeper emotions. Or maybe my image of her as a famous person clouded my view so that all I saw was what I was expecting to see: confidence. I didn't think a celebrity would be worried about whether another person wanted to be friends or not, so I didn't see it. Either way, I know what my answer is.

"Yes, Aviva. I forgave you yesterday for your lie. And whatever drama there is, I'm sure I can handle it." I tentatively smile, and she breaks into a relieved grin in return.

"Okay. Cool."

I laugh and imitate her. "Cool." Then I open the car door. She pushes me out, both of us laughing, and I find my own car – the only other one in the parking lot – and wave good bye to her as she pulls away.

My car is frigid, and I spend a solid five minutes running the engine just to warm up the interior before I decide I can move my fingers enough to drive safely. I drive home, clothing bags in the passenger seat, happy.

Whatever preconceived notions I may have had of celebrity are fading away. It was initially hard to understand that Brynn was Aviva Jersey, but now, one day later, it's easier to accept. I'd been raised in a world mostly separated from all possible interaction with fame, so the only contact I'd had with that lifestyle was through magazines and online articles, which had led me to believe that nearly all celebrities are party-hungry, promiscuous, drug-and-alcohol-consuming rebels. Somehow I don't think that Aviva is the only famous person who doesn't fit that label. I thought I understood before that magazines exaggerate everything, but the information they provided still sank into my subconscious.

At least I know now. As the stereotype fades away, so does most of my awe at the celebrity lifestyle. I think that it will be easier for me in the future now, to see that fame is just a label that society places on people. But even if a person is famous, they're still just a regular person. I'd been referring to Brynn as a 'regular' L.A. girl, but Aviva is 'regular' too; just maybe a bit more well-known. And regular isn't a bad thing to be.

5

Chapter Five

Somehow, even though I'd used it as my excuse to go home, I never managed to complete any of my schoolwork. My brain was too wrapped up in thoughts of celebrity and disguises and wondering how society has put so much pressure on famous people that some feel the need to put on a wig just to experience regular life. I knew that I had a lot of schoolwork left for the end of the weekend, but every time I tried to write so much as a word, my mind drifted elsewhere and then I couldn't remember why I'd been writing that word in the first place.

When I wake up Monday morning it's with the realization that my week is going to suck, all because I was too distracted to do homework when I actually had some spare time. The only highlight is that I get to wear some of my new clothes from Aviva today, so at least I know I'll look good. The outfit is so different from those that I usually wear that I do a double take when I catch a glimpse of myself in the mirror.

I'm wearing one of the two dresses I'd picked. This one is periwinkle blue, with iridescent straps criss-crossed all down the bodice until the waist, where the straps condense into two braids that continue down either side of the skirt. It hits just below the knees, and is somehow reminiscent of both the '20s and '80s, and yet is still totally modern. I love it.

I tie my hair up into a messy bun and drive to school. Maybe a dress wasn't the best outfit to choose for March, but I can suffer for the sake of fashion.

I get several compliments on the dress, so it was definitely worth it. I even see Asher studying me more carefully at newspaper editing, and realize that I don't feel much at all over it. Definitely a good sign.

Unfortunately, my preoccupation and contemplation yesterday was definitely *not* worth it. I have to spend all my free time working on essays and projects, because university takes no breaks. I'm just happy midterms happened before I met Aviva, because even if I can complete a reading or writing assignment, I still can't focus well enough to study and remember test material. I cross my fingers that my distractions will pass before final exams next month.

I get a text from Aviva that night, and when I look at the time, I realize that I'm too late to go to the gym. The text is asking if I'm coming to work out tonight. I reply with the news of my doom.

Hey. SO MUCH HW. Won't be able to go to gym nxt few days, srry.
She responds with a simple, *It's ok.*

I click my phone off and return to my work.

Tuesday passes in much the same way, but by now I'm seriously beating myself up, because I'd completely forgotten that in addition to the work that I have to hand in, I also have readings to catch up on. I don't hear anything from Aviva, and don't have enough time to text her so much as an apology for being a bad gym buddy.

Wednesday comes, and it looks as though the end of my work sentence is finally in sight. At eleven p.m. that night, I sit back in relief, having emailed in my final assignment and finished my final torturous Latin reading. Unfortunately, I've also finished a bag of chips. I sigh. At least I can go to the gym tomorrow to start to work it off.

That's when I realize that I haven't spoken to Aviva since the weekend, and haven't texted since Monday. I was drowning in too much schoolwork to notice before, but now I think that it's kind of odd. Even on days when we weren't at the gym or together elsewhere, we communicated somehow.

Oh well. She's probably been as busy as I've been, with her job. Which reminds me that I still don't know what exactly she's here in Toronto for – is she filming a new movie or something?

I vow to ask her tomorrow, then fall into bed, exhausted.

The next morning, when I actually have a chance to catch up on social media, I see that I've gained several new followers on Twitter and Instagram, and they're all fan accounts for Aviva. I shake my head in wonderment at the amount of attention these accounts must pay to Aviva's every move in order to catch every time she follows a new person.

The day passes faster than usual, now that I'm more relaxed, knowing that I no longer have hours of additional work after classes to anticipate. There are some new readings assigned, but that's to be expected.

I arrive at the gym ahead of Aviva tonight, excited to be somewhere other than my house or my classes. I start my workout, planning to go a bit longer than usual in order to make up for my sedentary last few days and the junk I ate while I worked.

Except that Aviva doesn't show up. Even as I'm cooling down after my extra-long session, she's still not here. Maybe she came earlier in the day? Or maybe she's taking a day off? But then why wouldn't she let me know? Well, I didn't tell her I'd be here today... maybe I should have.

Whatever. She probably has a bunch of relevant, time-consuming things to do for her job. Or maybe when I was busy with my homework, she found someone else to hang out with. The unbidden thought puts a curl of fear into my stomach, but at the same time, I feel almost as though I expected it. Should I text her? No. I don't want to bother her, in case she's doing something important. Maybe she'll come tomorrow.

I leave the gym feeling slightly dejected.

The next morning, I wake up in a much better state of mind. It's a Friday, which indicates the week is ending, and I also got eight hours of sleep last night – a first, for this week.

I now realize how stupid I'd been last night. Aviva is my

friend; she wouldn't ditch me because I had a schoolwork overload for a few days. Would she?

I send her a text before I lose my nerve.

Hey, r u goin to the gym tn?

Her response arrives on my way out the front door. *Yes.*

Okay, good, so that's settled. I'll see her today, and I can complain about all my homework and she can tell me more about her job. Everything will be normal again.

Except that it's not. When I arrive at the gym that night, Aviva is already there, dressed as Brynn, so at first I think that we're back to our familiar rhythm. Except that every time I attempt to start a conversation, her answers are brusque and to-the-point. We make small talk, but Aviva is not acting like herself. She is usually the one to start conversations, and at points where I may have difficulty filling the silence, she's always the one to elaborate on a point or bring up a new one. And our topics are almost always in-depth or analytical or at the very least, fun. This polite small talk is anything but *fun*.

The majority of the time spent working out today is silent, and I don't know how she's interpreting it, but on my end it feels awkward. I don't know what to do about this, and I don't really know what happened to incite this change. Of course I figure it had something to do with my absences from the gym this week, but what in particular is causing this cool shoulder? Did something happen to her that I don't know about? I really wish I could get a good look into Aviva's mind, but I've never been good at reading her.

When we've finished our cooldowns and are packing up to go, I know that I have to attempt something in order to negate the possibility of future sessions as uncomfortable as this one has been. Maybe if we have some more time to talk, where neither of us are distracted by exercise, we can return to our usual easy banter. With that thought in mind, I stop Aviva before she leaves and ask, "Hey, do you want to come over to my place tomorrow?"

It's like my words lift a huge weight off of her shoulders. I can actually see her straighten slightly, rolling her shoulders back and assuming the confident position that she'd had every other day I'd known her but today. She smiles, and this time it's a real smile, not one of the fakely bright ones she'd been shooting toward me earlier. "I'd like that," she says, releasing a long breath.

I smile in return, happy to have broken through her shield but still unsure as to what had forced her to put it up in the first place. "Okay, great! I guess I'll see you tomorrow, then."

I begin to head toward the exit, but stop when Aviva loosely grabs my arm. She looks around warily, though there's no one here but the two of us, as usual. She still looks like the girl I know, not the stranger from earlier, but the smile has been replaced by a more serious expression as she asks, "Have you told anyone? That I'm... me?"

I shake my head. Is this what had been bothering her? Had she been angry over a false assumption that I'd spill her true identity to the first person I encountered? I suppose it would explain her earlier attitude, though not the breakthrough at my invitation. Oh well. Maybe tomorrow she'll be more open with me.

She's still looking at me expectantly, so I add a verbal answer to my initial headshake. "No, Aviva. I can keep a secret." I mean to say it earnestly, but it comes out with more irritation than I'd intended. I've told her multiple times that she can trust me with her secrets. I hope that she can begin to believe me soon. It's been about three weeks since we first met, and I haven't dropped a single detail that she's entrusted to me. I hope it doesn't take another three weeks for her to see that I'm serious about secret-keeping.

She nods slowly, looking off to the side. She directs her gaze back to me to say, "See you tomorrow," then takes off. I'm left alone in the gym, confused by the whirlwind of emotions brought on in such a short amount of time.

6

Chapter Six

I'm not sure what to expect Saturday morning. I don't know if Aviva will come over as herself or as Brynn, and what the implications would be either way, since my whole family is home today and will undoubtedly see her. I also don't know if she'll retain the cool demeanor from earlier yesterday, or show the more open side that started to peek out again towards the end of the workout.

I'm in my room, trying to focus on my assigned readings, when I hear the doorbell ring and Mom call out, "Naya! Your friend is here."

I trip over my feet rushing downstairs but right myself before it becomes embarrassingly noticeable. Standing in the front foyer is Brynn. Okay. That should make things less complicated. I quickly make the introductions, making sure that I don't falter when I state Brynn's name, even as the voices in my head shout *Aviva!* and dare me to trip up.

I lead Aviva up to my room and close the door behind up, hoping to keep some semblance of privacy in the busy house. Downstairs, I can hear pots and pans clattering and figure Mom is starting on lunch. I know that Dad's in the garage, doing some repair work on his car. That means the only variable unaccounted for is Connor, but as long as he's not in my room, I don't really care what he's getting up to.

I sit back at my desk but clear away my textbooks, since there's no way I'll get any more reading done right now. I gesture for Aviva to sit on my bed, and she happily flounces onto it. We start off with small talk, but I can already tell that Aviva is back to herself. Her facial expressions are varied and more exaggerated, her voice ranges tones, and her posture is relaxed. I dive straight into my complaints about my hellish week, and she listens as I list off every last assignment and reading I'd had to complete with a slight frown on her face.

She pauses once I finish, and the frown is deeper. I'd originally thought the frown was one of concern for me after my homework overload, but now I realize that it pertains to whatever it is she's about to say.

"What?" I ask.

She takes a deep breath. "I didn't think... I thought the homework was an excuse. I thought that you might not have wanted to be friends anymore."

The concept is so unexpected and unexplored on my end that now I'm the one frowning. It eases as her explanation puts the questions of her coolness and sudden personality switch yesterday into place. Then I'm giggling, and I don't know why, and I can't really control it, but then Aviva joins in and I don't have to worry about it anymore. We laugh together and I can feel tension seeping out of my body.

When enough humour drains out of my body for me to maintain a straight face, I say, "I think we've both been overthinking our sides of this relationship."

For whatever reason, this makes her laugh again, albeit somewhat more drily than before. At my questioning look, she explains, "I'm not used to relationships being this uncomplicated. There's always some type of drama in L.A."

I raise my eyebrows in feigned shock. "What? The City of Angels' residents aren't all angelic?"

She smirks. "'Fraid not."

"Oh, do tell all."

And our conversation dissolves into a very enjoyable gossip discussion. She mentions several names, although only one – Sierra – does she call her friend. Some of the situations she mentions are serious, though most are simply funny. As she trails off at the end of yet another wild tale, a sad smile remains on her lips.

"Do you miss L.A.?" I ask impulsively.

She adjusts her wig. "Some things I miss. Others, not so much."

I wonder what she prefers about Toronto, then remember the inquiry held in the back of my mind for the past couple of days. "What are you doing in Toronto, anyway?"

She grins at me impishly. "Work."

Just as aggravation is about to overpower me, I register the glint in her eye and realize she's joking. Not about the subject matter, but about her secrets. I smile, crossing my legs and raising my eyebrows and wait until she continues.

"It's a top-secret project," she teases.

I bite my lip and pretend to look irritated. "Details, please." It feels so freeing to ask for more information and know that she'll actually give it to me, now that I'm in on her big secret.

She smiles excitedly. "Okay. I'm technically legally bound not to give anything about the plot away – or the project in general, actually – but as long as you promise not to say anything..." she trails off, looking at me expectantly.

This sounds interesting. I make an X over my heart, giggling as I say, "Cross my heart and hope to die."

That seems to be good enough for her. Or maybe she's just been bottling everything up so much that when the opportunity arises, the information bubbles out like it's been brimming over for weeks.

"Have you ever heard of Hayden Landen?" she asks. The name sounds familiar, and I realize that I saw the name in the same place as I'd seen Aviva's, almost a month ago: the school newspaper.

"She's a director, right?"

Aviva nods, wide-eyed, reminding me of a bobblehead. I've never seen her this excited about something. "Yes! She's relatively new to the Hollywood scene, but her work is phenomenal, and she always has strong female leads."

That does sound like something to be happy about. "And you're working with her?"

Her eyes dart around my room like she expects people to be

spying on us before she grins again and says, "Remember, secret. But yes! We're still in pre-production, but I'm so excited for this role."

"Why are you so excited for this one? What's different? Just the director?"

She tilts her head, considering. "Not just the director. I am excited for that, definitely, because there aren't many female directors, and to work with such a talented one will be awesome. But also the character! She's strong and badass and doesn't have to rely on men to solve the problem for her." She leans in closer to me and whispers, "This is the type of role I love to find. The type that I wait and wait for. A *good* role."

I recall what she'd said before, after I'd first realized Brynn was Aviva Jersey. After her ex-friend Ivy had leaked her relationship with Callan to the press, she hadn't gotten any *good* roles for a while. It sounds like she's gotten past that now. As I look at Aviva now, beaming at me, I realize just how much she loves her job. She'd attempted to describe it before, but it's one thing to hear about it and another entirely to see it. I smile back at her.

"So it's filming in Toronto?"

She nods. "Yeah, although we're not there yet. Still have a lot of stuff to take care of." She leans back on my bed. "I really like being attached to a project this early, and to be part of pre-production, and casting."

I grimace. "Sounds like a lot of work to me. But hey, if you enjoy it..."

She stares up at my ceiling blissfully. "I do."

I wrack my brain for other aspects of a movie actors are expected to fulfil. "So will you have to do a lot of promotion, too?"

She nods. "A lot of it will be based in Toronto, since we're trying to get Canada excited that this huge movie will be filming in your quaint little country." She winks at me, and I laugh. She smirks, then says, "No really, I love Toronto. I haven't been here a lot though, other than promo for other movies, or awards shows. I'm looking forward to being here for a while. Although I do hate the cold," she confesses.

I snort. "Don't we all? So when will you actually start filming?"

She shrugs. "A few months. Right now we're aiming for June."

My eyebrows shoot up. "So you'll be here for a while." She'd said she'd be spending some time here to work, but I'd expected maybe a month or two. According to her though, they wouldn't even have started filming by that time. The thought makes me very happy.

"Yeah. The estimate was just set. It's later than I'd expected, but you don't get opportunities like this one every day. And honestly, I'm enjoying the break. It's like working and not working at the same time. I still have to do some meetings, but I don't have to wake up at five every morning to get to set for hair and makeup."

I frown. "Hold up. Five a.m.? Ew."

She laughs. "That's not as bad as night shoots. You have to flip your whole sleep schedule so you can film from eleven p.m. to four a.m. It's just lovely," she adds sarcastically.

I gape at her. "Not gonna lie. Totally didn't think acting was that difficult."

A burst of laughter escapes her. "That's why you have to love it." She sits up, sighing. "I have to go."

"What? You just got here..." It feels that way, at least, but looking at the clock, I see it's been over an hour.

She twists her lips. "I actually have a meeting later. For the movie. But I'm glad we did this. I'm glad we... it's good we both know where we stand."

I nod, and stand as she does. She must see the disappointment in my face, though, because she pauses at the doorway before leaving my room. She chews her lip for a second before hesitantly saying, "I'm going to a movie premiere next weekend."

The topic change throws me for a second, but I recover quickly. "Oh. Cool! In Toronto?" I hope she won't be leaving again. Not only do I miss our conversations when she's gone, but the gym is much more enjoyable when she's there too.

Luckily, she nods. "Yeah, in Toronto. Do you want to come?" Her voice is steady, but I can see a glint of vulnerability in her eye.

I freeze for a second out of shock. Then I realize that she's waiting for an answer, and my silence is probably freaking her out, so I quickly choke out, "Yes! Um, definitely yes!"

I can see the signs of relief as her shoulders drop a bit and she takes a deeper breath. "Great. Because those things suck to go to alone."

I laugh. "What about your boyfriend?"

She shakes her head, eyes exaggeratedly wide. "He refuses to come to Toronto just to go to a premiere. I have no idea why..." She smirks.

I giggle. "Okay, point taken. What's the movie? What's it about?"

"It's called *Stormy Night*. It's maybe or maybe not a ghost story

– you can't really tell from the trailer – but spooky stuff starts happening in this old motel when a huge storm takes out the power."

I tilt my head. "That sounds pretty good."

She grins. "Yeah! You can check out the trailer online." She starts listing names of hugely popular actors who star in the movie as I open my bedroom door. I'm preparing to walk downstairs to let Aviva out when Connor bursts into my room, almost hitting Aviva and successfully cutting off her flow of words. I can see his features shift as he prevents himself from swearing – his usual response when something doesn't go his way – and he smiles charmingly instead, sticking out his hand for Aviva to shake.

"Hi, I'm Connor," he says. Aviva automatically takes his hand and I glance over at her face. She looks surprised, but open. I'll have to warn her about the perils of knowing my brother before she leaves. Looking back at Connor, I roll my eyes, but neither of them notice. I've seen this routine before, and unfortunately, it usually works. Connor sees a girl he likes, Connor goes after a girl her likes, Connor ends up with the girl he likes, Connor dumps the girl he used to like. At least Aviva has a boyfriend. Based on the length of time Aviva and Callan have already been dating, and the way she talks about him, I feel pretty safe in assuming that she's not looking for anyone else.

I focus back on the present in time to hear Aviva introduce herself as Brynn and Connor apologize for almost hitting her with the door. Well, that's a first. I can't remember the last time I heard Connor apologize for... anything, really. I sincerely hope that Aviva isn't falling for his gracious act.

"Okay, now that we all know each other," I say, cutting off Connor's attempts at starting a conversation and pushing Aviva out the door as I do so, "it's time for – Brynn – to leave." I grimace, very aware that I almost said *Aviva*.

Aviva seems surprised, glancing back at me as I keep pressure on her back all the way to the front door. In the entryway, I force myself to calm down a bit. "Thanks for coming," I tell her, and I mean it. I can feel Connor's presence behind me, and I press my lips together. "I'll text you," I tell her as she exits the house. "And I'm really excited for the movie!" She smiles and departs, leaving me to face my brother.

He's been slowly making his way down the staircase until he stands beside me, peering out the etched glass set into the door. "That's Brynn?" He sounds incredulous. "Damn, she's hot."

I bite my cheek. "And totally taken. Sorry." I force my voice to sound light and airy, as if I'm positive there's no way he'll ever get with her. Which is *true*, so it shouldn't be as hard as it is to sound carefree.

Still focusing on the window, Connor shakes his head slowly. "Not for long," he says, turning toward me. "Because I'm planning on getting to know her better."

I roll my eyes, not even deigning that worthy of a response. I head back up to my room, closing the door again and cursing my lack of a lock, and pull out my phone.

Hey, I text Aviva. I'm not sure if she'll see it yet, since she may already be driving home, in which case I'll have to wait at least fifteen minutes. Luckily, she must not have left yet, because I receive her response almost immediately.

Um what was that about lol??

I grimace and attempt to explain, in as little detail as possible without sacrificing my full meaning, Connor's womanizing habits. Once that's sent, I pause and then begin to type again.

Not that I think you'd cheat or anything, I'm quick to add. *Just thought u deserved fair warning that he's after u :/*

The moment of silence after I send my paragraph increases my heartrate until I can feel the blood pulsating through my face. My phone vibrates and I fumble it as I read the response.

Haha thx for the heads up. But dw im kinda used to scaring guys off by this point.

Yeah, I guess I should have figured that. I can't even imagine the number of guys who attempt to pick Aviva up when she's out in public. Or hell, even at private parties. She has the type of personality that attracts people to her, including, I'm sure, other celebrities.

Ok cool. Well I guess I should let u go then... and ive gotta get back to my hw :(

K, ttyt!

I put my phone down on my desk and blankly stare at the pile of papers in front of me before finally sighing and digging back into my work.

The next day, I realize that I swept Aviva out my door so quickly that I didn't get to ask anything about premiere etiquette. I had a chance to look up the movie, and the trailer does look good. It's something that I might actually pay to see in theatres, so I'm excited that I get to go early with Aviva.

I finish – actually *finish*, not just rush through – my readings, and have enough time to watch TV for once before heading to the gym. I see the star of *Stormy Night* making a guest appearance on a popular show, although not one I watch often, and realize that I may actually be *meeting* her in less than a week. I'm not so much starstruck as weirded out. It's so strange to see her on my little screen and then potentially be introduced to her, as I'd be introduced to anyone else, in real life.

When I arrive at the gym, I'm a bit earlier than usual, because I finished my readings. Usually I try to complete all my work at once (although not usually succeeding), which leads to me arriving here after Aviva. Today I'm all alone, but instead of feeling lonely, it's freeing. I look around and decide to try something new today. Sure, the elliptical trainer is good most days, but I'm in the mood to try something different. However, the weights and most of the other ambiguous-looking machines still intimidate me, so I go for something familiar, if not routine: the treadmill.

Aviva arrives a few minutes later, after I'm already huffing and puffing, sweat streaming down my temples. I smile at her, but she doesn't return it at first. Actually, her face looks strained as she stares at me – paler than usual, with a look in her eyes that I don't recognize, and definitely don't like. But then a large grin takes over her face, erasing all trace of what I thought I'd seen, and I'm left off-balance. She quickly strides over to her usual elliptical.

"Do you want to join me over here?" I quickly call out, hoping the invitation will allow me a closer look at her, assuaging my ill-ease.

She's already setting up her elliptical, though, and her fingers don't stop moving until the machine beeps, indicating it's ready to go. I'm worried she's just going to completely ignore me, because I know there's no way she didn't hear me, but after she starts moving, she finally looks up at me again.

She flashes me another huge grin and says, "No." The word is hard and flat, and contrasts with her smile. She seems to realize it, because she quickly amends, "I'm good over here."

"Okay." My voice is quiet, but still rings out in the room, offset only by the sounds of my feet padding on the treadmill, and the squeak of her elliptical moving. The noisy silence continues throughout our whole workout, and I don't know how to break it, or if I should, considering the amount of effort it would take to be heard across the room. In the end, I don't say anything until my hour is almost up and I'm finally walking, and not gasping anymore so much as loudly panting. God, I hate the treadmill. I am definitely going back to the elliptical tomorrow.

"So," I say. Aviva looks up at my voice, and it seems as though she's back to normal. Not harsh, but not forcefully happy, either. Just neutral, and maybe a bit tired. "I watched the *Stormy Night* trailer."

She smiles, just a fleeting, unconscious tip of her lips, and asks, "What did you think?"

"It looks good," I tell her. "I'm looking forward to it. I just had a few questions about, like, what is expected at a premiere."

She nods, looking lighter. "Fire away."

I smile, trailing to a stop and taking a gulp of water before continuing. "Okay. Well, what should I wear?"

"Semi-formal is fine. Most girls will be wearing dresses, or maybe jumpsuits." Okay. That kind of makes me nervous. I file it away for later, knowing in the back of my mind that I'll likely be spending hours searching through all my clothes – old and new – for something I may deem appropriate. Just knowing that all the other people there will be wearing designer clothes notches up my anxiety even higher. I know next to nothing about fashion. Sure, I can tell what looks good on me, but that doesn't mean it's the height of style.

"Right. Okay. Um, how long does the whole event usually take?"

"A few hours. This movie starts at six, I think, so we'll show up for 5:30. And we'll probably be out by eight or 8:30."

I frown. "So should I have an early dinner beforehand?"

She shrugs, breath hitching as she answers, still moving with the elliptical. "If you want. Or we could go out for dinner after."

I grin. "That sounds good. And, uh, how will we get to the building? Where is it, anyway?"

Aviva licks her lips, quickly, before answering. "I can give you a ride. Usually I just sneak in the back door, but I have to be seen on more carpets now, to garner more interest in my current activities, so that I bring more publicity to my new project." Her face brightens at the mention of her new movie, although I can see the signs of tiredness in her body as she finally begins to slow down and cool off.

"Oh. Okay... So, should I just meet you inside?"

She looks down and plays with the lid of her water bottle. "Well, actually, I was hoping... that you would walk the carpet with me."

A strangely high-pitched laugh escapes my throat, and I stare at Aviva. "Wait. Seriously?"

She lifts one shoulder and tilts her head in a *Why not?* gesture.

My mouth hangs open for a second before an adamant "No!" comes out. "No. No, I do not think that's a good idea."

Aviva tilts her upper body to face me. "Why not?" Her voice is curious, and it gives me pause. Why am I so vehemently against it?

"Well, first of all, I'm not always *photogenic.*" I grimace. "And, um, I'm a nobody; why would anyone want me on the carpet? Would I even be allowed? And wouldn't that expose our friendship?!" My voice has risen to a pitch much higher than my regular speaking voice by the end.

Aviva twists her mouth to the side as she considers. "Well, first of all, of course I'm not going to force you to do anything. *But–*" and here she raises an eyebrow and gives me a mischievous look "–the photogenic thing can be fixed. You don't think stars look so good all the time naturally, do you?" To be honest, I kind of did. "They all have photography and publicity training."

"Okay, but–"

She shushes me jokingly. "I'm not done yet. Secondly, *you are not a nobody.* You're just as relevant as any other person on that carpet."

"That's not what I meant–" I begin to say.

Aviva nods. "I know. And to answer what you really meant, yes, you'll be allowed on. You'll be with me. Although I still don't know why I'm allowed on." I giggle at the openly dubious look on her face. "And... I'm okay with our friendship being in the public as long as you are. But it's fine if you're not okay with it." Her last sentence comes out slightly rushed.

I take a moment to consider her words before finally relenting. "Okay." I hurry to tack on my conditions before her gleeful shriek drowns me out. "*If* you help me pick out an outfit, and teach me how to be more photogenic."

She grins. "Yes! Definitely. You can borrow one of my dresses, if you want. Unless you already have something in mind?"

I bark out a laugh. "No, one of yours would be appreciated, for sure."

"Okay. Well, the premiere is on Saturday, so how about you come over to my place on Friday? You can pick an outfit and I can media train you." She says the *media train* bit in an intentionally awful British accent, and I smirk.

"Sounds perfect, darling," I reply, in an equally unimpressive accent. Then, in my regular voice, "How about I come over after newspaper editing?"

"Yeah, sure. I've got the whole day off," she explains, looking positively gleeful, "so whenever you can works for me."

It's only after we part ways and I'm driving home that I realize I never asked about her strange reaction when she first walked into the gym. By this point I'm wondering if it ever really happened, and if it did, if it was really something to worry about. I should probably just forget about it.

This school week seems to fly by for me, a welcome reprieve after the monotonous drag I'd almost become accustomed to. It's not until Thursday that I realize I haven't thought about Asher in a while. I dig deeper into my emotions, trying to understand them. I really think I'm done with Asher by this point. I'm no longer just saying that, either. There's a difference between saying that you're over someone, maybe even convincing yourself of it, but still continuously thinking of them, and truly getting over them and forgetting to think about them at all. I think I've finally reached the latter. I wonder what that means in terms of potential future romances. I decide to put off the thought of new relationships, for the moment, at least. It will happen when I'm ready; I'm not going to go actively seeking one.

Friday enforces my realization about Asher. I've been anticipating going over to Aviva's apartment all day, and now that I'm at newspaper, the combination of excitement and nerves is making it hard to concentrate on the editing work in front of me. I'm so distracted, with the division of my thoughts between tonight and tomorrow, and the papers I'm attempting to edit at the same time, that at first I don't even realize Asher is talking to me. When it finally registers that my name is being called, I look up sharply.

"What?"

Asher grins at me lazily, a piece of his blond hair falling forward, blocking the blue of one of his eyes. "Oh, I get it, I'm not important anymore, since our breakup. I was just asking what's up?"

I frown in confusion for a moment at this totally unexpected attempt at initiating a conversation, then look back down at my work as I reply. The sooner I finish this, the sooner I can get to Aviva's. "Um, nothing much, you?" My response is automatic and disinterested, and I hope that he doesn't think I'm trying to be rude. I just really want to get out of here soon, and his random question is prolonging my stay.

"Oh, good. Just school, you know," he complains in a familiar tone, probably expecting a laugh. I give him a quick smile instead, then focus back on my work. "I just noticed that you've been... different lately, Naya. Not in a bad way or anything. I just wanted to know if everything was okay."

That's enough to grab my attention. I raise my head and face him head-on, one eyebrow raised. "Yes, actually, everything's been great. Thanks for your concern," I say coolly, then go back to ignoring him.

"Oh, good." I detect a trace of surprise in his voice, though I don't bother analysing in depth what it could stem from. "Any reason life's been so *great*?" he continues, semi-sarcastically.

If I really wanted to get rid of him, I could answer somewhere along the lines of *I haven't been with you*. But even if I no longer want to be with Asher – even if he's actually starting to annoy me – I really should try to stay on good terms with him. So instead I shrug and say, "New friends. It's refreshing." I may be exaggerating a bit by pluralizing 'friends', but it's not like he can ask for proof.

There's a short silence, during which I rapidly mark errors in red pen on the paper in front of me, before he says, "You have any plans tonight?"

Now this is something I don't mind answering. "Yeah, actually. I'm hanging out with a friend as soon as I'm done here." I'm not going to say who yet, because even if Aviva's okay with outing our friendship, I have no evidence that we're actually friends right now, aside from her phone number, which I would hate to call just to prove to some people from school that I'm friends with a celebrity.

"Oh? Someone I know?" His voice sounds off, somehow. Not

angry, exactly, and not curious, either. I'm so thrown off by his tone that it takes me a second to recognize the significance of his question. When I do, I snort a laugh and say, "Not likely."

I finally place the tone of voice. Is Asher... *jealous*? Of what? Maybe I'm wrong, but even so, the thought amuses me. Asher could use some jealousy. He'd certainly provoked enough in me.

Finally, I reach the end of the last article I'd been proofreading, and jump up, forcing Asher to jolt back a half-step. Whoops. I hadn't realized how close he'd been. I gather up my backpack and papers, and while turning back to check I got everything from the desk I'd been working at, I realize Asher is still next to me.

I stare at him a half-second, wondering if there's something I'm forgetting to do, or a paper I need to give him, but I don't think so. "Kay. Bye." I say, and turn and walk out the door, finally leaving him behind me.

Hmm. It's interesting that now that I no longer have feelings for him, he's starting to get on my nerves. He's kind of pushy, and nosy. And that whole following me business? Weird. But whatever. I'm just happy that I've finally reached another weekend, and now I get to go to Aviva's.

I drive straight to her apartment building, and this time the man at the front desk doesn't even look twice at me. I smile and stand a little taller. I greet the people in the elevator with polite hellos and a smile, and they return it, looking slightly surprised but entirely welcome. It's not until the cube starts moving that my nerves from earlier hit me again. I'm sure I'll be welcome anywhere that Aviva says I'm allowed, and I'm sure it will be fun to be with her, in public and when she's actually displaying her true identity for once, but the knowledge doesn't unknot my stomach at all.

By the time I reach her floor, I'm the last one in the elevator. I step off, onto the soft carpet leading to her door, and knock. She lets me in, looking almost as excited as the other, non-nervous part of me is. She leads me straight back through her bedroom and to the giant closet-room containing all of her clothes. We go to a section that contains a level of formality somewhere between summer-chic and prom-wedding. There's an assortment of outfits, all incredibly different, yet retaining the same label of semi-formal. I see mint-green wraps alongside sparkly black pantsuits and red-hot mini dresses. Aviva begins to dig through them all, muttering under her breath as she does.

Finally she selects one, asking, "What about this?"

I look at it. It's a burgundy velvet dress that looks like it would hit about mid-thigh. Normally I'd have no objections, but this dress has so many pieces cut out that I can't imagine it would cover anything important. At my hesitant look, Aviva injects, "The best way to feel confident is wearing something that makes you feel that way."

I make a soft noise of objection. "That's the last way I'd feel in that."

Aviva frowns and turns back to the rack, ruffling through until she pulls out another dress. This one is a soft gold, but upon closer inspection I realize that it's actually two pieces: a top that ends just below my breasts, and a skirt that begins just above my belly button, thus revealing almost my entire midriff. I swiftly shake my head.

Aviva sighs. "Naya, you have a great body. You've been spending so much time on toning it, why not show some off?" I don't reply, because I have no answer. I'm just so used to insecurity that it feels weird to even think about being confident enough to show off my hard work. "Trust me, it took me long enough to accept my body," she continues in a near-whisper. "And life is so much better once you have. You need to do the same."

Um, what? From what I've seen of Aviva in movies and magazines, she's always been super-slim. She had no reason to ever have been insecure. "What are you talking about?" I ask incredulously, but she just shakes her head and turns back to the dresses.

"It was a long time ago," she finally answers in that same soft voice, before pulling out another dress for me to see. "How about this one?" she asks at a regular volume, sounding perfectly cheerful once again.

I examine her face, looking for more information, but all I can see is her excitement over yet another potential dress. I bite my lip. I really should know better than to search an actor's face for answers. She could put on any character she wants. With reluctance, I turn to the dress, and inhale sharply. It's *gorgeous*. Seafoam blue, with shoulder straps that continue down to cross over the chest, then wrap around the waist as a belt. The skirt goes down to just above my knees. It's significantly more modest than the others, yet still breath-taking, so I go to the bathroom to try it on. When I come out, Aviva is beaming. She leads me to a full-length mirror back in the closet-room. I look... and my mouth actually drops slightly open.

I don't look like cute little Naya, or even pretty Naya. I look like *sexy* Naya. The dress is tight and clings to every curve, no matter how small, while flowing effortlessly over my stomach, making it look perfectly flat. I do a little spin, admiring the way the fabric shimmers under the lights. "God *damn*, Aviva," I finally get out.

She laughs. "I think we've found the dress that gives you your confidence." I just nod in agreement. She demonstrates how to walk and stand with good posture, pushing shoulders back, back arched, and chin up.

"Just keep your face natural," she explains. "If you don't feel like smiling, give them an intense look. If you do feel like smiling, don't fake it. Just smile like you would at a friend, or laugh if you can. It looks so much more natural."

I attempt it, but feel so awkward practicing in front of Aviva and the mirror that I end up groaning with my face in my hands. She chuckles and grabs my shoulders from behind, forcing me to straighten up again. We look into the mirror as she talks. "You need to pick out a mantra. You don't even need to tell me what it is if you don't want to. Just look in the mirror and pick out some features that you love about yourself. And just keep repeating them in your head."

She steps back and I study my reflection. I've always loved my eyes, with their mixture of ivy green and hazelnut brown. I also love how long my hair has gotten; it's almost reached my midback. As for my body… I hadn't really realized it, but my many hours at the gym have actually started to make a difference. Of course I'd been hoping that they would, but I hadn't taken the time to look at myself in the mirror, as I'm doing now. My calf muscles are more defined, and I'm starting to look closer to an athlete than a couch potato. Okay. As long as I can keep that in my head, it should definitely be easier to retain confidence. *I love my eyes. I love my hair. I love my calves.* I smile and nod at Aviva.

She gasps excitedly. "Let's do a faux carpet walk. I'm going to put on my outfit!" She ignores my half-hearted protests because honestly, it does sound kind of fun. She returns five minutes later in a dark pink pantsuit that offsets her blonde waves beautifully. She's also holding a (hopefully fake – or else majorly expensive) diamond-studded clutch. When she joins me in front of the mirror, we actually look like we belong together. Of course she always looks carpet-ready, but now I look good enough to be seen with her and not be mistaken for her assistant.

"Ready?" she asks, and I just laugh and shake my head. She grabs my hands and drags me into a clothing-free section of the room that forms a mostly-straight path, and we strut down it, making cheesy faces and posing like we're at a modelling agency audition. Finally we collapse side-by-side on the floor, giggling.

"What should I tell people when the pictures of us together come out?" I finally ask.

"Well, I'd prefer that you don't tell them I'm Brynn. I'd like to hold onto her as an escape route for as long as possible."

I nod. "So then how did we supposedly meet?"

Aviva snorts. "Um... the grocery store? Maybe we met in line and started talking." We both laugh at the absurdity of the normalcy, but agree on the story, even hashing out which grocery store it was and which cash register we'd been in line for. "It'll just be better," she continues, "if we don't mention the gym, because as much as I love my fans, I'd rather not be mobbed by them during my workout."

My stomach growls, reminding me of the time, and I realize I should get home for dinner. I stand up and reluctantly gather up my regular clothes to change back into before leaving. It physically pains me to strip off the dress, but I know it will be safer here with Aviva than in my car, or at home where my parents might see it or Connor might be able to reach it. When I return, Aviva is back in her regular clothes too, hanging up her outfit again.

"What time should I come back tomorrow?" I ask, reluctantly relinquishing the dress.

"Four? That should give us enough time to get dressed and for me to do my makeup. And yours." She tacks on the last sentence a second later.

I shake my head in amusement. "Deal." I'd much rather leave that job to her. This whole situation is starting to feel somewhat surreal, augmented by the fact that I'll be wearing someone else's dress, with someone else doing my makeup. Even the thought makes me feel like *I'm* the celebrity in this relationship. "And what time will I be back home by? I need to give my parents some sort of estimate."

She raises an eyebrow. "That depends. Are you interested in going to the afterparty?" She reads my hesitation correctly and says, "It's okay. Next time. How about we just go out for dinner after the movie's over and then take you home? So, probably 10 or 11?"

I nod, relieved. If a premiere already makes me this nervous, where I know there will be some fans who bought their way in, I can't even imagine how scared I'd get for an afterparty, where I'd be just about the only one who isn't an actor and who wouldn't know anyone. I'm happy to postpone that for as long as possible.

I leave, hugging Aviva goodbye and promising to be back tomorrow by four on the dot. On the drive home, my thoughts wander to tomorrow's events. I'm curious as to how many other people Aviva will know at the premiere. If there will be very many, why would she have invited me? I'm terrified that Aviva will get caught up with other celebrities and leave me somewhere, where I'll be ignored by everyone else. I catch the negative drift of my thoughts, and attempt to stop it – just because I'll be surrounded by famous people, doesn't mean they'll all be snobby. I really should know this by now. But what if Aviva is an anomaly? What if the premiere is miserable? Just because I'll be looking good, doesn't mean I'll belong there.

I sigh. I guess I'll find out tomorrow.

Chapter Seven

I wake up on my own for once, not jolted out of sleep by my school alarm as I usually am, and finally feel refreshed. I stretch out in bed, just enjoying the quiet relaxation spreading throughout my body, until with a jolt I remember what's happening later today.

The premiere.

I'd actually enjoyed our Friday family night last evening. I'd gotten so caught up in our game of Monopoly and fighting with Connor over properties that the insecurities I'd felt during my time with Aviva had been swept away. In fact, I'd even forgotten to mention my plans for tonight to my parents. Now, I can still feel the worries niggling at me, but they seem less valid than they did yesterday. Another benefit of a full night's sleep, I suppose.

I click my phone on and immediately realize why I feel so rested: it's nearly noon. I need to be at Aviva's by four, and I still have other things I need to do today. I shoot out of bed and hurry downstairs for breakfast – or is it lunch?

Mom's at the kitchen table, sipping a coffee and flipping through the newspaper. She looks up at me through her reading glasses as I dash into the room, smiling at me bemusedly. "What's the rush, hon?"

"Is there any food left for me?" She shakes her head, and I get out the toaster, bread, and peanut butter as I answer. "I, um, have plans tonight. And I have stuff to do before I go. I need to get my homework done, and Savannah emailed me yesterday about doing some extra editing work this weekend."

She raises an eyebrow. "I hope your 'stuff' also includes cleaning up your room."

I freeze. "What? No! Come on Mom, it's not that bad..." my voice trails off, though, because I can't even kid myself about that. But as long as it doesn't bother me, I don't see why it should bother her.

She shakes her head, returning her gaze to the newspaper. She tucks a strand of her short brown hair behind her ear. "Sorry, Naya, but you're not getting out of it this time. I can barely walk in your room, there's so much clutter on the floor."

"Why do you need to walk in my room?"

"Naya." Her voice sounds tired. "You're cleaning your room today, and that's final. If it's not done, you're not going anywhere tonight."

As much as I'd been afraid of going to the premiere, I'd never considered backing out. And I'd certainly never considered that my mother might be the reason I'd have to miss it. "But Mom, this is important!" I burst out.

She glances up at me curiously, and I'm afraid she'll be mad that I lost my temper. Instead, though, she just seems interested. "Okay," she says calmly, folding the newspaper in half. "Why?"

How do I explain this without giving away everything I promised Aviva I wouldn't? I settle on just telling her what the event will be. "I'm going to see a movie. And then out for dinner after."

Her eyes narrow, and I can almost see the thoughts swirling through her head. "Is it a date?" She nearly sounds excited, which is surprising. After my breakup with Asher, she'd never spelled out anything specific, but I could tell her thoughts on my dating life through little comments she would make – i.e., that it shouldn't exist. Not because she didn't want me to be happy, but rather, she hated to see me so unhappy. If one relationship could cause that, what could additional breakups do? Now, though, the glint in her eyes suggests that her aversion is over. I consider agreeing just to make things easier, but I really don't want to lie. Withholding information is already hard enough.

"No, I'm just going out with Brynn," I say carefully, watching her face. It doesn't change much, and I realize that maybe it isn't dating she wants from me so much as simple social interaction.

"Brynn seemed nice," she muses. "But maybe next time you bring her here you can do homework instead." I don't mention that Brynn isn't in school, because I don't know if my mom's opinion on her would change if she found out. Rather, I just nod and smile, tight-lipped. "Okay," my mom says finally, opening up her newspaper again. "You can clean your room tomorrow. But only if you're back by midnight tonight at the latest."

I release a shaky breath. "Thank you," I tell her genuinely, and, toast now slathered with peanut butter, sit across from her at the table. We eat in silence, but it's comfortable, and I'm happy.

Time seems to be passing at a faster rate than usual, and Savannah's left me a lot more editing work than I'd anticipated. By the time I finally emerge at the other end of it all, I have half an hour before I should leave for Aviva's, and I can't fathom the thought of doing more work. Instead, I Google *Aviva Jersey Toronto*, curious as to what will come up.

There are several images from TIFFs of years past, and a few of her walking the streets in high-fashion garb, but none that I can see of us coming out of the gym two weeks ago. I guess none of the pictures taken were good enough, or nobody bothered posting them. I'm not sure how to feel about that. I mean, they wouldn't have been the best shots of me or Aviva, all sweaty and tired, but that also means that tonight is really the first time we'll be acknowledged as knowing each other in public. If some photos had leaked of us together before, maybe the pressure wouldn't be as high tonight.

With butterflies once again rising in my stomach, I realize that it's about time to leave for Aviva's to get beautified before we go out. I call goodbye to my mom and Connor, although only my mom responds.

When I arrive at the huge parking lot outside of Aviva's apartment building, I push myself out the car door and lock it behind me before I can decide that I probably should clean my room tonight, actually. The man behind the desk barely gives me a second glance today, and I smile shakily to myself on the way up the elevator. There are several other people in the silver box, and the white noise caused by their shifting, clothes brushing and zipping, and feet stepping helps to centre me. Silence is too oppressive right now.

It's not until Aviva actually opens her door, however, that I calm entirely. Seeing her again pushes away all my stupid fears and worries that she'll abandon me, on purpose or not. She hugs me and pulls me inside, grinning widely. "Are you ready for your makeover, darling?" she asks, once again affecting that intentionally bad British accent. I just raise my eyebrows in response, indicating my hesitation. She laughs and pushes me toward the bathroom to change, where I see the beautiful dress I chose yesterday hanging on the back of the door. I slip it on, instantly feeling more confident as I study my reflection over the sink before I walk back out to Aviva.

She takes me to her bedroom and sits me down on a white chair facing a dresser littered with dozens of makeup products, half of which I couldn't even attempt to name. Before I can protest, she spins the chair around so I can no longer see the mirror, which means I won't be able to say no if she starts to go overboard with my face. I grimace, but can't bring myself to complain more, lest it ruin her joyful mood. And, honestly, her glee is beginning to rub off on me too.

She chatters to me rapidly as she applies foundation, concealer, and a multitude of coloured powders to my face. She only pauses her rapid-fire speech while she's leaning in close to work on my eyes. My face feels so much heavier than I'm used to, and I'm starting to wonder if agreeing to let Aviva do my makeup today was really such a good idea. Finally she steps back, as I blink and squint, trying to become accustomed to the feel of false eyelashes.

"Can I see now?" I grumble for the umpteenth time. This time, however, she agrees, spinning me around with a flourish. It takes me a second to orient myself, and when I see my reflection, I nearly look around again to be sure that *yes, that is really me.* Aviva leaves the room as I study the look in the mirror.

I'd been expecting something completely over-the-top, glittery and bug-eyed. But this look is... well, I couldn't say subtle, because there is a slight pop of sea-foam blue applied to my waterlines that matches my dress. But the lines are sleek and blended, nothing harsh or too dark. My cheekbones seem much more defined, and I decide that perhaps I should look into learning how to contour them myself, because the sharper face shape makes me look older, or at least closer to my age than *cute Naya* usually seems.

I hear Aviva enter the room again and look over to see her watching me smugly. She's wearing the same magenta pantsuit she'd tried on yesterday. "Good, right?" she asks.

I nod. "Definitely good. Definitely great, even."

She grins and playfully shoves me off the chair. "I have to do my makeup now, 'cause we're running out of time before the car comes to pick us up."

She applies her makeup much more quickly than she'd done mine, although equally expertly. I wander over to her white leather couch and sit, careful not to crumple my dress, and scroll through my phone as I wait for her to finish. Suddenly her cell starts ringing, and I hear it cut off as she answers.

"Okay," she chirps, then enters the room I'm in, gripping her phone. "Our ride's here," she mumbles, attempting to apply a sheer nude lip gloss with her other hand at the same time.

Butterflies fill my stomach again. *I am so sick of this. I will* have fun tonight. I look awesome, Aviva looks awesome, and it doesn't matter that I won't know anyone else. We're going to a movie, not a job interview. No one's main objective will be to judge me.

With that in mind, I follow her out of the room and into the elevator. A wave of apprehension rolls over me when we get to the ground floor and I see that the *car* Aviva mentioned is actually a *limo*, but I don't let it show. I keep walking confidently forward and slip into the spacious back, next to Aviva. There's a mini-fridge situated across from us that I curiously crack open.

"Help yourself," Aviva murmurs, as I realize that it's champagne. Hey, I could use a bit of relaxation right now, and it's free alcohol. I take a plastic flute and pour from the bottle in the fridge, marvelling at the smoothness of the limo ride as it coasts onto the busy street. I grab another plastic cup and prepare to pour for Aviva, but she stops my hand, just shaking her head and shrugging with a half-smile, so I put the bottle back into the mini-fridge and lean back in my seat to drink mine.

I feel the bubbly hit my stomach and belatedly realize that perhaps drinking with not much in my stomach wasn't the best idea. Oh well. I just won't have any more after I finish this glass. My hands, which I hadn't even noticed were trembling, settle as the last of my nerves drain away, leaving me only with excitement for the night. I smile as I look over at Aviva, but she's staring out her window. I take the moment to study her.

Something is off, but at first I can't place it. She looks fairly normal, legs crossed, hands in her lap, face stoic. After a moment, I realize that her top leg is jiggling up and down, and that's what had initially caught my attention. Then I also see that her casually-crossed hands are clenched together a bit too tightly to really be considered casual. I've never noticed Aviva to have any unconscious tendencies. She's always so tightly in control of her body. Even now, I can't read anything in her face; the only reason I even notice anything off is because I've been around her enough by now to pick up on anything abnormal. *Is Aviva nervous too?* The thought catches me off-guard. Here I'd thought I was the only one who had something to worry about, thinking that Aviva would be used to the carpet and other celebrities and attention by now. Maybe she is. Maybe she's worried about something else. Either way, it helps me to realize that I'm not alone in feeling out of my element.

I don't say anything. I don't want to press her before we have to put on our best faces for the cameras. Instead, I finish my drink, put it down, and begin asking questions unrelated to the event in an attempt to get her to loosen up. She gives me anecdotes from previous films she's shot, tells me funny stories about crazy directors, and her experience working with male models while helping a friend shoot a music video (the way she relayed it to Callan afterwards, it wasn't any fun at all; the way she relays it to me, it was one of the highlights of her career).

Suddenly I realize that the limo is slowing down; it's hard to tell, with such a smooth ride. I look out the window and all I can see are flashing cameras and hubs of people spreading out in every direction. Aviva's door is cracked open by a burly man wearing all black, but before she gets out she flashes a huge grin at me and whispers, "Confidence."

I scooch across the seat and follow out her door, where she's waiting for me with her hand out. I grab it instinctively, needing some sort of comfort in the face of all this strangeness. She leads me, flanked on each side by bodyguards, toward a roped-off building entrance. Recognizing her, the guards in front of it unlatch it and let us walk up the stairs and into the much emptier, although just as loud, red carpet. She stops in front of a slightly older woman wearing a blazer and dress pants and leans her head in for a quick discussion. Nodding, Aviva pulls back and, looking over at me, invites me closer with a quick wiggle of her fingertips. I walk slowly towards them, feeling completely out of place.

"This is my publicist, Shona." Aviva has to project her voice in order to be heard over the buzzing of the crowd. "Shona, this is my friend Naya."

Shona grips my hand and shakes it firmly. "Nice to meet you. I was just letting Aviva know who she's talking to tonight." Her eyes drift over the top of my head and her attention is snatched away. "Oh! Gotta go. Blake just got here. I'll talk to you later, love," she tells Aviva, patting her shoulder as she walks back toward the entrance.

I'm not quite sure what just happened or what to do, so I just follow Aviva docilely as she leads me down the carpet, and halt when she does. I stare at Aviva, just trying to figure out what to do, and see that her physicality is completely different from when we were in the car. She's owning the carpet, and only then do I remember the lessons she attempted to give me in preparation for this moment. I can't remember all the technicalities, but I do my best to keep good posture and not look as overwhelmed as I'm feeling.

Cameras flash from every direction, and suddenly I realize

that *I'm on a freaking red carpet*. I begin to giggle, and Aviva looks over at me and smirks. Not even the distinct "Who's she?" I can hear from the crowd can affect my newly buoyant mood. I'm still grateful for Aviva's proximity though, partially because I'm afraid if she leaves me here alone I'll be kicked out by security. Aviva leads me up the carpet in several short jags, then stops and poses again at every stop. Every time we move along the carpet, Aviva mutters something funny in my ear to help me to relax. It's usually something stupid or easily apparent, about an over-the-top outfit or a new piece of dating gossip. Once she even tells a knock-knock joke. Slowly, the lessons begin to trickle back into my brain. *Shoulders back. Back arched. Chin up.* Even though I doubt I'll look as good as Aviva when the photos come out, I feel good. This is super scary but also a lot more fun than I'd expected.

Once we reach the other end, we're shown into a darkened room. As soon as the doors close behind us again, the noise from the carpet becomes muffled and everything inside sounds like it's coming through cotton. It takes a few more moments before my ears to stop ringing and noises begin to sound natural again. I continue to follow Aviva, this time to our seats in the theatre. She slumps down, miming an exaggerated sigh of relief. I giggle, partly as a release of nerves, but we don't have time to say much before someone climbs onstage, addresses the audience and introduces the movie, the lights go out completely, and *Stormy Night* begins on the huge screen.

It's good. Really good. The old motel *does* turn out to be haunted, and the guests staying in it when the power is cut off by the storm have to band together to figure out how to defeat the spirit terrorizing them. I'm actually frightened at some points, and movies almost never scare me. Maybe that's because the only horror movies I've seen have had bad acting, though. The acting here definitely convinces me. When the credits roll and the lights come up again, I stare at Aviva with wide eyes. She returns the look and we hold it for several seconds before bursting into giggles.

"That was terrifying," I mumble, carefully wiping under my eyes so that my tears of laughter don't ruin my makeup. Everyone around us is beginning to stand, but we wait a few more minutes so that we'll have more room to exit the theatre. As we begin to file out along with the others, Aviva says reluctantly, "And now for the business part of the night. Interviews and networking." She greets nearly everyone we pass by as we approach a larger room where everyone seems to be congregating. I stay with her for a bit, but my eyes catch and linger on some benches sitting alongside the wall. When she says she has to go talk to some reporters now, I indicate the benches. She nods and smiles apologetically, and we head off in opposite directions.

The benches aren't entirely empty, so I won't particularly stand out by sitting off to the side. However, I choose a spot with no one else nearby. I'd rather people-watch than converse with someone now, without Aviva here to act as mediator. I look around curiously, finally getting a chance to take in the crowds around me, since I wasn't able to see before the movie started and we were plunged into darkness. I see many familiar faces, including a few that actually make me catch my breath. This is definitely an A-lister premiere. And – *oh my god* – is that Karl

Logger? I used to have a celebrity crush on him in high school, and the fact that I'm so close to him at this moment feels surreal.

When I feel as though I've looked around enough, my mind starts to wander. No matter how good I may look and feel tonight, it's not enough to actually get up and insert myself into some celebrities' conversation. I don't see Aviva yet either, and none of my bench mates appear too friendly, so I pull out my trusty old phone and connect to the free WiFi.

I find a semi-interesting article on a new anthropological trend that I figure may help me with my Anthro class. I click on it, but the connection is slow. I'm so excited by the fact that it's *finally* loaded that my mind doesn't register that a figure has sat down beside me until he speaks in a low voice.

"I may actually have to sleep with my lights on tonight."

Surprised, I look up – and blink. The guy who'd spoken is *seriously* attractive. He looks somewhere around my age, maybe a few years older, and has thick, wavy brown hair, green eyes, and a sharp, clean-shaven jawline. I realize that my face is frozen into whatever expression I'd been wearing while waiting for my phone to load, and quickly adjust my lips into a smile.

"I know," I agree, nodding emphatically. "Might take me more than just tonight, though, to be able to fall asleep without picturing that ghost in the bedroom."

He grins, revealing straight white teeth, and holds out a hand. "I'm Jace," he says.

I shake his hand. "Naya." When I pull my hand back, it tingles, and I flex my fingers unconsciously.

Jace. I don't know of any celebrities named Jace. He doesn't look familiar either. Maybe he's a plus-one, like me? It's not like I could just casually bring it up, either... *Nice to meet you, are you famous?* I could ask if he came with someone... but then that would make me sound like I'm asking if he has a girlfriend, and I don't want to come off as desperate in my first impression. Whatever. Just the fact that I've never heard of him before makes him much less intimidating than half the other people in this room. The fact that he's also smoking hot doesn't deter me from talking to him, either.

"So, what did you think of the movie, Naya?"

My name on his tongue is incredibly sexy and renders me temporarily speechless. I try to make it look as though I'm just giving the question some good thought.

"Well, I'm no expert, but I really enjoyed it." I tuck a piece of hair behind my ear, hoping that answer conveyed my lack of knowledge without making me look stupid.

He nods, looking satisfied with my answer. *Phew.* "I really liked it too. That climax scene where Marissa dies... incredibly done. The mise-en-scène was really great, with the fog outside the window. It could've been really cheesy, but they pulled it off. Actually, the mise-en-scène was great throughout the whole movie. Maybe it was the rapid cross-cutting that made the climax so good. Or the focus of the shots..." he trails off, looking at my face sheepishly. "Sorry. I get kind of carried away talking about movies. I love them," he laughs awkwardly, "if that wasn't already obvious."

I try to pretend like I understood half of what he just said, but honestly, the only thing I focus on in a movie is the plot and the acting. I didn't really mind listening to him, though. Watching anyone speak with so much passion is fascinating. The fact that I also got to unabashedly stare at him throughout his monologue didn't hurt either.

"No, that's cool," I assure him. "Do you study film in school?"

He shakes his head. "No, I just know a lot of people in the industry, who've taught me quite a bit." He smirks. "I would like to go to university in the future. I just need to figure out what I'd study first."

I nod. That's definitely something I can relate to. I know I enjoy writing, but I'm still not sure what I want my future job to be, exactly.

He grimaces. "Also, every year that I'm away from school, the less I want to go back. I'm twenty-one," he explains at my questioning look.

I nod. "I'm in first year at the University of Toronto. Like, I know education is important, but trust me, all the work is not so enjoyable."

His eyes widen slightly. "U of T, eh? Nice."

I smile. "It is nice. Most of the time. I've lived in Toronto my whole life, so it just seemed sort of natural to go to university here too."

He smiles. "I was born in Toronto, but my parents moved my family to the States when I was still little. Now I kind of switch back and forth."

"Where in the States?" It's comfortable talking to Jace. I don't feel awkward at all, and the more we exchange questions and answers, the less self-conscious I become.

I become so caught up in our conversation that I don't even notice the time passing. My phone has long since fallen asleep again, article forgotten, and the only thing I'm focused on is Jace.

Suddenly I become aware of another presence though, hovering over me. I drag my gaze upwards to see Aviva standing and biting her lip to hold back laughter, eyes on me. Immediately I blush, but hopefully the foundation she applied earlier covers it.

"Hey, Naya," she says. Our rapid-fire conversation trails off as Jace turns to look at her too.

"Hey," I reply, pushing down the disappointment at her interruption. "All done with your interviews?"

"Yeah. Sorry they took so long. I'm starving now. Although it looks like you managed to occupy yourself." She eyes Jace curiously.

There's a moment of awkward silence before I realize I should be introducing them. "Oh! Sorry. Aviva, Jace. Jace, Aviva," I say, gesturing to each of them in turn, face flaming. I'm quite sure that there's enough heat in my face now to melt away my foundation entirely.

Jace nods. "I just saw *Darkness Rising* in theatres," he tells Aviva, referencing her latest film. "Actually, I saw *Marido* recently too. Great films."

Aviva smiles with real happiness, as only mention of one of her two loves can produce. "Thank you!" I'm suddenly very happy that her love other than acting, Callan, has taken her off the dating market. My eyes flick to her, and she must receive the correct message, because she quickly tacks on, "We're actually about to go out to dinner. You're welcome to join us." My stomach flips hopefully, but then sinks as he shakes his head reluctantly.

"I have work in the morning, so I'm just going to go home. Thanks for the offer, though. It was nice to meet you," he says, then turns back to me. "Naya. Hopefully we'll run into each other again."

I can only nod as his eyes bore into mine, leaving my mind blank. Then he leaves, and I heave in a deep breath, suddenly finding myself in dire need of oxygen. I turn back to Aviva, eyes taking a moment too long to focus on her, to find her biting her lip again. I flush one more time (*Stop. Stop. God, stop it, Naya.*) but she doesn't comment, instead grabbing my arm and leading me toward the exit. I'm lost in my thoughts and don't even realize that we're getting into another limo until I'm seated in the soft leather seat, staring out the window, and Aviva speaks.

"So, I have this great place in mind for dinner."

"Okay," I murmur, "sounds good."

"No preference for type of food?"

This question requires more brain power, enough that I turn away from the window, coming back to myself. "No. Anything should be good." I smile.

She looks supremely amused. "Okay. I think you'll like where we're going, then."

Ten minutes later we pull up in front of what seems to be, at first glance, an old warehouse with a long line of fancily dressed people winding along the side. It's only as we step back into the cold air, approaching the front doors, that I begin to be able to hear muffled voices coming from inside.

"What is this place?" I whisper to Aviva, curiosity finally piqued.

"It's called Warehouse," she tells me.

I snort. "How original."

We approach the front doors, surpassing the line, ignoring

the grumbles, and my eyes register a burly man standing before them. He's wearing all black and had been blending in with the building until now, especially since it's dark outside. It's always dark so early in the winter, even if we have recently turned the clocks forward an hour. At least it's not as frigid as it was last month.

Aviva stands on her tiptoes to say something into the man's ear. He's well over six feet; Aviva is at least 5'7", and she's wearing heels. The man nods stiffly and points around the building, to the opposite side of the line. Aviva chirps a quick "Thanks!" and then grabs my arm again and pulls me in that direction.

"Where are we going?" I ask confusedly. "Shouldn't we join the line?"

Aviva pauses and shoots me a wink, the moonlight glinting off of her shimmery eyelid. Then she walks a few more steps forward, reaching a side door that had also been effortlessly blending into the wall. She sharply raps on it three times and waits. Within two seconds, it cracks open, and she smiles at whoever's inside. I inch towards her, trying to get a better look. The door opens all the way, and I follow Aviva in, grateful to get into the warmth.

The woman holding the door open eyes me suspiciously, but her look relaxes when Aviva grins at me widely. The lady closes the door behind us, and I hear the lock automatically click into place. Like the bouncer outside, she's wearing all black: a tight midnight turtleneck, and wide-legged dress pants. The only thing to separate her from the darkness outside is a bronze nametag labelled "Dana", which I can barely read in this dim lighting.

"Aviva," Dana says in a low, smooth voice. "It's good to see you again." She brushes her lips over each side of Aviva's face, ensuring she never actually touches skin so as not to smudge her bright red lipstick.

"Dana." Aviva smiles fondly. "This is my friend Naya."

Dana turns to me and I smile awkwardly. "Hi."

Dana doesn't seem to notice my discomfort. She smiles at me warmly too, then proceeds to do the same air-kiss routine as she'd just done with Aviva. I stand still as a statue, smile frozen on my face. When she pulls back, she turns to Aviva again, asking, "Just you two tonight?"

At Aviva's nod, she leads us through a doorway into a vast dining room that takes up almost the entire interior of the warehouse. Glancing around, I recognize several familiar faces, both from onscreen, and from the premiere. Wow. Apparently Warehouse is tonight's hot spot.

We're seated alongside one mauve-painted wall with fanciful white trim. The table between us is rectangular and made of heavy, glossy wood, and the chairs are velvet in a similar shade of purple to the walls. The occupied tables are scattered throughout the room, so that the space feels full without anyone being close enough to overhear others' conversations unless they put in a concerted effort. Which I'm grateful for when, barely a few seconds after Dana hands us our menus and leaves, Aviva begins to ask questions.

"So, how did you enjoy the premiere?" I open my mouth to answer, but before a single syllable can leave my lips, she interrupts with, "Don't you dare just tell me about the movie. You know that's not what I mean."

I pause as Dana returns to drop off a bread basket and fill up our water glasses. Service here is *fast*. I use the time to formulate my answer.

"The red carpet was, uh, *interesting*. Kinda intimidating. I don't know how you do that by yourself."

She smirks. "There's a reason I invited you. I don't feel as stupid just standing there and posing when someone else is doing it too. But that's still not what I mean."

I decide to play dumb. If she wants specific answers, she'll have to spell her questions out. "Well, you already said you didn't want to talk about the movie, but I don't know what else to say, so..."

She rolls her eyes playfully. "Okay, fine. So, *Jace*. Let's talk."

Don't blush, don't blush, don't... damn. "Oh, okay. Yeah, he seems nice."

"Nice, huh?" She raises an eyebrow and narrows her eyes, but I can see a smile dancing in them.

"Are you ready to order?" We both straighten up a bit, surprised by the new voice. Aviva gives a more formal smile to the server, greeting her with, "Oh hi, Virginia. Sure." She lists off her order as I frantically scan the options, not having paid the menu any attention since its arrival.

"Naya?" Aviva asks. I look up. "Do you know what you want?"

"Um... sure. I'll have the..." I point out an item randomly. "That. The fettucine alfredo."

The girl – Virginia, apparently, although I can't see a name tag – writes it down on a small pad of paper. "No appetizer, then?" she asks.

I hadn't even thought about it, but it's already late for dinner, so I don't want to eat too much. "No. That's all."

"We'll also get some wine," Aviva adds. I nod, and allow her to choose it from the wine list Virginia provides. I don't drink much wine, so I figure Aviva will know what's best, especially since she's been here before. Virginia nods approvingly at Aviva's choice and assures us she'll be back soon, then disappears as suddenly as she'd shown up.

I dig into the bread, dipping it into the oil and vinegar provided since apparently it's too fancy here for plain old butter, and avoid Aviva's eyes.

"Naya," she chides, and I sigh. I don't know what I'm hoping to accomplish by not admitting to liking Jace when it's obvious that she already knows I do. I've already dumped all my Asher problems onto her and she actually helped a lot with those. With her connections in the industry, maybe she might know some of the same people Jace does, and be able to give me another opportunity to see him. Maybe I just don't want to jinx the possibility of anything happening by putting the option out into the universe. I never really tell anybody that I like someone because I'm deathly terrified that they'll let the person know, or that it will somehow get back to them. But I trust Aviva. I know that she won't tell anybody something I ask her not to. We've been through enough and I know too much about her for her to risk that. Not that I'd ever tell her secret identity, even if she did let my crush slip out.

"Okay, fine," I murmur, swallowing my mouthful. "I *may* like him." I can feel the heat rushing through my face but ignore it, instead reaching for another piece of bread.

She claps excitedly and I glare at her. "I knew it!" she stage whispers. "This is great. I already like him better than Asher."

"I don't know that he likes me, too," I mutter.

She raises her eyebrows. "Well, he was acting like he did. He was definitely more interested in you than me."

I sigh. "Okay, well, still. I may never see him again."

She shrugs. "The industry is smaller than you'd think. Everyone knows everyone, or they know someone who knows everyone. If he was at that premiere, chances are he knows some industry people."

That's what I'd been hoping. "But you've never met him before? Or even seen him?"

She joins me in grabbing some bread, carefully dribbling oil over it as she considers. "No, I don't think so." At my frown, she continues. "But maybe some people I know have. I can ask, if you want?"

"No!" I say, more emphatically than I'd been aiming for. I clear my throat. "I mean, that's okay. You don't need to." She smirks again, and I get the feeling she's enjoying this conversation a lot more than I am. "Shut up," I mutter, and she laughs outright.

"You should've gotten his number," she mentions, just as our wine is delivered. The glasses are large and round, and mine feels heavy in my hand after the liquid is poured. I take a grateful sip and wait for the server to leave again before responding.

"Maybe he was just being friendly," I say. "He seemed like an outgoing person."

Aviva shrugs. "Well, maybe the intrigue will be enough to convince you to walk some more carpets with me in the future."

The idea fills me with simultaneous dread and excitement, and I waver. "Maybe." I can decide later. Honestly though, the thought that Jace could potentially be there too is definitely incentive.

Our food arrives, and we finally move onto other, less uncomfortable topics. I complain about textbook prices and how I'll likely never use them again after this April. Aviva laughs, and it sounds half-relieved, half-wistful.

"That's something I don't have to worry about," she says, expertly slicing her steak into even strips, "as long as I'm working and not in school."

"Do you think you'll ever go to post-secondary?" I ask curiously.

She nods and chews her first strip, closing her eyes momentarily in apparent bliss. I take the first bite of my pasta. Wow. This food is incredible. I look back up at Aviva's voice.

"I definitely want to go back, in a few more years. But I just graduated high school, you know? I want to take some time for myself."

I nod. "I wish I could take some time off. But then I'd need to get a job, probably something minimum-wage involving physical labour, and I'd rather do schoolwork than that right now."

Aviva nods thoughtfully, then smiles. "I forget, sometimes. How lucky I am to be able to do what I love."

"And that you *know* what you love. What you want to do for the rest of your life."

Her eyebrows raise. "Do you not know?"

I chew on my lip, then take another bite of pasta as I formulate my answer. "I know what I like to do. But I don't know if doing it in a work setting would take the enjoyment away from it. Or if there's another job out there somewhere that I would enjoy even more."

She nods slightly, staring intently at the wall behind me. Then she looks me in the eyes and says, "I don't have the answer for this one. I've always known what I wanted to do. But I hope you find your thing soon. Because everyone deserves the opportunity to have their dream job."

The conversation is beginning to feel stifling, so I quickly shuffle through my brain for a topic change. "What kinds of questions did those reporters ask you?"

The rest of our dinner out is dedicated to lighter conversation, and we stay long after we finish our meals and drinks. I haven't felt this simultaneously relaxed and yet emotionally high in a very long time. I'm not even worried about the work I know I'll have to do tomorrow, which is a change, because usually even just the thought of it stresses me out.

Aviva calls for the limo around eleven, because everyone else is starting to clear out – probably headed for the after-party, or the after-after-party – and I need to be home before midnight, as per my mother's conditions. The car comes pretty quickly, and I reluctantly stand. Virginia immediately swishes in and removes our remaining dishes from the table as we meander toward the exit.

We walk at a much brisker pace toward the limo, the winter air chilling us through our thin clothing. We tumble into the backseat, Aviva rubbing her upper arms to create friction. I slam the door closed with relief, then sit on my hands to warm them. The driver takes us back to Aviva's apartment building, where my car is parked. We wave the limo off, then she waits, shivering slightly, as I get into my vehicle. Any trace of alcohol has long worn off by now.

"I'll let you know when we can go to another premiere," she says.

"I said maybe," I remind her.

Her eyebrows flash up and down once quickly as the corners of her mouth lift into a restrained smile, and she just murmurs, "Mhm."

I roll my eyes, fighting back a smile of my own. "Good night, Aviva."

"Night." She waves through my window after I slam the door shut and crank up the heater. I pull out of the parking lot, tiredness beginning to creep into my body. Tonight was busy. More emotionally and mentally than physically, but it was still draining. A bit of my euphoria from earlier is still left over, and I let out the grin that had been building inside. Tonight may have been nerve-wracking, but it was also exciting and fun. Better than I'd expected.

When I wake up the next morning, my good mood is still in place, if a bit toned down. Light is already brightly streaming through my window, and I feel well-rested, so I figure it's later than I usually wake up. Cleaning my room, which usually stresses me out, seems like a small job to me now. I decide to start on it as soon as I consume some brunch.

Unfortunately, the job proves more time-consuming than my happiness had tried to convince me it would be. Not only do I have to pick up and put away everything on my floor, but I make the mistake of beginning to sort through all of my high school assignments I'd kept in a drawer in the corner of my room. By the time I've cleared my floor and am a third of the way through the papers, it's already been an hour and my back is beginning to hurt from crouching. I pick everything up and continue at my desk, trying to decide which papers I could possibly use in the future versus which are no longer relevant.

When I finally finish, satisfaction fills me. There's no way Mom can reprimand me about the cleanliness of my bedroom now. I check my phone and my stomach drops. It's already four p.m. and I still have the rest of my homework to complete. Reluctantly, I bring up my message thread with Aviva and type.

Hey, so I won't be able to get to the gym tn. Too much hw.

Her response is almost immediate.

Aw, that sucks :(What about tmo?

I breathe a sigh of relief. Just planning everything out is already helping to lower my anxiety over my homework.

Ya, I can do tmo. Right after newspaper?

Kk! Ttyt.

I turn my phone off then stand up and stretch, deciding I can take a short break before moving onto my schoolwork, now that I no longer have to worry about making time for the gym too. I walk downstairs to the kitchen, where my mom is already preparing dinner. I sit at the table.

"How was last night with Brynn?" she asks.

I smile. "Really fun. The movie was good, too. And then we went to this fancy restaurant after."

Mom raises her eyebrows. "I hope that didn't cost too much."

I think back. I hadn't even thought about the cost, as there were no prices listed on the dinner menu. I can't recall pulling out my wallet, either. With a jolt I realize that Aviva must have put it on her tab, or else paid somehow without me noticing. Now I'm also hoping that it wasn't too expensive, since Aviva treated me and I didn't even notice. I have to remember to thank her tomorrow.

"Brynn treated me," I say blithely, hoping Mom won't press further. Luckily, she doesn't. "We may go out again soon," I add.

She nods. "As long as you keep getting your homework done, and keeping your room clean," she says with a pointed look at me, "then that should be fine."

"Oh trust me," I mutter, "my room will be clean for much longer this time. It's practically bare now."

She smirks. "Somehow I doubt that."

I just shrug. It's not like I can argue. Even if it's relatively clean, it's still far from empty. "When's dinner?" I ask instead.

"Whenever your father and brother come home. They're at the movies. Seeing some new film that apparently only entered theatres this afternoon."

"Oh really? Do you know what it's called?"

She pauses in her stirring the pot on the stove to recall. "Uh, *Stormy Night*, I believe."

I start to gasp then begin to cough as I choke it back. That's the movie I saw last night. Mom gives me a weird look as my breathing calms down. "I'm fine. Just... dust or something." She looks dubious still, and I'm not in the mood to try and dream up more excuses for how ordinary Brynn and I managed to get into a star-studded high-budget movie premiere, so I say that I should start on my homework now and leave the kitchen, nearly sprinting back up to my room.

Ugh. I hate lying to my mom. Or, in this case, omitting critical information. But I have no way to tell the truth without giving away that Brynn is Aviva, which she specifically asked me not to do. And as good of a friend as she's been to me thus far, I don't want to hurt her. So instead of putting myself in a position where I might be forced to spill information I don't want to, I stay in my bedroom and do my homework until dinner, then quickly return and work some more after everyone is done eating. I actually manage to finish my assigned readings, including the ones I'd needed to catch up on, before ten thirty, after forcing my mind to focus solely on school. I take a brief moment to mourn my missed gym time yesterday and today, but I'm too happy about the fact that I actually get to sleep for more than eight hours two nights in a row to worry about it for long. I've engaged my brain so much today that it remains blissfully blank as I settle into bed, allowing me to drift off peacefully.

I don't know whether it's from attending a high-profile premiere two nights ago, or if Aviva's confidence lessons and lectures are finally beginning to sink into me, but I feel totally comfortable as I go through my Monday classes. Usually it takes me a while to get back into the swing of the school week after being off for the weekend, but I feel as though I completely belong among my classmates today.

Even newspaper editing, previously a large source of anxiety, due to Asher and Savannah, doesn't affect me today. It's such a huge relief to walk in without shaky hands and butterflies erupting in my stomach. I smile and say hello to several other editors. They return the greeting immediately, if a bit confusedly, since I don't normally say much by this point in the day. I notice that neither Asher nor Savannah are here yet, but I don't think on their absences further.

I sit at my desk, but really don't feel the urge to work. I decide to check my email on the school's computer before I start, and quickly sign in. There's nothing important, so I just flip through the store advertisements until I feel a presence behind me.

"Slacking off, huh?" A familiar male voice asks amusedly. "That's not like you, Naya."

I roll my eyes, although he can't see from his position, and reply, "Everyone needs a break once in a while, Ash." The nickname slips from my lips before I can restrain myself. That's the first time I've used the shortened version of his name since our breakup. I shrug it off. It's just a name, and I've been silly to have avoided it for this long, anyway.

"Oh yeah?" he asks. "What's the matter, hard weekend?"

I reluctantly sign off of my email, since it seems that he's not just making passing conversation, and turn to face him. "Nah," I return, not really wanting to talk about the good portion of my life with him, the cause of my hard portion. "I just spent a lot of time doing homework yesterday and really didn't want to continue the trend today."

"This isn't homework, Naya," he tells me cajolingly. "It's a job."

"Pretty sure you need to get paid in order to consider something a job," I tell him. "But I'll get on it anyway." Then I turn back to the computer screen, pull up some articles, and wait for him to leave. I don't actually need these articles for my editing work today; I just want him to let me be. I patiently wait to hear his footsteps retreating, but am quickly disappointed when he continues talking.

"Aw, I'm just teasing you, Naya," he says, and comes around to lean on my desk, blocking half of my computer screen. "Don't take everything so seriously."

I grit my teeth and paste on a saccharine smile, returning, "No, it's good that I start now. I actually have plans after this, so the sooner I'm gone, the better." I hold eye contact with him, hoping that he gets the message to *leave, already*.

"Plans, huh?" he asks. "With the same person as Friday?"

Oh, that's right. I'd told him that I was going out Friday. "Yup, same person," I tell him. "Same person as Saturday, too."

Something flickers in his eyes, and I decide that if he's planning on staying here a while, I really should start on my actual editing work. I pull out several papers from my backpack, and place them on the other side of the computer, as far away as they can get from Asher while still being on the desk. I ignore him as I get to work editing, but he doesn't seem to be paying much attention to the work I'm doing, or the fact that it's different from the pages on my computer screen.

"So are you and this *person*... getting close?" he finally asks, and I smother a laugh. It's obvious that he thinks this *person* is male, and that by *friend* I actually mean much more.

"Yes, actually," I reply, smiling down at the pages in front of me as I tick away in red pen. "*Very* close," I can't help adding, looking up at Asher with a grin. He's frowning, but as soon as he notices me staring up at him, he quickly replaces it with a cocky eyebrow raise.

"Good, good," he mutters. "And what about tomorrow? Do you have any plans then?"

"Why?" I ask nonchalantly.

"Do you want to get dinner or something? Just like the good old days?"

I take a beat to think over my response before answering. Why is it that just when I'm finally over Asher, he begins to show interest again? I'd never wanted to break up in the first place; it had been entirely his decision. But after seeing what happiness apart from Asher is like, I want to continue experiencing it. I know that if I don't resist, I could easily get sucked back into the whirlwind a relationship with Asher resembles. But I don't want that anymore. I *want* to resist. Especially since meeting Jace... I have no idea whether a relationship with Jace is feasible or not, but if it is, there's no way I'm returning to Asher and effectively ending any chances at it. I still don't want to piss Asher off, though, since I will have to continue seeing him at newspaper every school day, so I reply carefully.

"That sounds nice, but I can't," I tell him, a smile frozen on my face. I have no real excuses beyond *I really don't want to go back to that relationship*, and I don't want to make anything up, so I leave it at that. He can fill in the blanks with whatever excuses he wants.

He stiffens slightly, but retains his swagger as he says, "Next time then."

I smile again but don't respond beyond that. A *yes* would give him too much hope, while a direct *no* could ruin any chances of civility between us for the rest of the school year.

"I really do have to get on this," I tell him, indicating my editing work with the pen in my hand. He begins to frown darkly, so I quickly tack on, "It was nice to talk to you, though."

He nods, handsome face blank of emotion, and walks away, still owning the room as he usually does. I sigh silently, then mentally congratulate myself on avoiding that trap. Aviva was right, as she often is. Asher didn't treat me well when we were together, and our breakup may well have been the best thing for me. I'm finally realizing what Aviva has been able to see all along.

When I get to the gym about an hour later, Aviva isn't here yet. I'm surprised, because this is the time I usually get to the gym, and Aviva almost always beats me, or at least arrives near the same time. I wait ten minutes, but she still doesn't show up, so I decide to begin my workout. I send her a text first, asking where she is, but receive no response. I shrug it off, figuring she's just a little late, and pull up my music instead, since she isn't here to distract me from my burning muscles with witty conversation. Remembering her odd response to the treadmills, I decide to return to the elliptical trainers. They're more enjoyable, anyway, or at least don't make my lungs burn quite so badly.

Half an hour later, Aviva still isn't here. This is way past the time she usually arrives, so I cool off a little bit and check my texts. There's still no response from her, so I pull up her contact on my phone and hit the call button. This is the first time I've called her instead of just texting, so I'm a bit surprised to hear her voicemail. Primarily because it's not her voice, but a masculine one – Callan's, perhaps?

"Hey, you've reached Aviva's phone," the recorded voice says humorously. "If you've managed to get to this point in your call, I think you'll know what to do next." Then the beep sounds.

"Hey, Aviva," I say nervously, "it's Naya. I was just wondering if you were still coming to the gym tonight? I hope you just forgot and everything's fine... I'm only going to be here for another half hour, so it's okay if you can't make it, but let me know your plans as soon as you can." I pause awkwardly, wondering if there's anything else I should say, before hurriedly finishing up with, "Okay, bye!"

I cringe as a press the *End Call* button, but hopefully that message should be enough to spur Aviva into telling me where she is. I increase the speed on my elliptical trainer once again, hoping to expel the pent-up energy I now have from the anxiety of making the call.

At the end of my workout, there is still no word from Aviva. I try not to let it bother me, but now that my mind is no longer focused on just breathing, it has plenty of room to wander about. I try to distract myself with meaningless activities on the way home, like picking up the mail. There are only some bills in our mailbox, so I also pick up a rag mag from the FREE NEWSPAPERS box next to it, chuckling at the quality of these 'newspapers'. I drive the rest of the way home, then enter the house slowly, taking a closer look at the free magazine. I usually don't pay these types of magazines any attention, but I'm actually glad I picked this one up, because in huge bolded letter, the cover proclaims, *BURNING EMBERS: FROM BOOK TO MOVIE!*

Burning Embers is a hugely popular book series, one that I actually enjoyed reading. It's not just the romance/action plotline that usually gets picked up for the big screen; it has many psychological elements, and I'm very curious to see if they'll be transferred to the filmic version. I hope so. I find the article on page 21, but it contains more speculation than actual facts. It does mention that the characters have been cast, but not who the actors are. I grunt, disappointed. I want to see if they'll match up to my mental images of the leads.

I turn the page, but just find some silly quizzes and horoscope predictions. I begin to recall why I don't often read this type of magazine as I flip through page after page of relative nothingness, until my eye catches on a crimson headline. It reads *RED CARPET FASHIONS OF THE WEEK*. Both hope and reluctance fill my chest as I slowly scan down the page. *There*. It's Aviva, in her pink pantsuit from the weekend. I quickly skip over her to the snatch of blue visible at the edge of the image, and a burst of air escapes my lips. *That's me*. Well, sort of. It's my dress, at least; the majority of my body, including my face, has been cut out of the image. I don't know how to process this. It's not as though I'm the one this magazine is focusing on; hell, they don't even care about my dress. But I'm still in the picture. It feels surreal.

I tear my eyes away from the tiny bit of blue and look back over at Aviva with more focus now. She looks perfect, as she does in almost every image I've ever seen of her. There's a small box of text to her other side, which I read now: *For more on Aviva Jersey, check out page 36!* I automatically turn to the suggested page.

It's all about her new movie, the one directed by Hayden Landen. The article explains much of what Aviva told me last week, including that her character is a strong female lead, and that Aviva is involved in casting the other characters. I bite my lip.

Didn't Aviva say that all this information was top-secret? Maybe I misunderstood, and she only told me the amount the public could know, keeping the high-clearance stuff to herself. I shrug it off, and start up my laptop instead, really curious to see if I can find any other pictures of Aviva and me together at the premiere. Maybe even some that include my face.

I type 'stormy night toronto premiere' into my search box and scroll through the image results, but there are so many results that I can't even spot Aviva, let alone myself. I add Aviva's name to the search terms, which helps a little, but the majority of images are from other premieres she's attended. Well, it has only been two days. I suppose I'm lucky I got to see even just the one image in the rag mag.

I end up only finding one image of Aviva at the Stormy Night premiere, and it looks to have been taken during one of her interviews, when I wasn't present. I would keep looking, but when I pause on a photo of a brown-haired man on the red carpet, I realize that I've been subconsciously looking for Jace too. I sigh. Best not to get too invested in Jace, considering that I don't even know if I'll ever see him again. I shut my computer down, simultaneously disappointed and relieved.

Dinner is good, but I don't have much to add to the conversation. I'm still in the good mood that I'd felt all day, but my lack of contact with Aviva has left me feeling slightly off. She nearly always responds to my texts immediately, which are less noticeable than a call, which she'd also missed. I don't know why she wouldn't reply, especially after missing our scheduled gym time and receiving my slightly worried voicemail. Maybe her phone died, and she hasn't had a chance to recharge it yet? But wouldn't she find some way to communicate with me? Even a call from a landline, or a message over social media sent from a computer? But maybe she hasn't been home yet. Maybe something came up earlier, and so she had to go to the gym tonight instead.

Well, I already texted and called her. I don't want to keep sending her messages, especially if she's just not receiving them yet. I don't want to flood her. I decide to push her out of my brain for the moment, and focus back on my dinner.

"This is really good, Mom," I tell my mother with a smile, emptying my mind of everything but the taste of the homemade lasagna on the table in front of me.

8

Chapter Eight

I'm slightly worried to see Asher at newspaper editing the next day. I hope I didn't screw up our working relationship by turning him down. I think that was actually the first time I ever said no to spending time to him. Luckily, he still seems to be trying to win me over, all smiles and winks and inside jokes I'd nearly forgotten about. I wouldn't mind being friends with this Asher. As long as he remains jovial and doesn't get too deep or try to ask me out again, I can enjoy my time around him.

I still haven't heard anything from Aviva. I keep checking my phone at newspaper, which leads Asher to ask, "Waiting for a call?"

I shrug. "Maybe. Hopefully."

He squints. "Lovers' quarrel?"

I look up sharply and snort. "Definitely not." I mean that Aviva and I are far from lovers, but if he wants to take that as

I have a boyfriend with whom I am very happy, he can. He attempts a smile, although it looks a bit sour, and walks away. I put my phone into my backpack instead of just my easily-accessible pocket, determined to finish up my editing work. If I still haven't heard anything from Aviva by the time I get home, I'll try sending her another text. Maybe she's just forgotten to reply by now, and a new message will remind her.

On my way home, I realize that I actually miss Aviva. It's only been a few days since I last saw her, but I've become accustomed to seeing her every day, and spilling out all my stress and secrets to her. It feels as though I have pressure bottled up inside of me now, just waiting to be relieved.

I still have no new notifications on my phone, so I formulate my text message as I drive. My voicemail was already serious enough, so I don't want to be too heavy in this text. Just something light-hearted. A conversation starter.

When I've parked in the driveway at home, I send a quick *hey* before I even leave my car. I wait impatiently for two minutes, but decide that staring at the screen won't help her to respond any faster. I get out and go inside the house, unpacking all my books from my backpack onto my desk. I keep my phone turned face-up beside me as I attempt a reading.

Twenty minutes later, there is still no response, so I decide to ask a question, if a simple greeting isn't enough to trigger her reply. I recall the rag mag from yesterday.

I saw news of ur movie is out. I thought it was a secret lol?

I replace my phone on my desk and turn back to my textbook. I don't even have enough time to finish the paragraph I'd started when my phone vibrates with a new message. I jump, almost surprised to have finally received something.

It's from Aviva. *We need to talk. Can we meet in person?*

I stare at the message, not breathing for a short beat. I'm thankful she replied, so I know that she's not seriously injured or that something else terrible had happened to her, but her message sounds ominous. I can't decipher the emotions behind the words, so I make my reply cheerful, hoping that will set the tone for our conversation.

Sure! Will u b at the gym tn?

Her message takes less than thirty seconds to arrive at my phone from the time I sent mine. *Not the gym. Sooner. Like now.*

When I don't immediately reply, staring at my screen in confusion, wondering what could possibly be so urgent now but not twenty minutes ago, when I sent my greeting text, another message arrives from Aviva.

Can I come to your house?

I pause for a second but then reply quickly, fingers fumbling over the tiny keys.

Ok.

I stare at my phone as the message sends. I wait a minute for any new texts, but receive none. I guess that means she's on her way over here now. I'm suddenly very happy that my bedroom is now clean. She's seen it before, but after not seeing Aviva for a few days, and then being unable to clearly interpret the tone she was using through text messages, I'm feeling more vulnerable than usual.

I find my mother downstairs and let her know that Brynn is coming over for a bit. She nods and says that she can stay for dinner, if she likes. I don't know what we'll be talking about though – is Aviva mad at me? – so I give a noncommittal shrug and say I'll ask her when she gets here, then return to my room. I leave the door open so I can hear when Aviva comes.

Five minutes later, the doorbell rings. "I'll get it!" I shout, running from my room. I open the door cautiously, then slam it back shut in panic when I see who's behind it. It's Aviva. As in, blonde, no-wig Aviva. I take a surreptitious glance over both shoulders, ensuring no one is nearby, then open the door again quickly.

Aviva looks pissed, but I can't tell if it's because of our pending conversation, or because I just slammed a door in her face. I usher her inside and up the stairs, noticing that Connor's door is slightly open, but he must be busy inside, because he doesn't come out to see us and blow Aviva's cover.

Once in my room, I close the door and lock it behind us. I take a deep breath and turn back to Aviva, saying, "Sorry. I told my mom that Brynn was coming over. I didn't know you'd..." I gesture weakly at her hair.

She doesn't acknowledge what I just said. Instead, she sits primly on the end of my bed and clasps her hands in her lap. She nods at the chair by my desk and I fold back into it, feeling suspiciously like a naughty student at the principal's office.

She pauses for another moment, further heightening the anticipation in the room, then slowly says, "Naya, I have a few questions to ask you, and I want you to tell me the complete truth."

She seems to be waiting for something, so I answer, "Okay..." It comes out sounding more like a question than a reply, though. I have no idea why she would preface our conversation with that statement. I have always made it a point to tell her the truth.

Aviva nods. "Are we friends?"

I pause, thrown off by the query. Her face is expressionless, and she doesn't seem at all unsure of herself. The question seems more like a test than a genuine concern. I cough to cover up my moment of silence. "Yes, of course." I think I hear a noise outside of my room then, and my head whips around to look at my door, but then Aviva says my name softly and I quickly turn back. Her voice, although low in volume, is extremely commanding.

"Did you enjoy the movie premiere?" she asks next. I'm beginning to feel backed into a corner, but I don't know why. Her line of inquiry seems so unassuming on the surface, but I feel as though if I say just one word wrong, I'll set off a landmine.

"Yes," I reply hesitantly. "Well, you know. It was kinda intimidating at first," I laugh nervously, "but I had fun."

She blinks at me impassively. Her face is so devoid of life, it's almost frightening. "Did you talk to many people there?"

"At the premiere?" I confirm with raised eyebrows. At her nod, I say, "Um, not really. Like I said, intimidating. I think it was just you and J-Jace." I stutter over his name and blush.

Aviva seems to consider everything I've said so far. She leans forward slightly, breaking her perfect posture, and I can sense that she's building up to the most important question yet. "Did you talk to the press about my new movie?" she asks, and I can see the slightest bit of strain entering her face.

My brain goes blank. *Did you talk to the press about my new movie?* I can easily translate that sentence to say *Did you break my trust?* "No, of course not!" I say adamantly. My volume level is higher than expected, and Aviva's eyes widen barely perceptibly, the first response she's given to any of my words. "Why would I do that?" I ask in shock.

Her face transitions back to the mask she had on previously. "I hear they pay good money for celebrity secrets," she says idly, as if the conversation isn't important. As if she's not accusing me of selling her out. As if this isn't the biggest fight we've ever been in.

Her apathy is triggering a different response in me, as the surprise drains away. I'm hurt, yes, but more than that, I'm *angry*. I take a deep breath before replying. "There are better ways to make money than selling out your friend's secrets," I say stiffly.

Aviva shrugs, and although the movement itself is casual, I can see that it's calculated on her part. "Better, maybe, but not faster. Not easier. University is expensive." She stares at me straight-on. "Or so I've heard."

I stand up. I refuse to cower in my seat like a scared little girl when I've done nothing wrong. Now I tower over Aviva. It feels wrong, since she's taller than me, but it also feels *right* for the moment. "Yeah, Aviva, school is expensive," I tell her, my voice frosty, "but I'm not in debt. Why would you just assume *I* told the press about your movie? Like, really. After everything I told you? You know a lot of my secrets. Pretty much all of them, actually." I cringe, hoping this reminder won't spur her to let my personal details slip in public as some sort of revenge, but I want her to see what is so obvious to me. The kind of relationship that I thought we had.

"Your secrets—"

I wait a second to see if she's planning on finishing that sentence, but she just presses her lips together tightly. It's enough, though. I know what she was going to say.

"Oh, that's right," I remark scathingly. "*My* secrets aren't as important as *yours*, because *I'm not famous.*"

She scowls at me, but I know that's what she was thinking. At least now she's dropped the ice queen façade, and I can actually see what she's feeling, even if all she's feeling at this moment is anger. It's better than not knowing at all.

I take one more deep breath, physically forcing some of my frustration out of my body, and pushing my shoulders down to a more normal position. "I don't know who told your secret, Aviva," I finally tell her, staring her down. Her eyes shift away for a few seconds before returning to mine. "But it wasn't me."

She studies my face for a few moments after my declaration, and I can see some hesitation creeping beneath her skin.

"Obviously someone else found out," I say, my voice now just sounding tired. "But whoever it was, it wasn't my fault."

"But you were the only one who–" Suddenly her voice catches and confusion infuses her features.

"*Not* the only one who knew," I correct. Obviously I couldn't have been the only one, because someone else had ratted her out to the press. Aviva remains silent, so I sigh and rub my hands over my eyes, smudging whatever makeup I have on my eyes right now, but I can't bring myself to care. I drop back into my seat and rest my head against one hand.

"I did–" I look up at Aviva's words, and see her face is twisted into an amalgamation of emotions. I can barely discern one from the next, and I'm not sure I want to; they all look negative. "I did tell Sierra," she continues quietly.

Sierra. I remember Aviva mentioning her before she told me about her movie. Sierra was the only person Aviva had actually called her friend while telling me stories of Los Angeles. *Shit.* If Sierra was the only other person who'd known – and Aviva seemed pretty sure of that, at least – that meant someone else she had trusted had betrayed her. "I'm sorry," I tell her quietly, eyes firm on hers. "I didn't tell. So I'm sorry that she did." I can't bring myself to say Sierra's name out loud, because I've never met her, and it feels odd to make such a definitive and negative statement about a girl I know almost nothing about.

Aviva's face twitches slightly, and I can see hurt entering her expression, breaking past her fury. "Where is the washroom?" she asks stiffly, pulling her phone out of her purse. I sigh and put my face into my palms. I'm done. I'm just so done with this conversation at the moment.

"I think you should go, Aviva," I tell her, keeping my voice neutral. If all she wants is to make a call and then come back and talk some more, I'd rather pass for now. Even if she came back and apologized, my emotions are too tangled up to handle it. I need some time to cool off and figure out everything I'm really feeling.

She presses her lips together and nods, then stands without speaking and walks swiftly toward my door. The instant it opens, I see a frozen Connor standing on the other side. His eyes widen enormously as he takes in Aviva – *double shit* – but she doesn't give him long to look. She turns her body to the side, passing by him without touching him, and leaves my view. I hear her staccato steps down the stairs, then the sound of the front door opening and closing with a resounding *thud.* Connor is still in the same position outside of my door but for his head, which has swivelled to watch Aviva's every move until she's out of the house.

I get out of my chair, trying to escape the fog of the conversation through a change in seating. I flop onto my bed, but it doesn't help as I'd hoped it would. I close my eyes, and thus hear rather than see Connor enter my room. I groan and pinch my nose between my index finger and thumb. "Connor, get out! I am *so* not in the mood."

His footsteps keep approaching, so I open my eyes reluctantly and glare up at him. "Why were you outside my room, anyway? Did you need something?" I ask pointedly, hoping he can just take what he requires and get out.

"Mom said you had Brynn over," he mutters. He must be in shock. He rarely says anything quietly; he likes to be the centre of attention too much. "She sent me to ask if she wanted to stay for dinner. But when I got up here, I heard you guys fighting, so I thought I should wait for you to finish before interrupting."

Hold on – wait for us to finish? He was *eavesdropping* on us? I'm about to accuse him of it when he opens his mouth again quickly and bursts out, "You said *Aviva*. That was Aviva Jersey, wasn't it?"

I try to think over my answer quickly, because Connor is staring at me expectantly. I can't really deny it now – *oh no, she was just Aviva Jersey's doppelganger, whose name also happens to be Aviva* – and the photos of us together at the premiere are available now anyway, if someone really wanted to go searching, so there's not much I can do beyond nod. It's a slight movement, but Connor is staring at me so intently that he sees it and reads the meaning immediately.

He squints at me incredulously. "How did you even meet?"

I recall the story Aviva and I had agreed on before the premiere, if anyone asked. "Grocery store," I tell Connor, hoping against hope that he won't question it.

Unfortunately, he does. "You never go grocery shopping alone," he accuses me, suspicion evident in his voice.

I shrug, mind racing. "I did. Once."

He snorts. "Yeah, okay. And what exactly did you buy?"

Finally the answer comes to me. The one sure-fire way to cut my brother off of this line of questioning. "Feminine products," I tell him succinctly. I see him withdraw slightly, but not as far as I want, so I add, "Urgently needed," with a false grimace.

His face is almost comical, and he takes several more steps backwards, towards my bedroom door. "Well, um," he tries to recover himself, "why was Aviva here instead of Brynn? Or is Brynn her nickname?" His tone is belittling.

"No, no," I say quickly. Even if I am mad at Aviva, that doesn't mean I'll let loose even more of her secrets. Actually, this incident gives me even more incentive to protect her secrets, to show her that I am reliable even in the face of high tension. "Brynn cancelled."

He looks dubious. "In the time between when you told Mom she was coming and the time Aviva arrived?"

"Um. Yeah. That's what I just said, isn't it?"

"And what, Aviva was just conveniently on her way over here? You never mentioned anything to Mom about a second person coming too."

"Brynn sent Aviva in her place," I say, making my story up on the spot.

"So Brynn and Aviva know each other?"

"Yes," I say defensively. I just hope he doesn't ask what Brynn and I were planning on doing that so easily replaced Brynn with Aviva, because I would have no idea how to answer.

"Hm." His eyes flicker as he processes my words. "So what is Aviva doing here?"

At first I freak out, thinking he's asking the very question I'd hoped he wouldn't, but then he tacks on, "in Toronto?" and I take a deep breath and re-centre myself.

I pause momentarily, wondering if I still shouldn't say anything about Aviva's new movie, but considering the news has already been published in print, I think I'll be safe from any future wrath. "She's making a film," I finally tell Connor, deciding not to say anything more than that.

Connor takes a moment before finally bursting out, "But why would she even want to hang out with *you*?"

I wince, the comment hitting too close to home. It's very similar to the thoughts I'd been having myself not too long ago. But I don't let my resolution waver, simply replying, "Believe it or not, some people actually like me."

Connor snorts in response and I frown at him. He just shrugs unapologetically and slowly begins to exit my room. "Well, as long as she keeps coming over here," he tells me, taking measured steps backwards, "I'm fine with it."

"I wasn't asking your permission!" I call after him, but he just rolls his eyes. "And we had a fight. As you heard. So who knows if she'll be back..." I sigh and rub my eyes wearily.

"Make up with her," Connor tells me over his shoulder. "She's got to be even hotter than Brynn."

I snort, first for the obvious reason – *Is Aviva hotter than Aviva? Or the other way around?* – and then because Connor's never even seen Brynn. He's basing his whole perception of her on what I've previously described. I fall back onto my bed and move my hands to my temples, attempting to alleviate some of the tension I can feel building up in my head. I don't want to focus on my fight with Aviva. I know that right now, I'm still angry, and I think it'd be better if my mind were clear of negativity when I analyze our conversation. I can't focus back on schoolwork now, though, so I put in my earbuds instead and close my eyes, letting the lyrics resound through my skull.

When I open my eyes again, Connor is at my door. "Didn't I tell you to leave?" I mutter, my mouth full of cotton and my vision not quite clear. I blink and it focuses.

"That was over an hour ago."

Oh. I must've fallen asleep. I take a deep breath and sit up. I actually do feel somewhat better now. "So why are you here again?" I ask him.

"Dinner's ready." He turns around. "What do you think, I came to hang out?" He snorts and walks away. I roll my eyes.

My music is still playing through my earbuds, so I stop it. I drop my phone onto my bedside desk and go downstairs. My mind does feel clearer, although I'm still tired. It's enough that I can successfully finish my schoolwork downstairs after I eat, while Connor goes out on a date with a new girl and my parents watch a movie in the family room. Normally I'd be too distracted down here, but I prefer the different location right now. I think I'd be more distracted in my room, with memories of the afternoon still so fresh. And my tiredness motivates me to finish my work quickly, so I can return to my bed.

I scrub my face and brush my teeth in my bathroom, then grab my charger and plug my phone into the wall in my bedroom. I don't focus on the screen. I don't want to see if I have any notifications. I just want to sleep.

When my alarm wakes me in the morning, it's from a beautiful dream where I was lying on the hot beach, sunbathing. I open my eyes to my window, where snow still lies in patches on the ground, remember I have to go to school again today, and a frown overtakes my face. I snuggle back under my comforter and check my phone. I'm momentarily surprised to see that I have three missed calls from Aviva, until I recall yesterday's argument. I heave a sigh. I don't have enough energy or motivation right now to have this conversation. I don't bother listening to the messages, figuring I'll just call her later and she can tell me everything she left in my voicemail anyway.

My Anthropology tutorial seems to drag on for at least half a day, although the amount of time the clock shows actually passing is significantly smaller. I'm pretty sure I fall asleep several times, back ramrod straight. When the T.A. finally releases us, I bolt upright and scurry outside into the (cold) sunlight as quickly as I can without outright running. I buy some lunch and take it into my car, where I blast the heat. Once I'm warm and full, I decide it's time to call Aviva back.

She picks up on the first ring. "Hey!" Her voice is bubbly as it usually is, but I can hear a tentative edge in the short breath she took before her greeting.

"Hi," I reply.

There's a moment of silence before she continues. "So, uh, did you get my messages?"

"Got them, yeah," I say, picking at my fingernails. "Didn't actually listen to them yet though."

"Oh. Okay. Um, well..." I stare down at my lap as she gathers her words. "I'm sorry," she says finally. I take a deep breath, the words hitting something inside of me. When I don't immediately reply, she tacks on, "for accusing you. I know you didn't do it now."

My frustration is draining away, and my hurt, although not erased, has been mended by her apology. I don't want to hang onto those negative emotions. I want us to be on good terms again. I look at my empty car and at myself eating lunch in it, and grimace. After all, Aviva kind of is my only friend.

"It's okay," I tell her. There's another brief silence, but this one feels much less tension-filled than the first.

"I called Sierra," Aviva finally says. I perk up, extremely interested. "She, um... she admitted to selling the story." Her voice breaks on the last word.

My mind explodes with a "*duh!*" but I refrain from saying it aloud. "I'm sorry she did that," I reply simply instead.

"Yeah," she agrees, drawing in a ragged breath.

"But why would you believe so easily that I would sell out on a promise like that? I thought..." I trail off. I don't know how exactly to end that sentence. *I thought we were closer than that? I thought we had more trust than that? I thought you knew me better than that?*

She gets the gist of my message anyway. "Do you remember when I told you about Ivy?"

I do. Ivy had been her best friend when she was sixteen. Ivy had been the one who had leaked her relationship with Callan to the press, which led to Aviva missing out on some good roles. *Poison Ivy*, I remembered calling her. "Yeah. I do."

"Look, I know that you and Ivy are different people. Vastly different," she tells me, "but it can still be hard for me to trust people. Especially because Ivy and I were so close when she broke my trust. She wasn't just a casual friend. She was my *best* friend."

Again, I feel that there's more to Ivy's role in breaking Aviva's trust. There's something behind Aviva's words that feels loaded with pertinent information I'm not able to grasp right now. Whatever it was, it must have been huge.

"Okay, but why me? You were close with both me and Sierra, right? So why didn't you suspect Sierra at all?"

"I'd known Sierra longer. Years longer. And, um... this is going to sound bad. Look, Sierra doesn't need any money, okay?" Her voice is pleading.

I grunt in exasperation. "But why didn't you just call me and *ask*?" All I hear from the other end of the phone is silence, so I continue. "I will never lie to you Aviva. Okay? That's my promise from now on. If it will take total honesty for you to trust me, I'll give it. No white lies, no surprises, nothing."

I hear her sigh, but I can't tell what emotions triggered it. "Okay," she agrees. "I promise too. I'll never lie to you."

I notice she left out the *total honesty* part, and recall all the times I'd had suspicions that she was hiding something. I don't care, though. I'll accept it until she's ready to trust me entirely. As long as she always tells me the truth about present matters, the past doesn't matter.

"So, then, are we good?" she asks cautiously.

I nod into the phone, although I know she can't see it. "Yes. We're good."

I can hear a smile in her voice now. "Ah! Okay. Good." I smile too. "In that case, there's another movie premiere this weekend, if you're interested. And, if you get sick of me, Jace might be there."

"Oh my god," I groan, covering my red face, although no one is around to see it.

"Well, he might," she says teasingly. "I can't guarantee it, but I can't guarantee he *won't* be there either."

"Yes, okay, fine," I laugh. "But my mom said she'll only let me keep going out with Brynn if she sees us studying together too."

"Ooh, really?" she says excitedly. "What will we be studying?"

Wow. If I had the option of being out of school, I don't think I'd be this excited about studying. "Um, there are a few options," I tell her. "But I probably need to study for Latin the most. It's just a lot of memorization."

"Okay," she agrees cheerfully. "Learn me some Latin."

I snort at her intentionally bad grammar, until I hear her mutter something about her wig. "What was that?"

"Just... the wig. It's annoying."

"Well, I mean, my brother's already seen you at my house, so the cat's kind of out of the bag about us now anyway. I could tell my parents I'm going out with you, not Brynn."

"Um, yeah," she says hesitantly, then, "Okay!" with significantly more enthusiasm.

"Okay," I agree with a smile. We plan for Aviva to come over to my house once I'm done at newspaper editing tomorrow.

"And I'll see you at the gym tonight, right?" she asks.

"Yes. Definitely."

"Okay. Bye."

I smile again. "Bye." I tap the screen of my phone to end the call, noticing the time as I do. I need to get going in order to make my next class – Creative Writing – in time. My feet don't seem to drag as they did this morning though. I feel a bubble of lightness elevating my shoulders and head, keeping my grin glued to my face. I go with it. It feels good.

Chapter Nine

My Thursday morning class – Creative Writing tutorial – is easy, but I actually have to focus for my afternoon class – my Science tutorial. My head is still immersed in equations when I get to newspaper editing, so I don't initially notice Asher staring at me as I work. I attempt to ignore him, although my focus goes out the window every time I feel his eyes on me. When I finally finish all of my work assigned for today, I make a beeline for the exit, hoping that my single-minded focus will convince Asher to leave me alone.

Unfortunately, it doesn't. "Hey, Naya! Wait up."

I contemplate pretending not to have heard, but considering every pair of eyes in the office has turned to stare at us, I don't think my excuse would fly. So I slow down and say steadily, "I've got to get going, Asher. If you want to talk, walk with me."

He falls into step smoothly, his longer stride allowing him to maintain an easy pace as my legs move swiftly. We've just gotten out the door when he asks, "So, what are you doing tonight?"

That sounds like he's going to ask me on a date. That *definitely* sounds like he's going to ask me out. "Study date," I tell him meaningfully, hoping he'll move on.

"Oh?" he asks airily. "Is it with your *friend* who I don't know?"

I smirk. "Yes, actually."

"Are you dating him?" he finally asks. His tone is calm on the surface, but the words are rushed.

I sigh and turn to face him. "My *friend*," I tell him, giggling, "is a girl."

I can see the mask of confidence return to his face. "Oh," he says, laughing too. "Well, Naya, I didn't know you swing that way."

That cuts off my laughter. "I don't!" He keeps chuckling. "Ash, you know I don't. God, why does everyone keep saying that?" I mumble, recalling Connor's previous comment. "We're literally just friends."

He shrugs, predatory glint back in his eyes. I cast around my mind for something else, anything else, to deter him from asking me out again. I suddenly wonder if I should mention Jace, or even that I'm interested in someone else now, but the truth is that I don't know if I'll ever see Jace again, so I just keep walking away. When I reach my car, Asher is still lingering.

"Do you have the time?" he asks abruptly.

"Um..." I turn on my car's engine and wait for the display to appear. "Oh, shit!" I'm late. I'm seriously late. "I have to go. See you," I mutter, waving a hand in his general direction as I peel out of the lot, leaving him standing awkwardly at my now-empty parking space.

When I get within view of my driveway, I see Aviva's car already parked in my usual spot. I curse and quickly park on the side of the road instead, hoping that she's not unbearably uncomfortable in there, that my mother isn't currently telling embarrassing stories of me, and that Connor hasn't started trying to flirt with her yet.

I slam the front door open, announcing my arrival, and hear my mom and Aviva call greetings from the kitchen. I walk in quickly, wiping the beading sweat from my forehead, and see them seated across from each other at the dinner table. I take the seat next to Aviva and smile awkwardly, apologizing for being late. "Newspaper ran late, and then, um, *someone* kept trying to talk to me," I say, side-eyeing Aviva, hoping my mom will just assume it's someone she doesn't know.

"It's okay," Aviva assures me with a grin. "Your mom and I were just talking."

I turn to Mom with raised eyebrows. "Oh? What about?"

"Aviva was telling me all about a movie you're planning on going to this weekend," she replies, and I grimace and cut in.

"Yeah. About that–"

"And I said that you can go," Mom continues.

I blink at her for a moment before saying, "Oh? Really." Aviva smiles at me encouragingly.

"Yes," Mom says. "You can go because you're doing your homework now. I'm very glad you're making time for schoolwork too."

"Okay. Great." I smile. I'd thought that it would be much

more difficult to get permission to go to another movie premiere, but it looked like Aviva had done all the work for me. "Well, I think that's our cue to leave." I grab Aviva's hand and pull her towards the stairs.

"Oh, and Naya?" Mom calls behind us. I pause and wait for the other shoe to drop, as Aviva just giggles silently next to me.

"Yes?" I call back.

"I'll want to hear all about the movie. It sounds quite good."

I freeze, waiting to hear more, but she seems done. "Okay Mom!" I reply. "I will, I promise!" Then I pull Aviva the rest of the way upstairs.

Once my bedroom door is pulled firmly shut behind us, I turn to Aviva with wide eyes. "She loved you!" I stage whisper emphatically.

Aviva leans back onto my bed and fluffs her hair up dramatically. "What can I say?" she replies in a posh accent. "All parents do."

"Seriously, though," I say, "Sorry for being late. That must've been awkward." I indicate downstairs with a hooked thumb over my shoulder.

"No, seriously, it was fine. Your mom is pretty chill."

"Yeah, well, with you, I guess so." I begin to take out my Latin notes, spacing them out over the surface of my bed. Aviva picks up certain pages, asking me questions, and telling me about a role she played several years ago in which she had to speak a witch's incantation in Latin.

"I just learned it phonetically," she tells me conspiratorially. "I had no idea what it actually meant."

I snort. "Do you still remember it? Maybe we can translate it."

As she attempts to recall the spelling of each word, I reflect on how easily we've slipped back into our normal routine. Joking, teasing, self-deprecation, and the occasional tidbit of real talk. We seem to have moved past our huge blow-out.

I have to use an online translator for a few of the words, but we eventually determine that Aviva's spell had been to help plants grow. She laughs hysterically at this, because it was apparently supposed to have been a curse she placed on her mother. Then I move to my desk so I can't read the notes on my bed, and she quizzes me on verb meanings and conjugations. After about an hour, I think I know everything as well as I ever will. I'm afraid that Aviva would be getting bored, but she actually seems to be enjoying this. Well, I suppose when you're not the one who actually has to remember everything, studying would just be optional learning.

"Okay, that's enough," I finally say. "Thanks."

She shrugs and says to me, "Naya, if you don't ace that test, I will be very disappointed in you." Her voice is serious but she adds a wink at the end, so I snort.

"Yes, mother."

We move on to talking about the premiere, because, as I point out, my *real* mother currently knows more about it than I do. Aviva tells me that this movie is a dramedy about a man in witness protection, and his desire to meet his favourite band, who are about to retire.

"Who's in it?" I ask, and she lists several names I don't pay any attention to. "And, um, who will be there?" I pretend to wonder aloud.

I can tell Aviva isn't fooled by my feigned aloofness. "I still don't know who Jace is," she tells me with a sympathetic smile. "I don't know if he's an actor himself, or if he's friends of someone, and if that someone will bring him or not. I really don't know if he'll be at the premiere. And you said you didn't want me asking around about him, so..."

I shudder. "Yeah. That's still a no." I could just imagine how stalkerish that would seem, after meeting him only once. "I mean, I obviously don't know who he is. In case you didn't notice, I'm not really into the whole celeb scene."

"Yeah, kind of got that when you didn't know who I was at first, even after I took my wig off."

"Yeah," I agree. "But, I mean, he did say hopefully he'd see me again, so there's got to be at least a chance that he'll be attending more premieres."

"Very true," Aviva says with a smile. I can't tell if she genuinely agrees or if she's just being placating, but either way, a girl can hope. And I have another two days before I'll find out for sure.

"Do you want to come over tomorrow to choose a new outfit?" she asks hopefully. I can see her desire to turn me into a human doll for her to dress up once again.

Despite my reservations, I relent. "Fine. But you'd better make me look good Saturday. Like, *smoking* hot."

"Deal!" she squeals, and I shake my head, laughing. We move onto other topics – I tell her about Asher's apparent new fixation with me, and she tells me about how much work actually goes into the pre-production of a movie, since she's only been involved in the filming before. Time flies by.

My Friday classes drag on, as they usually do. By the fifth and final day of the school week, all I can think about is leaving and enjoying my weekend. And despite my reluctance yesterday, I really am looking forward to picking out a dress with Aviva this afternoon. When I'm finally let out of my English tutorial, I just can't picture doing any more analyzing of writing today. I usually do enjoy newspaper editing, or else I'd have quit long before now, but I can't bring myself to go today. Instead, I nearly skip towards the parking lot, feeling like a rebel – *You're so lame, Naya* – and drive straight to Aviva's apartment building.

I'm early – nearly an hour early, actually – but the thought that Aviva might not be here actually hadn't hit me until now. I walk into the lobby, wondering if I should just go up to Aviva's floor and knock on her door, or wait down here, where we'd planned on meeting. I settle on finding a seat on the lobby couch and sending Aviva a text. I wait awkwardly until she replies a few minutes later.

Hey, yeah im out but ill be back soon! Gimme 2 mins :)

I can feel the desk clerk's eyes on me, so I pretend to text as I walk casually back out of the building. I'll just meet Aviva out front.

I'm still fake texting when I hear her voice and look up sharply. "Hey," she says, giving me a side hug and turning us towards the building entrance. "Have you been waiting long?"

I hear several clicks from behind us and turn to look, but Aviva is already pulling me through the door, so I ignore the noises. "Um, no, just a few minutes," I tell her. "Sorry, I know I'm early."

"Yeah, what happened?" she asks as we pass the clerk – *Remember me now? I'm not just some weirdo hanging around* – and wait at the elevators. "Newspaper cancelled?"

"Not exactly," I admit. "I may have skipped it."

She turns to look at me face-on, a mischievous grin on her lips. "Naya? Skipping? No, never."

I shove her playfully as the shiny elevator doors open before us. "What can I say? I must've been overtaken by a demon or something." We laugh before I continue. "I don't know. It's the weekend. I wanted to start it already. And you know, do you the extreme favour of letting you dress me up."

She snorts, and then grows more serious, although a smile remains on her lips. "I was just out with Hayden Landen," she informs me.

"Oh! The director?" At her nod, I ask, "How'd that go?"

"She's... disappointed that the news came out early. But she's not mad at me. I explained what happened. It's not like I was the one who leaked it, or was even careless with the news. I just trusted someone I shouldn't have."

"Well, that's good, right?"

"As good as it can be for this situation."

The elevator dings as we arrive at Aviva's floor, and she unlocks her door. Once inside, she flops onto one of her white couches, and I follow her lead and plop myself onto the one opposite.

"Just a second," she tells me. "I need to check something." She pulls out her phone and starts tapping away at the screen, so I shrug and do the same. I'm checking my email when she asks, "Do you want to do a Snapchat story?" We joke around for the short video before she posts it with my username for all her fans to see.

"You have no idea how weird it is to me that you have fans," I tell her, exercising our new total honesty policy.

"You have no idea how weird it is to *me*," she retorts. "Like, who cares what I'm doing every hour of every day? I don't even care!"

"Is it ever creepy?" I ask as Aviva get up and heads to her room full of clothes.

"No..." she calls back. "Not creepy. Sometimes I wonder how, exactly, a fan got a certain picture of me when I don't remember ever posting it, or how they know something about me that I don't remember ever saying publicly, but I know it's because they care about me. None of my fans want to hurt me. Of course, the haters–" she snorts derisively, "–that's another matter entirely."

I consider that. I hadn't even thought Aviva had any haters, but of course, being a successful actress, there had to be at least a few. "And those ones are creepy?" I ask, getting up and meandering over to her, where she's pulling a few different racks of clothing to the front of the room.

"Those ones can be *scary*," she tells me with wide eyes. "Death threats on social media are not fun."

"Understatement much?" She shrugs, but I don't know how she's taking this so calmly. If anyone ever threatened to kill me, even online, I would probably call the police.

"Now," she says brightly, obviously trying to change the subject. "What style of dress are you thinking for tomorrow night?"

"Well, uh, I was thinking something kind of sexier this time."

She pauses in her riffling through the clothing items, and

turns to face me directly. "I'm all for showing off your hard-earned muscles," she tells me, waving a hand in front of my body, "but last time, you wanted to cover up more. So is this change because you're feeling more confident? Or is it in case a certain someone whose name rhymes with *lace* might be there?"

Heat floods my face, and I'm not wearing any foundation today to cover the redness I know has overtaken my complexion. Ugh. I *hate* blushing. I couldn't lie even if I wanted to as long as my face flames up at the slightest embarrassment.

Aviva sees it and shrugs with a half smile. "It's up to you. You can wear *that* if you want–" she tells me, indicating a wrap that appears to be nothing more than a few strips of fabric pinched together in key locations, "–but there are better ways to impress a guy than with skin."

I nod, giggling awkwardly.

"So, with my lecture out of the way," she continues with a wink, "let's find you a dress."

I end up with an outfit that I adore. The dress is tight and black, and shows off quite a bit of leg; however, it also extends all the way up to my chin in a turtleneck style. Sexy and classy combined. Aviva has also somehow talked me into wearing four-inch black stilettos. I was more unsure of these, because I never wear heels, but after looking at myself in the mirror, I couldn't say no. With the short cut of my dress and the heels, my legs appear to go on for days, which is a rarity for me, considering my height.

As I stare at my reflection in the mirror in awe, Aviva flounces up with a pleading pout on her face.

"What?" I laugh, knowing this expression means a request is coming.

"Well, since you're already all dressed up, will you let me do your makeup too?"

"Tomorrow?" I ask. I'd assumed she would do it again for the premiere anyway.

"No. Tonight. Right now." She enhances her pout, popping her lower lip out, making it look ridiculous in comparison with the top one. "I want to do a Snapchat tutorial."

I shrug and agree. I really don't mind having my makeup done, and Aviva is pretty much an expert – at least in comparison to me. "I just have to take off my makeup first," I tell her, referring to the mascara I'd put on for school. "And it has to be a subtle look. I'm not going home with prom makeup on."

She grumbles good-naturedly before agreeing to my terms. As I use her face wipes to present her with a clean, bare face, she sets up her huge makeup collection in front of the dresser in her bedroom, the same place I'd sat while she did my makeup before the last premiere.

Before beginning on my face, she does a little introduction to her phone camera. "Naya has agreed to let me do her makeup," she says, eyes on the lens, so that every viewer would think she's speaking directly to them. "So I thought I'd do a little tutorial for you guys." She smiles sultrily and winks before ending the video and posting it to her Snapchat.

"You're different with your fans," I comment.

She looks up, surprised. "Am I?"

"You're much more... concentrated." At her confused look, I elaborate. "Like, you're you, but more so. More personality, more flirting, more energy."

She looks off to the side, and I can see that she's turning over my words. "I guess... I guess I feel like I owe them more of me. I wouldn't have the career I've always dreamed of if it weren't for them. I want to give them my all. And I guess... I'm kind of scared that if I don't give everything, they won't like me. As much, or... at all anymore." She shrugs with a small sad smile.

I stare at her. This is the first bit of insecurity I think I've ever heard from her. "You have to know that's not true. Your fans want to see the real you more than they want to see you on high alert all the time."

She lights up again, but it's with the same energy from her introduction video. A false energy. "Stop trying to distract me," she tells me jokingly. "It's time to start your makeup."

I don't know if she believes me or will take my words into consideration, but I know that she doesn't want to dwell on it now. So I also take off my serious mask and allow her to introduce different palettes and brushes to the camera then apply them to me as I try to keep my face looking normal and relaxed.

"And... done!" she finally exclaims gleefully. The camera has become less of a distraction as she continued to film different steps of this makeup look, especially since sometimes I couldn't actually tell if it was recording. Aviva hammed it up either way, to me and to her viewers.

"Can I actually see now?" I ask with overdone exasperation. She's kept me facing away from the mirror the entire time, same as when she did my premiere makeup before.

"Anything you'd like to say before you see your final look?" she asks.

I look directly into the camera. "I better not look like a clown."

Aviva bursts into laughter and spins me around. She quickly taps her phone again to record my reaction as I see myself. I take a second to study my reflection before smiling. I look nice. Like myself, but smoother, my individual features more defined.

"Why are you an actress?" I ask Aviva, turning to peek at her. "You should be a makeup artist."

She seems to find this hilarious, although I'd been mostly serious, about the makeup part at least. "Pose!" she tells me, and I oblige, beginning with a serious face, then transitioning to sultry, then silly. Soon I'm up out of my chair, attempting the high fashion model poses I've only ever seen within the pages of *Vogue* or *Elle*. Aviva is laughing so hard that she takes a moment to breathe and apologize for her shaky filming.

"Why are you laughing?" I ask with mock offense. "You don't think I'm a good model?" This sets her off again, and I join in, until we're leaning on each other, crippled by our humour.

Aviva films one final video of us saying good bye to post. It's only when she puts a filter containing the time over our faces in the video that I realize how late it's gotten.

"I need to go," I tell her, grabbing my regular clothes to change back into. "What time do you want me to come over tomorrow?"

"Same as last weekend?"

I agree and head out after reminding her that I won't be able to go to the gym tonight if I want to go out tomorrow.

As I'm exiting the apartment building, I hear several more clicks and I could swear I see a flash. *Are those cameras?* But just as quickly as the noises had appeared, they disappear, and I'm left to wonder what, if anything, just happened.

When I get back to my house, my mother mentions that I look lovely today – *well thank you, Aviva* – before reminding me of my chores. Tonight, neither the housework nor my homework can bother me. I'm too safely wrapped in the happiness of today and the exciting potential of tomorrow.

Although I want to sleep in the next day, my body won't allow me to. Every time I close my eyes, they end up open again five minutes later. When I finally give up on going back to sleep, my phone informs me that it's ten a.m. I sigh and rub my eyes, getting out of bed. I can already feel the adrenaline pumping through my veins in anticipation of the premiere tonight.

I've left myself the most mindless chores to do today, which I complete after eating my brunch. At 3:45 p.m. on the dot, I leave my house to drive over to Aviva's. We perform the same routine as last weekend, with Aviva doing my makeup, then finishing her own just seconds before the limo arrives. She uses only black on my eyes today, smoking out the lash lines and attaching heavy false lashes to my upper lids. We clamber into the limo and drive the thirty minutes to the premiere location, which is different from that of last weekend. Again, I drink one glass of champagne, letting it assuage my nerves, and Aviva turns hers down.

Once we arrive, Aviva and I are ushered through the security together; apparently they'd been forewarned that I would be with her again, since no one seems surprised to see me or attempts to verify my identity.

I feel more comfortable on the red carpet than I did last time. I still feel as though I don't belong, but since I knew what to expect ahead of time today, I was able to mentally prepare myself. I smile genuinely for several shots. Aviva seems to catch some of my energy, and her eyes become less cool, her smile less perfect. She puts her arm around me and squeezes me to her side at one point and I giggle in surprise.

"Not as bad, right?" she asks me quietly, eyes knowing. She scans the crowd of fans and reporters in front of us, screaming as loud as their lungs will permit, and I can see her desire to head towards one particular woman holding a microphone toward her.

"Do you know her?" I ask, looking between Aviva and the reporter.

She startles, then replies, "I've talked to her before. She's from The Peony."

The Peony is a magazine that I've read before, although it's not my first choice. It's a celebrity magazine, but it actually does contain more fact than fiction.

"You can talk to her if you want," I tell Aviva, although my stomach curdles at the thought of being left alone on the carpet.

"I'm sorry," she says to me. "I know we didn't discuss this."

"No, it's fine," I tell her. "I get it. It's your job. I can just head inside." Although that would be less nerve-wracking than staying on the carpet in front of all the flashing cameras and screaming fans, I still feel uncomfortable at the thought of doing so alone.

"No, don't be silly!" I look over at Aviva, and she looks nearly as uncomfortable at the thought of being alone in front of everyone here as I am. "We can do just one interview." She indicates the woman from The Peony. "Then we can go in together."

My stomach drops at the thought of going over to be interviewed. "No, no, I don't want to talk to her–"

"Then don't." Aviva grabs my arm and pulls me behind her towards the female reporter. "I'll do the talking, you can just keep me company."

I grimace but oblige. It is better than being alone, at least.

The reporter's smile grows wolfish as Aviva approaches, hand still firmly secured to my arm, pulling me along behind her. I stop a step behind Aviva as she greets the woman by name – Vicky.

"This is my friend Naya," Aviva tells Vicky, and Vicky shoots me a quick, obligatory smile before turning back to Aviva.

"So Aviva," Vicky begins in a husky voice, like she smokes two packs of cigarettes a day. "What can you tell me about your new movie with Hayden Landen?"

Aviva rattles off the description of the movie she'd originally told me, somehow making the words seem fresh, like it's the first time she's ever said them. Once she's done, finishing with a mischievous "And you'll have to watch it to find out more," Vicky asks, "I heard that the news of this movie came out early. Is this true?"

I freeze, unsure how Aviva will answer. But she just gives a blasé smile and says, "I accidentally let it slip a bit too soon. But it's okay, Hayden isn't *too* mad at me." And she winks, prompting Vicky to laugh.

"How is it, working with Hayden Landen? Are you nervous to work on a new project with her, considering the critical acclaim her past two films have received?"

"Absolutely! But I know that if Hayden and I work our very hardest on this film, it has to turn out well. After all, as Edison said, success is 1% inspiration and 99% perspiration, right?" At Vicky's satisfied nod, Aviva adds, "Anyway, we should get inside," and starts to back away with me.

"Just one more question!" Vicky shouts over the din, and Aviva releases my wrist again to step forward again. "How is your relationship with Callan Nyler? Are the engagement rumours true?"

My head snaps up at that. I hadn't heard any engagement rumours. I'd known their relationship was serious, but surely Aviva would tell me if she got *engaged*?

Aviva laughs. "Nope, no engagement ring yet," she tells Vicky, holding out her hands as proof.

Vicky points out a prominent blue gem embedded into a silver ring shaped like a rosebud. "What's that one?"

"Haven't I shown this one to you before?" Aviva asks.

"Nope. Trust me, I'd remember that," Vicky tells her, a tinge of jealousy colouring her words. I try to hide my smirk.

"This *is* from Callan, but it's not an engagement ring. It's a promise ring. But I've had it for six months; nothing new. Sorry, no gossip there," she says directly to Vicky's camera with a little shrug.

I'd seen the ring on Aviva's finger before, but I hadn't really thought anything of it. I hadn't known it was from Callan, or even that it was any sort of real, valuable gemstone; I'd just assumed it was plastic, or maybe dyed quartz.

"Well folks," Vicky says, also turning to the camera, "that's Aviva Jersey." She turns back to Aviva and thanks her, and Aviva smiles sweetly before once again pulling me away. I'm actually really impressed with the way Aviva was acting through the interview, considering how uncomfortable I know she gets at press events like this. Maybe acting is all it was, but she really handled herself well. And it didn't *feel* like she was acting, like it had when she was doing the Snapchat introduction yesterday. She had felt more real today. Whether that was because she'd actually thought about what I'd told her, or whether it was just easier for her to interact in person than through an electronic device, I don't know.

We walk at a leisurely pace past the remaining reporters screaming Aviva's name, although every instinct is telling me to run. "Just smile and wave," Aviva tells me from the corner of her mouth, and I follow her directions, acknowledging the crowd as we pass. A few people, probably fans, watch me with wide eyes and open mouths, and scream when I smile at them. This is weird. I'm not the famous one, and yet even just being on the carpet is enough for some of these fans to freak out over me.

We make it inside the building, and the wave of noise washes away as the heavy doors close behind us. Aviva instantly turns to me. "Sorry about that," she says, indicating outside the doors. "I wasn't planning on doing any interviews, but with the news out early, Hayden thinks we should try to hype it up as much as we can, so..."

"It's fine," I tell her, shaking my head slightly. "I told you to do it."

"Okay. Well. I guess we should find our seats, then." My head is swivelling as she speaks, eyes scanning the crowd, until with a jolt of electricity, I see him.

Although I'd been hoping he would be here, had just been looking for him specifically, I'm not sure I'd actually expected him to be here. But there he is. *Jace.*

Probably because of my lack of response, Aviva follows my gaze and sees him too. I turn back just in time to see a flash of humour cross her face, before she grabs my wrist again and starts leading me in his direction.

"What are you doing?" I hiss in mortification, studiously staring away from Jace, who, as far as I know, hasn't spotted us yet.

Aviva just shushes me. She's not looking directly at Jace either, but instead at an empty spot a few metres away from him. Once we're there, she releases me. I don't stop though, instead using my momentum to turn at a ninety-degree angle and keep walking away. Aviva rolls her eyes but doesn't attempt to stop me. Instead, she pastes a concerned look on her face and says at a volume slightly higher than usual, "I'm sorry I have to leave you here while I do more interviews."

Wait... what? I turn back slowly and she raises her eyebrows at me, encouraging me to play along. "Well, um," I say awkwardly. "As long as you only do a few more." I have no idea what expression currently resides on my face, and if it even fits our current conversation. I'm not a good actor, unlike Aviva, whose concern hits just the right notes, neither under- nor overdone.

In my peripheral vision, I could swear I see Jace's head turn towards us, but I continue to stare studiously ahead, so I can't be sure.

"There are plenty of people in here," Aviva continues. "I'm sure you could find *someone* to talk to." The emphasis on *someone* is so slight that I'm not sure anyone but me would be able to detect it. Then she pulls me in for a hug and whispers "You're gold," into my ear with a self-satisfied smirk. Then she releases me, shoots me a wink that anyone not looking at her face-on could easily mistake for a blink, and heads for the doors.

Oh. She's actually doing more interviews. I am actually alone. I look around awkwardly, first to my left, where everyone seems to be involved in conversation, then to my right, where I see Jace looking back at me. My heart stutters when he smiles, says goodbye to the person he's been speaking with, and strides the last several meters between us. I smile automatically, hoping it doesn't look goofy.

"Hi," I say as he reaches me. I feel jittery.

"Hey, Naya," he returns. *Oh, thank god.* He remembers me. "You're here with Aviva again?" He looks off towards the exit, where Aviva had just disappeared.

I nod. "Yeah," I agree. "I don't know if you heard about her new movie with Hayden Landen? The news came out kinda earlier than expected, so they want to use that to their advantage as much as possible."

Jace nods. "I did hear about that. Good for her. I've only seen one film by Hayden Landen, but it was amazing."

Oh, right. He's a big movie buff. Of course he would keep track of upcoming blockbusters.

"I'm okay with staying in here," I admit. "The red carpet is fun for about two minutes, but then the lights and screaming start to get to me. I don't know how actors do it so often." I shudder.

He laughs and my smile widens even further. "I certainly can't stand it," he confides. "Maybe we just need to get used to it."

"Maybe," I agree. My nerves are settling, and I recall how this happened the last time I saw him, too. There's something about Jace that just calms me.

"So are you excited for the movie tonight?" he asks, and I smile sheepishly.

"I don't know much about it," I admit. "Aviva told me the basic plot, but that's about it."

He raises his eyebrows. "Do you want to know more?"

I raise my eyebrows too. "Do you know much more? You better not tell me any spoilers."

He chuckles. "I don't know *that* much. But my friend had a minor role in it," he says, indicating the guy he had been talking to earlier, when Aviva had started her charade to attract his attention.

"Oh cool!" I say. "Okay, yeah. Let's hear it." I smile, not even caring anymore whether I look silly or not.

He begins with a summary of the plot similar to the one Aviva gave, then moves on to second-hand stories from set, and cast gossip. The room is beginning to thin out around us as people leave to take their seats, but I barely notice until Aviva finally flounces back inside, face shiny. She spots us and hurries over.

"Sorry I took so long," she tells me with a barely noticeable smirk.

"That's okay," I say, looking at her for an extra beat, trying to express that it *really is* okay. "Um, Aviva, you remember Jace?" I ask innocently, remembering my manners this time.

"Yes, of course," she says with a smile. He offers his hand for a shake but she brushes it aside and pulls him in for a short hug instead. "Sorry, I'm a hugger," she says with a shrug as she pulls back. I frown slightly, not seeing her play. Aviva is not a huge hugger. She'll hug me, sure, but she doesn't go around regularly hugging people she barely knows. I've seen the promise ring from Callan though, and I know she's not interested in Jace, so I don't know what she's doing. I make a mental note to ask her later.

Jace smiles easily, going with it. "No problem," he says. "We really should find our seats now, though." I nod in agreement, and we head into the screening room. Try as we might, however, we can't find any three seats in a row. We find a pair together, and then Aviva spots a single one a couple of rows back.

"You guys sit here," Aviva says, indicating the pair of seats. "It was my fault we were late, so I'll take the single seat." Then she disappears into the darkness before I can protest. *Would* I have protested?

The movie begins to roll, sound blaring. I stand awkwardly for a moment before Jace sits in the chair further from the aisle, grabs my arm, and pulls me gently toward the second seat. *Oh my god.* My heartbeat doubles as I stumble forward and find my seat in the dark. I look up at Jace once I'm properly positioned, and he places a single finger over his lips, which are curved up at the edges into a smile. *Shh.* That's why he grabbed my arm – so that he wouldn't have to yell over the movie to get my attention.

I can't take my eyes off of his lips. He's still looking at me, too. Someone a few seats down drops their popcorn and swears loudly, and the sound jolts me back to awareness. Slowly I blink, and when I open my eyes again, I make sure they're facing forward.

The movie is entertaining, but try as I might, I just can't manage to give it my full attention. I am hyperaware of Jace in my periphery; every minute shift he makes is enough to snap my focus away from the screen again. When he leans forward and places his hands under his chin, I realize how tense I've become. I take a slow, silent breath, forcing myself to relax back into my chair as I exhale. I place both arms on my armrests and look back at the movie just as the protagonist finds out his favourite band is planning on retiring. His face is comically screwed up, and I hear Jace chuckle beside me; just like that, my attention swings away from the screen. I sigh. This is going to be a long movie.

I keep my eyes forward even as I register Jace leaning back into his seat. Then something manages to break through my façade of calmness: a touch on my hand. I start and look to see that Jace has grabbed the hand I'd left on our shared armrest. I look up at him, and I know my eyes are wide, but I can't seem to control them anymore.

Jace looks back at me carefully. He seems almost... uncertain? The thought is almost laughable to me. How could he be at all unsure of my feelings towards him? I don't think I've ever been good at hiding my crushes, and I have a huge one on him. Maybe Aviva's lessons in confidence have had the side effect of making me less approachable, or maybe less readable? Whatever the reason, I give Jace a big smile, simultaneously enjoying and trying to ignore the multitude of sensations running over my body as I do. The butterflies previously contained to my stomach are travelling up my throat, and a warmth is running up my arm, stemming from Jace's hand in mine. I look down at our hands intertwined, and the sight sends a shot of adrenaline through my body. Feeling more daring, perhaps because of the darkness, I squeeze his hand, then return my eyes to the movie.

He squeezes my hand back, and my breath hitches in my throat. I keep my eyes on the screen, but I still can't pay enough attention to the film to really appreciate it. I just can't bring myself to care about the movie anymore.

10

Chapter Ten

    I can't say what the latter half of the movie is about, or if the main guy ever even ends up meeting his favourite band before they retire. My mind is too busy whirring away the whole time. Holding hands is a good sign that Jace likes me back, right? I mean, friends don't do that platonically. But what will happen when the movie ends? We'll have to let go, obviously. It's not like we're in an official relationship; he probably doesn't want other people to see. But will he want to see me again? Will he ask for my number? But what if he doesn't... should I ask for his? Can I build up enough courage to ask for his number?

    What if he doesn't actually care if people see us? What if he tries to kiss me? The thought puts a knot in my stomach, although I can't explain why. It's not that I haven't thought about kissing him, or that I don't find him attractive; I have, and I do. So then why don't I want him to kiss me right now?

The credits finally roll, and I am simultaneously disappointed and relieved. I feel Jace shift beside me, and I automatically drop his hand. He stretches his arms over his head, and my whirring mind suddenly becomes caught on the sliver of toned tanned stomach that shows as his shirt rises.

He turns to me, and I jerk my eyes up to his face. "That was a good movie," he comments, and I nod in agreement, although I know my enjoyment came less from the quality of the film and more from my contact with Jace.

"Would you be interested in seeing another movie with me sometime?" he asks in a low voice as the people around us begin to swarm out of the theatre. His fingers twitch, and I realize that he may be as unsure as I've been as to what is happening between us. I don't intentionally begin a mental comparison, but as I take in Jace's semi-concealed nervousness, I see the differences between him and Asher clearly. Jace actually seems to care about my response. Asher had always had a couldn't-care-less attitude towards me, but I'd been so blinded by his good looks and popularity that my infatuation convinced me he truly cared for me, too. I've only known Jace for a fraction of the time I've known Asher, but I already like what I see in him more than anything I saw in Asher.

"Yeah," I say, smiling shyly. "I'd love to."

As we're typing our numbers into each other's phones, he says, "I don't know if I'm going to any more premieres anytime soon..." He punches the final digit in and slides my phone back to me. "So how about a regular old movie and dinner?"

I laugh, returning his phone too. "That sounds really good." More than that, actually. The thought of Jace in a normal setting is odd to me, so locating our first official date away from all the flashing cameras and paparazzi should help me to remove any sort of starstruck-ness I associate with him. I'll also be more relaxed, without the pressure of formal wear and celebrities surrounding me.

"I actually have to run," Jace tells me, looking down at his phone and biting his lip – *focus, Naya!* "I have a meeting soon," he explains.

"Kind of late," I comment, and he snorts in agreement.

"The grind never ends," he replies, but I can see in the softness of his features that he doesn't mind it. "But I'll text you tonight," he says, and my heartrate instantly increases as my smile freezes on my face. I've heard that promise before, and it wasn't usually followed through on.

"Okay," I manage to agree cheerfully enough. Something in my voice must be different though, because he looks up from his phone again and studies my face.

"Okay?" he asks gently.

"Okay," I repeat softly. After a beat he nods, then passes by me, squeezing my hand as he goes. My breathing stutters, and I watch him walk away. Only when he's out of sight do I come back to myself and remember that there is, in fact, someone else I should be hanging out with right now. I turn back to Aviva's seat, which is easier to see now that almost everyone else is gone. She is still sitting, fiddling with her phone, but she must feel my gaze because her eyes shoot up to mine almost instantly. She stands and walks down the steps to me, and I smile giddily.

She smiles back tentatively, then more strongly as she reaches me and we walk out together. "I made sure not to spy on you," she tells me, eyes scanning mine, "so I need all the details. Pronto!"

I grin at her as we find the right limo. Once we've climbed in, I pour myself a glass of champagne and offer it to Aviva out of courtesy. To my surprise, she mutters, "Oh, why not?" and takes it. I pour myself a new one and we clink our chutes to a happy night. I'm bursting to spill everything this instant, but Aviva wants to hear the story all at once, and asks if I can wait until we get to the restaurant before beginning.

"Can we just order takeout back at your place?" I ask. "I've had enough excitement for tonight, I think."

She gives a relieved nod, muttering something about all the extra interviews she had to do while giving me a pointed look. I look back with wide eyes, all innocence.

We pick up Chinese food and eat it across from each other in Aviva's living room, each of us on a white sofa, sharing the table between us. I love Chinese food, and usually take my time consuming it, but I barely taste it tonight, my mind occupied by the night's events as I recount them to Aviva.

"So, what happened after I dropped that bait?" she begins, and I groan.

"That was so awkward," I mumble into my hands, rolling my eyes at Aviva's answering giggle. "But, genius," I consent. "It did work. He came over to me."

"And the conversation?" she asks, slurping up some noodles.

"Not awkward," I say, and she nods sagely.

"Always a good sign."

"Did you come back late on purpose?" Her only reply is a shrug, but I can see a smirk at the edge of her lips too. "Well, thank you," I say. "I don't understand your techniques, but they're quite effective. And I appreciate it." Suddenly I recall the question I'd had earlier. "Oh! Also. What was with that hug?"

Her eyebrows raise. "Oh, so you noticed that was weird? You don't think he noticed, did he?"

"No." I shake my head. "I just thought it was out of character."

"Okay. Let me try to explain this," she begins, chewing thoughtfully. "I figured that if I made him think casual touching was something we were okay with, like... he would be more comfortable with casually touching you, too." She looks up sheepishly. "Does that make any sense?"

I choke on some general tao chicken with laughter and end up coughing. "Kind of? I've just learned not to question you."

"And...?" she asks cautiously. "Was there any... casual touching?" She smirks.

"Well, I don't know how casual it was," I admit. "We held hands."

She shrieks and I jump, nearly spilling the rest of my chicken on the floor. "Details, details!" she encourages, and I oblige, face burning not only with embarrassment this time, but happiness too.

"And he said he'd text me tonight," I finish, my smile faltering slightly.

Aviva notices. "He hasn't yet?"

I shrug. "My phone hasn't vibrated." I dig into my handbag, where it's been resting all night, and click the power button. Nothing happens. I click it again before realizing the truth behind the lack of reaction. "Oh shit. It's dead." I look up at Aviva with panicked eyed.

"That could be a good thing! Maybe he has texted you!"

"I don't have my charger," I mutter, and Aviva goes hunting for hers. She brings it to me and I anxiously attempt to fit it into my phone, which is a different make from hers. With a little wiggling, the cable slips in, and my phone gives a short vibration as it begins to receive power. Aviva and I stare at the screen in silence as the phone powers back on and finds service again. Then two longer vibrations, as a notification for new text messages pop up on my screen. I attempt to type in my password but my fingers are shaky and I have to take a few deep breaths to release tension before I can unlock my phone.

I click on the new text messages and–

"They're from Jace!" Aviva yelps beside me. I don't reply, but a slow smile is beginning to spread across my face. The messages are simple: a greeting, and a request to text him back when I get a chance.

"Should I reply?" I ask, and Aviva looks at me like I'm crazy. "Like, now?" I clarify. "Or should I wait...?"

Aviva shakes her head slightly. "Why would you wait?"

"Um..." I don't know *why*, really. It was just something that Asher and I had often done. You take an hour to respond? I take two. I forgot to charge my phone? You left your phone at home.

Aviva must sense that I don't have an answer coming, because she shakes her head more adamantly. "There's no point in playing games. Games rarely lead anywhere helpful. Tell him you can talk now!"

I slowly type out, *im available now, if you can talk?* I pause and re-read my message, then send it decisively. I wait several moments, but he still hasn't responded by the time my phone begins to fall asleep. I frown and Aviva laughs.

"Give him a few minutes to read it and reply!"

I put my phone down on the floor by the outlet and we return to the couches to finish our dinner. Aviva tries to get me back into conversation, but it's tense for the first few minutes as my eyes keep wandering away from her and back to my phone's empty screen. Eventually I force my mind to focus and we return to our easy banter. That is, until my phone vibrates again and I jump up excitedly and run over to it.

"Is it him?" Aviva asks amusedly.

I nod several times, reading the message three times. "He's planning our first date," I tell her breathlessly. Aviva doesn't respond, so I look over to see her shaking her head at her noodles, softly laughing. I return to my phone.

He's asked if I'm available tomorrow. Reluctantly, I decline. I really have to use tomorrow for homework. We decide on next Friday instead, then Jace has to return to his meeting. I place my phone back on the floor delicately and flounce back over to the couches, this time flopping down on the same one as Aviva.

"Hi," she says.

"Hi," I return, and sit up. "Sorry if this boy drama has been monopolizing the night."

"Don't be sorry," she tells me, face growing more serious. "You deserve a chance at real love. Everyone does."

I also sober slightly. "You've helped me a lot. Ever since we met. So, thank you," I mumble awkwardly.

Aviva grins. "I haven't done that much."

I shrug. "It's been enough."

"Well, thank *you* for helping me settle into Toronto. New cities can be scary."

"I wouldn't know. I've lived here my whole life," I sigh dramatically, bringing us back to our earlier sillier mood. I stand up and return to my phone.

"I've got to take you with me to L.A. sometime," Aviva comments offhandedly, and I grin.

"That would be awesome." I check the time on my phone screen and sigh. It's getting late. "I have to go now."

We clean up the takeout boxes, then I unplug my phone, handing Aviva her charger back. She gives me a hug good-bye, and I leave her luxurious apartment, mind whirring away with all the events of tonight.

I spend the next day on homework, although the whole time, my mind is thinking *You could've been with Jace now. You could've been with Jace now*, thus making it difficult to focus. When I force my way through my final Latin reading, I allow myself a break for lunch, and find my mom at the kitchen table also eating. I serve myself some of the leftover pasta salad she's eating, and sit across from her. I smile in greeting, and she studies me thoughtfully.

"You look happy," she comments, and I shrug.

"Why wouldn't I be?"

"You haven't been so happy lately."

I chew a few noodles and swallow before responding. "It's good to have friends."

My mom frowns. "You've always had friends, Naya–"

"No, mom. Not after Asher and I broke up." I look off to the side, not wanting to see the guilt in her eyes. She has no reason to feel guilty over my lack of friends, or even not noticing that I had no friends, but I know what expression I'll find if I look back at her.

Finally, she sighs. "Well, that's in the past now. And you can look to the future."

A small smile crosses my lips as I contemplate my future. "Yeah. Yes, I can."

That night, I meet Aviva at the gym. After we work out, keeping up light conversation the entire time, we take silly selfies in the mirror, Aviva complaining that she can't post any because of her wig. I tell her to take it off then, but she just shakes her head with a half smile. "I'm okay being Brynn right now," she tells me.

It's getting warmer outside. It's finally April, which means my classes will be ending soon, although I'll then have to look forward to exams. I don't bother putting on my jacket while we walk to our cars. I grin, endorphins still pumping through my system, spring air filling my lungs, and wonder, as I say good-bye to Aviva, if this ideal life can really last.

Things are different on Monday. I got a good night's sleep last night, so I'm more observant in the morning, which is maybe why I can tell that something is off. I'm used to being invisible on campus. I'm not the most fashionable, or exceptionally beautiful, and I tend to keep my head down and just focus on getting to class, which means that no one pays me any attention. But today, as I look around, many people are staring back. I look down at myself, wondering if my shirt is stained, but I can't see anything different about me. When I look up again, I see someone's gaze just pass over me, and I breathe a sigh of relief, thinking that maybe I'm imagining things. That is, until they do a double take and stare back at me again, mouth slightly ajar.

I stop into the nearest bathroom I can find, thinking that maybe there's something on my face, since my clothes seem alright. I study myself in the mirror, but still don't see anything out of the ordinary. I take a breath and shake my head at myself, then dig out my phone to check the time.

My phone has thirteen new notifications since I left my house this morning. *What the hell?* Several new followers on Instagram and Twitter, a few DMs from strangers – nothing special, most just greetings – and a few Facebook pokes. I don't understand what is happening. Did a photo of Aviva and me at the first premiere finally surface? That might explain the notifications from my friends, people who would actually recognize me, but not the strangers following and DMing me. I don't know. Maybe it's just a coincidence. Maybe all the people staring are normal, and I've just never noticed in my regular tired, bleary-eyed morning state. I exit the bathroom and hurry to class.

In Latin, I receive a text from a friend from high school, Adeline. I haven't seen her since graduation, but we used to be close. She goes to a different college now, so I'm surprised to hear from her.

Hey Nay! Wanna hang out sooonnnn???

I'm touched by her reaching out. Maybe being happy and just living life attracts people back to you. Although I haven't thought about Addie recently, I used to miss her quite a bit. Immediately I respond, hiding my phone under the desk.

Yeah for sure! When r u free?

Her reply reaches my phone just as I'm about to put it away again. *Fri?*

My stomach flips in anticipation as I remember that I already have Friday plans. I smile and type back, *Can't, srry. Got a date that night :)))*

The flipping in my stomach drops as soon as I see her response. *Oh? Say hi to Asher for me!*

Not Asher, I quickly type. *We broke up. It's a first date actually, with someone new.*

Oh. Awkwaaaardddd! There's a short pause, then my phone buzzes again with her next message. *Saturday then? The mall?*

I smile, thinking of our high school mall days. *Sat @ the mall. 12 pm,* I agree. Then I slip my phone back into my backpack and attempt to catch up with the grammar structure we're studying.

Later that day, I leave my Science class and head straight for newspaper editing. Asher is already there when I walk in, which isn't unusual, but not entirely normal for him to be here so early either. I walk past him to my chair and sit down in it heavily, releasing a deep breath. There've been too many eyes on me today. It was weird. I sense someone approaching behind me and am not at all surprised to hear Asher's voice as he greets me.

I take a beat to regain my happy face, then look up at him and return his hello. Then I stare at him, not giving him anything more to work with.

"So," he finally says, "why weren't you here on Friday?"

Friday. I'd forgotten that I'd skipped newspaper on Friday to go to Aviva's. I'd been too excited for the premiere to sit through all this editing work. My smile is more genuine as I reply, "I had other plans."

He nods, but he doesn't seem satisfied with my answer. "With your *friend* that I don't know? What's her name, anyway?"

I pause momentarily as I consider. Should I say Brynn or Aviva? I've already told my mom both names, so I really could say either... but considering that Aviva's and my friendship has already been outed, on the red carpets and on her Snapchat story, it's not like I have to keep it a secret anymore.

"Aviva," I reply with forced casualness, hoping he won't notice my pause. Something changes in his face at the name, although I can't tell what; he still looks casual and cheerful, but *something* is slightly different.

"Well," he returns, "will you be hanging out with *Aviva* again this Saturday? Or are you free?"

I can tell where this line of questioning is heading. I don't know why Asher won't just accept that I'm not into him anymore. I'm about to lie and say I'm busy, but then I realize that I don't have to lie; I have plans now, with Addie. I tell him so, and he chews his lip.

"I didn't realize you and Adeline still hang out."

I shrug. "We don't, really. But we're going to on Saturday." I smile tightly.

"Alright. Then how about Friday?"

Dear lord, he just won't give up! I know that I can't just subtly discourage him anymore; I need to make it more obvious. So I widen my grin as I say, "Can't. Date night." He begins to open his mouth again, but before anything comes out I emphasize, "Not with Aviva this time. And *yes*, with a guy. Because, as we've already established, that's what I'm into."

His expression becomes much less casual now, and his smile seems forced. "Maybe another time, then," he states.

Ugh. I want to remain civil with Asher, since we'll continue working on newspaper together until exams start, but I'm just so sick of his advances. Especially since he was the one who ended our relationship! *Maybe another time?*

"Honestly, Asher, I don't think so," I tell him. His eyes snap up to my face, and I can read the shock in them. I savour it. Even after all of the discouragement I've been sending him over the past couple of weeks – months, even – he'd still honestly thought I would go out with him again. I'm not the same girl I was when we were dating. And I'm happy about that. Before I met Aviva, I would never have had the guts to tell that to his face. He seems like he doesn't know quite what to say now, so I turn back to my computer screen and begin my editing work. I can't actually focus on it enough to be productive until he leaves, but I can fake it.

That night at the gym, I tell Aviva about how Adeline reached out to me about getting together again. I expect her to be happy for me, since that's the kind of person Aviva is. She doesn't seem at all like the jealous type, so I'm very surprised when all she says is, "That's nice," in an unconvincing tone.

I consider dropping the topic, but I know that her reaction will haunt me at least for the rest of the night if I don't confront her about it. So I slow down my elliptical trainer, take a swig of water, and turn my head to look at her directly.

She looks over at me, sighs, and slows down too. "I just…

you should know," she begins, before taking a sip from her water bottle. "There was an article printed in that magazine we interviewed with on the red carpet."

"*You* interviewed with," I correct.

"Well, yeah. But they used a picture of the two of us on the carpet."

"Oh." I'm surprised. "Okay. Weird, but whatever. Isn't that good publicity for you?"

"Um, yeah. It's great. There are lots of photos of us together available for public consumption now, though."

"Is that bad?" I ask. "Didn't we agree to make our friendship public?"

"Yes, we did!" she agrees. "It's not bad. I just... want you to be prepared for the consequences." At my blank expression, she specifies, "I'm worried that your old friend only contacted you because she saw you in a magazine."

I shrug. "So what if it was? Maybe that's just what it took to get her to remember me."

Aviva faces forwards again. "Hopefully that's all it is."

I frown. "What's that supposed to mean?"

She speeds up, not looking at me as she says, "Maybe she's interested in getting some fame for herself too."

I stop short, ignoring the beeping coming from my machine. Anger surges up within me. "Not everyone is interested in fame, Aviva. Including you. Including me."

She presses her lips together before responding. "Yup. Hopefully that'll apply to your old friend too."

I'm furious. What, so the only reason Aviva can see for someone to want to regain contact with me is so that they can become famous? Not just to spend time with me? I don't want to say anything rash, so I step off of my elliptical trainer, grab all my stuff, and walk out, leaving Aviva behind, her machine still whirring away. I think I hear her protest as I let the door slam behind me, but I don't stop to listen.

Once outside, it feels like I have more air to breathe. I know that Aviva isn't trying to hurt me, but I know Adeline. She's *my* friend. Aviva's never had any contact with her, and doesn't know anything about her. It's not her place to say anything about Addie's character.

This argument runs through my head all night, including when I slip into bed. For some reason, I can't fall asleep.

The next morning, I wake slowly, the sound of my alarm pounding through my head. I roll over to switch it off, squinting at my new notifications afterwards. Tons more social media followers. I open up each app individually and adjust my notification settings on each so that I won't keep getting so many pop ups. I then check my texts and see one new one from Aviva. I sigh and read it.

I'm sorry. I hope I'm wrong.

I know that she's just trying to be considerate, so I'm not upset anymore. I'm also just too weary at this point to argue with her. I type back, *It's okay. Addie is different. It'll be fine.*

There's a momentary pause before her reply comes in. *Ok.*

I put my phone back down, squeeze my eyes shut one last time, then get up to face the day.

At school, all the double looks I'd started to notice take on a new meaning. Are these people really staring at me just because I'm friends with a celebrity? I had no idea that many people were so obsessed with the celebrity world. And why would they be interested in *me*? Aside from Aviva's suspicion that they wanted thirdhand fame. I can understand being a fan of Aviva, since she is a great actress, but there's nothing special about me. That's not me being self-deprecating, either. I know I'm not inferior, but that doesn't mean I'm superior to any of these people I pass.

One girl stares at me extra-long, and just as I think she'll pass by, she stops in her tracks and beelines straight for me. I quickly duck my head and pray she'll walk right on by. To my disappointment, she taps my shoulder. I stop and reluctantly raise my head. "Yeah?"

"You're Naya, right?" she's chewing pink bubble gum. I can smell it.

"Um. Yeah?"

"Are you really friends with Aviva Jersey?" She says *Aviva Jersey* like it's a single name, with no space in between. Her gaze is unsettling. I don't think she's blinked since we first made eye contact.

"Yeah?" It comes out sounding like a question, so I quickly amend, "Yes."

The girl squeals. She literally *squeals*. "Oh my god! Can I meet her? Or just like, get an autograph or selfie or something?" She sounds way too excited, and I'm feeling overwhelmed.

I don't know what to do. I don't know this girl. And since I'm not Aviva, I'm not about to offer things on her behalf. "Um, no, I don't think so," I finally mumble, before turning tail and hurrying off in the opposite direction of my class. I feel kind of bad, but realistically, I'll probably never see that girl again. And it's not like I'd ever want to become friends with someone who so obviously only wants to know me because of my association with Aviva.

I make a gradual semi-circle until I'm headed in the right direction again. When I finally make it to class, I slip into my seat with a relieved breath. At least in here, with everyone paying careful attention to the professor, I'm just as anonymous as anyone else.

When lunch comes, I decide to leave campus. There were some random people hanging around my car where I usually eat, in the parking lot, and I'm not about to be ogled like a zoo animal through my windows. They were trying to be covert, but considering the parking lot is not the best hangout spot, especially in the winter, their efforts at blending in weren't the most effective. So I drive away in search of some stress-relieving food.

I end up at a pizza place. I get a couple of slices and return to my car to eat. I just want to be alone in a quiet space right now. I lean back in my seat, feet up, and savour the carbs. After a few minutes, I begin to grow bored of my own company, and pick up my phone. I check my texts again, but there's nothing new. Should I text someone?

My eyes land on my previous texts with Jace, and a smile grows on my face, but it's quickly dampened as new thoughts intrude. Should I text him again before our date on Friday? Or should he text me? Has it been long enough since out last texts to message him again, or would I come across as too needy?

Ugh. Too much worrying. I think back to the last time I texted him, and Aviva's advice. What would she say about this? Probably to just go for it. Girl power and confidence and all that. No games. I type a quick *hello* into the little box, then send it, heart racing, before I can talk myself out of it. Then I slam my phone back down on the passenger seat and take a large bite of pizza, staring straight ahead.

My phone vibrates and I almost drop my pizza. Quickly I rebalance it, then slowly pick up my phone again, keeping calm. There's one new text message. My eyes skip over the words the first time I read them and I have to go back and scan more slowly. It's just a greeting and a *what's up* in response to my text, but a grin stretches across my face anyway.

On my lunch break between classes, I respond.

Oh? What're you taking?

I explain about my classes, and he asks for more information on my program and the university. We end up talking all about school, but instead of stressing me out as it normally does, it relaxes me. Jace seems just as enthusiastic about post-secondary as Aviva does, I guess because he's not taking any college yet either. Even through text, our conversation flows easily. There's never an extended pause and every response incites a new question.

It feels like hardly any time has passed when I remember to check my clock, but I jerk up in my seat the instant I see the digital number. I need to get back to campus *now* if I want to make my next class on time. I send a quick apology to Jace for having to cut off the conversation.

Dw about it, he writes back. *Sorry for monopolizing the conversation with talk of school :)*

I laugh out loud. *It's fine. I actually didn't hate it.*
So I guess I'll see you Friday?

I nod emphatically, despite knowing that he can't see me. *See you then :)* Then I click my phone off and start my car up again, officially de-stressed and prepared to face the rest of the day.

At newspaper editing later, Asher seems just as happy to see me as he had been yesterday. Good god, I don't remember him being this dense before. I wonder if I should make a shirt and wear it to newspaper from now on: ASHER, I'M NOT INTERESTED. I smirk at the idea but then sit at my desk, ignoring him as much as I can. Even when he sits at the desk next to me, I keep my eyes focused forward. Maybe I can just ignore him the whole time.

"Hey, Naya."

I grimace. I really don't want to be enemies, though, so I suppose I can't ignore a direct address. I turn my head a fraction towards him, reply, "Hello, Asher," coolly, and return to my editing.

"How was your weekend? We didn't get a chance to discuss it yesterday."

I smirk again, both at his downplaying of yesterday's encounter, and at the memory of holding Jace's hand at the movies. "It was *great*," I reply.

There's a pause, where I continue tapping away at my keyboard, before he asks, "What'd you do?"

I sigh, resigning myself to the fact that I'll probably have to talk to him until I go home. "Went to the movies," I say. Maybe if I give him the absolute shortest answers possible, he'll *finally* take the hint.

"With *Aviva*?" he asks.

Now that Aviva's warned me about the interview that's come out, I realize that he probably knows that my Aviva is Aviva Jersey. Oh god. That's probably why he won't leave me alone. Frigging attention seeker.

"Yup."

"What movie did you see?"

I actually have to strain to recall this one, but I can't come up with the name off the top of my head. The movie itself wasn't exactly the reason I'd gone to the premiere, after all. And I'd been too distracted sitting beside Jace to pay any attention to the movie. I laugh as I tell Asher, "I can't remember."

He bares his teeth in a poor imitation of a grin, asking, "What's so funny?"

I shake my head, still smiling. "Nothing." Then I turn back to my work with an air of finality that must finally transmit to Asher because after a moment he scrapes his chair back and leaves the seat next to me. Without his eyes boring into me, I'm able to work much more efficiently.

Chapter Eleven

Wednesday and Thursday pass in much the same fashion as the beginning of the week. My social media followers continue to grow, for whatever reason; I've now hit 5k on both Twitter and Instagram. A few people still stare at me on campus, but the number lessens each day, as I assume Aviva's Snapchat fades from their minds. Asher continues to be extra-friendly at newspaper editing, and I continue to be cordial and not an ounce more. And Aviva and I see each other each night at the gym.

Jace and I don't text on Wednesday, but Thursday at lunch we confirm our plans for the next evening. My stomach tenses up at the thought of seeing him again, and just getting back into the dating scene in general, but it's not so much anxiety as excitement.

On Thursday I inform my mom that I'll be going out to see a movie the next day. I don't clarify with whom. I think she assumes Aviva, and I don't correct it. It's not that I'm keeping Jace a secret; I just don't want to start gushing over the new boy in my life if our first date ends up being our only date.

I don't sleep well Thursday night. I'm jittery and anticipatory and my mind races with imaginings of our date to come. Even so, when my alarm goes off the next morning, I bolt upright, no room for sleepiness alongside the adrenaline that courses through my veins. My date with Jace is not until five p.m., and I have to suffer through my classes first. I already know that I won't be able to focus on learning anything new. At least it's a Friday; professors usually know that by this point in the week, no one's ability to focus is at an all-time high anymore.

I'm right. My classes drag; the minutes between classes drag; even lunch drags, since it's just more empty time to kill before I can go home. When I finally get out of my English tutorial, I know that there's no way I can go to newspaper editing too. I'm way too wound up to be productive, and I'm not in the mood to deal with Asher. Besides, if anyone wonders where I am, Asher can tell them, I realize, recalling how I'd told him earlier this week that I have a date tonight. Whether he'd tell the truth about my plans or not is debatable, but I really don't care. I laugh giddily, my spirits lifting now that I've given myself permission to go home and get ready for my date.

I arrive home by 3:30, and lock myself in my bathroom. I take a moment to just stare at myself in the mirror, euphoria bubbling up within me, combining with my nerves and forcing a giggle out of me before I take a breath and settle down. I've already done my daily makeup look for school, which is pretty much just mascara, but I want to add a little bit. I've only seen Jace in person twice before, and both times were at premieres where Aviva had dolled me up. I can't replicate those makeup looks, and I don't want to, since this is just a movie in a regular old theatre, not another fancy premiere. But I also want to look like I've made some sort of effort.

I swipe some soft brown eyeshadow over my lids and into my crease, and carry it down under my lower lashes too, then smudge it out a bit with my thumb. I stand back to study the look, and decide that I like it. It gives my eyes a bit more dimension, and also makes me look a little older. I add another layer of mascara onto my lashes and dig into my mom's makeup supply to find some bronzer, which I then apply under my cheekbones, the same way Aviva had done. There. Much better.

I chose the movie and the theatre tonight, so Jace is choosing the restaurant. That means that the location is convenient and I know that I'll enjoy the film, but Jace wouldn't tell me anything about where we're eating, so I have no idea how formally to dress. I end up deciding on a deep purple sundress, and add a small silver necklace to compliment it. That should be versatile enough for pretty much anywhere. The dress tucks in at my waist, then falls in gentle folds that end just above my knees. I obviously can't wear it out alone, considering that it still feels like it could snow outside (although it hasn't actually snowed in a few weeks), so I match it with a pair of tight black boots that reach just above my knees, just about meeting the bottom of the dress, and a plain black jacket. The jacket has pockets for my keys and a small wallet, which also provides the benefit of not having to carry a purse all night. When I look in the mirror, I look sophisticated. Older. Dare I say... sexy. Not in a bare-all-skin kind of way, but in a confidence-and-actually-making-an-effort kind of way.

I check the clock. 4:30. Even though I took a while to decide on my makeup and outfit, I still have some extra time, since I skipped newspaper. Screw it. It's only a fifteen-minute drive, but I can't wait here anymore. I'll just wait in my car if necessary. I yell a good bye to my mom, but slip out the door before she sees my date-night outfit.

There's some traffic, which means the drive to the movie theatre ends up being twenty minutes rather than fifteen, so it's actually lucky that I was running early. Even so, once I've found a spot and parked, I still have ten minutes to kill. I figure I should tell Jace that I'm here, even though I'm a bit early, so I shoot him a quick text letting him know I'm in the parking lot.

My phone vibrates with a new message almost instantly. *I'm inside, by the arcade machine. Wearing a baseball cap.*

I laugh under my breath at the thought that I might need a visual clue to remember him, as if he hasn't been the only thing on my mind lately. I step out of my car and straighten up, smoothing my hair down and locking my car behind me as I head inside. My boots have four inch heels, officially bringing me up to five feet and seven inches. The cold air, which I usually hate, feels surprisingly refreshing tonight.

I spot him the instant I step through the theatre's doors. He's facing a claw machine, but not actually using it. He's staring down at the floor, seemingly lost in thought. I stride up behind him and tap him on the shoulder, grinning. He turns, and for a moment his expression seems... exasperated, maybe? But then he takes me in and he grins back at me.

"Hi," he says, and his voice causes some sort of effect in my chest.

"Hi," I return, still smiling stupidly but unable to control myself. My brain freezes for a moment as I just stare up at him, my eyes on his green ones. I think I stop breathing. He looks *really* good in a baseball cap, which kind of surprises me, because I love his hair. It probably has something to do with his sharp jawline. His face is already so attractive that he doesn't need his hair to compensate for any features. Then I realize that I'm kind of blocking him in, between me and the claw machine, and quickly take a step back, blushing profusely.

"Uh, have you won any prizes yet?" I ask in an attempt to draw attention away from my red face.

He looks back at the machine and shakes his head. "Never tried it."

"Like, today?"

"No, like never." He laughs at my shock.

"Well, we have to do it, then!" Arcade machines are just as much a part of the movie theatre experience as the actual movie, in my opinion.

He shakes his head amusedly. "They're all just money traps," he says, indicating the row of beeping machines.

I shake my head with faux sadness. "That's because you're not just paying for the prize. You're also paying for the *experience*."

"That's only if you actually get the prize."

"Ah, and that's where the skill comes in." He still seems dubious, so I roll my eyes playfully and dig the correct coins out of my jacket pocket, then step towards the machine. I expect Jace to step aside so I have room to play, but instead he just shuffles back a few steps, so that when I find my position in front of the claw handle, I can *feel* him behind me with each breath.

"Which toy are you aiming for?" he asks quietly, but he's so close that I can hear him perfectly.

I swallow, eyes fixed forwards. "That one," I finally decide, pointing out a purple stuffed dolphin. Then I press the button to start the claw moving. Unfortunately, my usually A+ skills (okay, maybe A-) are not in effect at the moment, when all my focus is on the body so near to mine, and his *scent* – it must be some sort of cologne, but I've never smelled anything like it before, and it is making me think all sorts of thoughts that have nothing at all to do with stuffed sea animals. My time runs out before the claw picks up the dolphin, and I turn around slowly, giving Jace time to step back. He doesn't.

"Guess I was wrong," I breathe.

His lips part as he looks down at me, but then he blinks, eyes moving to the machine, and shrugs. "I think I understand now what you mean. About the experience." Then he does step back, to dig out some coins of his own. The air in front of me feels cold. I cross my arms and step aside, giving him a try.

He focuses intently on the game, and it's mesmerizing. His eyebrows draw down slightly in concentration, and his jaw clenches and unclenches every time his hand moves on the controls. I'm not paying any attention to the arcade machine until I hear something drop and Jace steps back in satisfaction, turning to face me. I blush again at being caught staring, and quickly look over at the prize chute, where the purple dolphin I'd been eyeing now sits.

"How'd you do that?" I ask in astonishment. I certainly hadn't won anything the first game I'd ever tried.

He chuckles and pulls the dolphin out of the machine. "Beginner's luck." He offers me the stuffed animal and I take it and thank him bemusedly. As I turn it over in my hands, Jace's phone buzzes. He pulls it out and reads the message on its screen, but then clicks his phone off again without responding.

"We should get our tickets now," he says, and I agree. We head up to the ticket booth, and I have to juggle my new stuffie as I pull the appropriate amount of cash out of my jacket pocket. I notice that the young ticket-seller is staring at Jace a seemingly inappropriate amount, and I hold back a laugh, very happy that I'm the one on a date with him. Jace is very polite and nothing more to her. He kind of avoids eye contact with her too, but that might just be me reading into things too much.

Once we have our tickets for the movie I've chosen, *Tell Me You Love Me (Or I Might Have to Kill You)*, we find the appropriate theatre room and sit about halfway back from the screen. Jace removes his hat and combs his fingers through his hair, placing his hat on his lap.

I snort. "Are you planning on just holding your hat for the rest of the night?"

He smirks. "Maybe you should hold onto it instead." Then he whips the cap onto my head, and I shriek. Someone a few rows back shushes us, although the movie still hadn't started. Giggling, I remove the hat and hand it back to him, then attempt to smooth my hair back down. He places it on the floor by his feet, then helps me to fix my hair, smoothing back a few stray strands behind my shoulders. My laughter dies as I register how large his hands are next to my face, and how warm they are in the cold theatre. My skin breaks out in goosebumps. His hands complete one final run over my hair, ending on my shoulders, where they remain for a charged moment before he removes them again. I swallow hard, but then the ads begin, filling the dark room with sound and light, and I turn towards the screen.

"You know," he murmurs in my ear after a minute, indicating the family in the ad onscreen. "Those kids are genetically impossible, if those are the parents."

I laugh, because he's right, and because it's such a strange thing to think of while watching an advertisement. "They're trying to sell something, not convince you that they're actually related."

"But why would I believe that that dish detergent is effective if I can't even believe that the family is real? Maybe it's all lies." He looks at me out of the corner of his eye, smirking again, and I really can't control my laughter. We're shushed again by the person behind us, and I roll my eyes, still giggling, although I do try to make it quieter.

"And this one!" Jace exclaims as the next ad begins. It shows a woman at a party, holding a bottle of champagne and smiling brilliantly at the other party guests. "How much makeup can they put on her?" he asks incredulously.

"Never insult a woman's makeup," I tell him, hitting him playfully. He catches my hand before I can take it back and smoothly laces our fingers together, eyes on mine the whole time. This time I'm certain I stop breathing, because when the need for oxygen finally registers in my brain again, my next breath sounds more like a gasp. I turn back to the screen, and our joined hands fall on the armrest between us.

Jace continues to make funny little comments throughout the ads, up until the lights dim and the actual movie begins to roll. Then he leans back in his seat, face growing more serious. Our clasped hands remain between us.

Despite the movie's somewhat comedic title, it's actually a drama. And although I enjoy holding Jace's hand tonight, it's not so new anymore that I can't concentrate on the movie, like last time. In fact, about halfway through the movie, when the main character learns that her husband is actually an assassin on assignment to get close to her and kill her father, I drop Jace's hand to lean forward and cover my gaping mouth with both hands. After a few moments, I lean back again, which is when I register that Jace's arm is now over the back of my chair. I look at him and smile, then lean in toward him as he loosely wraps his arm around me.

When the credits begin to roll, Jace puts his baseball cap back on and stands up even before the lights go up again. I guess he wants to beat the crowd out of the theatre. He offers me a hand, which I take, and helps me up. I grab my dolphin, then he leads me by the hand out of the room. We stop walking once we reach the foyer again.

"I'm hungry," he says, and I nod in agreement. "I was thinking we would go to Età Dorata. Do you like Italian?"

"Of course," I respond, but my brows furrow a bit. "Isn't that place pretty pricey though?"

He shakes his head. "Dinner's on me."

"No, you don't have to do that–" I try to protest, but he just shakes his head again, laughing a little.

"No, really, Naya. It's not a problem."

I had been planning on paying for my own meal, but Età Dorata really is out of my price range. And if he picked the restaurant and is insisting on paying, who am I to refuse? I slowly smile. "Okay. That sounds great, then."

He nods. "Okay."

We split for the drive, since we each brought our own vehicle. I follow his car to the restaurant, since I've never been there before. Once we're both parked and have met up again, Jace remarks offhandedly, "You know, we really should just bring one car next time. Much easier."

"And more eco-friendly," I comment in agreement, although on the inside I'm actually rejoicing. "So, you, uh – you see us going on more dates?" I ask in a serious tone.

He looks at me quickly, eyes slightly wider than usual, before he sees the teasing look in my face. Then he relaxes, and says, "You don't?"

I shrug. "I never said that." I meet his eyes. "Depends on how good the food is here, to be honest." My lips twitch.

His eyebrows flash up. "My restaurant choice better not disappoint then."

I nod seriously. "Can't go on more dates with a man who only picks tacky restaurants." Then we reach the entrance, I take in the formal atmosphere, and we both laugh.

"You're right, of course," he tells me. "I must pick somewhere a little less *shabby* for next time."

"Table for two, please," I tell the hostess. I look back at Jace with a smile, but see that he's focusing on some of the picture frames on the wall now.

The hostess nods. "Follow me," she says, sending a curious look at Jace. He doesn't look at her.

Once we're seated in a dimly-lit corner and the hostess leaves, Jace removes his baseball cap again. He jumps right into dissecting the movie we've just seen, and I enjoy hearing his analysis. I throw in a few things I'd noticed too, and he seems to really value my opinion on the matter, although I'm far from the film expert he seems to be.

"What was your favourite part?" he asks, and I recall the scene that had made me let go of his hand.

"The part where she finds out that her husband only married her so he could kill her father," I say, and Jace nods knowingly.

"The shots for that scene were actually designed to keep you on the edge of your seat," he says as some bread and balsamic vinegar arrive at the table. Jace keeps his eyes on the food the whole time, not even looking at our waitress as she introduces herself. I grin. He must not have been exaggerating about being hungry. We place our orders, and she heads away. Once she's gone, Jace picks up right where he'd left off, explaining about shot length and distance. His explanations are very interesting, not at all condescending. I can tell that he really loves the subject.

"How do you know so much about filmmaking if you've never been to college for it?" I ask, dipping some of the bread before shoving it in my mouth. From the first bite I know that my jokes about the food being bad won't be able to hold any water now, if this sample is any indication. It's amazing.

"Mom's a producer. I've been around industry people my whole life," he explains, also digging into the food. "That's part of why I haven't gone to university yet. I want to study something that I love, but that I can't already learn about in the field. I don't know what that would be yet."

Our server returns with our meals. Damn, service is efficient too. I guess that's what you get at such an expensive place.

"What's your favourite movie?" Jace asks once she's gone.

I think for a moment. "Probably 99 *Days*. I really like Hannah Carlson. She's a great actress."

He nods, smiling a bit. "I know Hannah."

My mouth drops. This is so weird. He laughs, and I quickly snap my jaws together again. "Doesn't she live in L.A.?"

He nods. "I lived in L.A. until I turned 18. Then I came back to Toronto. I still fly out there pretty often, though. It's where my family is. But, yeah. Hannah and I were childhood friends."

"I really want to visit L.A. sometime," I admit. "Aviva's invited me, but I just don't know when we'll actually have a chance to go."

"It's a great place, if you know which spots to hit. Most of the really good ones aren't on the tourist map, though."

"Maybe if we end up there at the same time, you can show me around," I offer, taking an intentionally nonchalant sip of my water.

"Maybe," he agrees. "So. Where else have you travelled?"

I don't know what it is about Jace, but he's just so easy to talk to. I never feel pressure to fake anything or play any games the same way I did with Asher. Sure, I wondered whether I should or not before Aviva and I talked about it, but that was because of my ingrained mindset, not because of anything Jace had done or said. Being Asher's girlfriend, I'd always felt as though I had to be on my toes. The slightest misstep would lead to some stupid punishment from Asher, like ignoring my calls for several days, or making me believe he was hanging out with some other girl even if he was really just at home watching TV. I don't feel any sort of pressure like that with Jace. Maybe it's too early to judge, and I really don't want to jinx anything, but I can't help but bask in this new atmosphere.

After we've finished eating and our server returns to take our dishes, she also asks if we want to order dessert. Jace looks at me, eyebrows raised.

"Yes," I say definitively, and he grins.

"Two dessert menus please," he tells her, although his eyes are still on me. She returns quickly with the new menus, and as she places them on our table, the overhead lights are dimmed. I check my watch. 9:30 exactly.

We each scan our menus, leaning towards each other to point out some particularly delectable-looking desserts.

"What about the fudge waffle combo?" he asks quietly.

"Where is that?" I ask, looking at his menu. I trace my finger down the list of desserts, scanning each one in an attempt to find it.

"Here," he murmurs, moving my finger to the right place. I freeze, then swallow and look at its description.

"That sounds good," I say, "but what about the chocolate peanut butter stack cake?"

He's looking right at me as he asks, "Where's that?" His pupils are huge, but the lighting is low, after all. I take his finger and move it to the correct point in the list. He turns his head to look, dropping his hand but grasping mine more firmly as he does. Our linked hands lie directly below his dessert menu, which is still clutched in his other hand. "Chocolate peanut butter stack cake it is," he affirms.

Our server returns at that exact moment, and I curse her ten times over in my head for interrupting our moment. Outwardly I paste on a fake smile and order the dessert to share.

Once the cake arrives, we place it between us and take bites from opposite ends. "This is so good," I moan, savouring the timeless chocolate and peanut butter combination. I look up to find Jace watching me. "You have–" I wave my finger vaguely around my lips, looking at the streak of chocolate on his. His tongue flicks out, removing it, and I watch the motion raptly. I find myself leaning towards him, completely unconsciously, and stop the motion. I sit back in my chair and stretch my arms behind my back, then take another bite of the dessert, very conscious of my movements this time.

When the server brings the bill, Jace swipes it off the table without even letting me see the total. He digs several bills out of his pocket and hands them to her, with a quick, "Keep the change." She riffles through them, making sure the amount is sufficient, then backs away, stammering *thank you*s.

I watch her retreating form, then look back at him. "How much did you–"

"Ready to go?" he asks. The question is abrupt, but his smile is genuine. I make a face. I don't want our date to end yet. He chuckles. "C'mon. Do you want to do something else?"

I shrug. "We could go for a walk." A romantic walk in the snow. That sounds like a lovely way to end the date.

He studies me dubiously, but ultimately agrees, after a *teeny* bit of wheedling on my part. We stand and grab hands. I don't know who initiated it; it felt more like our hands were magnets, drawn together by some unearthly, uncontrollable force. We walk to the exit. It's been dark out for a while now, and I'd apparently forgotten that winter plus nighttime equals fricking cold. But I'm not going to go back on my suggestion now, especially when I'd had to do some extra convincing to get Jace to agree. So I step through the doors bravely, feeling the (not so) lovely zero degree air hit me like a tidal wave. I look around slightly despairingly now. All I can see is darkness and concrete. I look over at Jace and see that he's biting his lip, obviously trying to hold back.

"Don't laugh at me," I grumble.

"I'm not," he quickly reassures me, but then he bites his lip again. I roll my eyes and drop his hand, walking off in a random direction since I don't know this area.

"Naya," he calls after me, and I can hear the humour tinting the word. He runs up behind me and grabs both of my wrists from behind to halt me, then spins me around. Now I'm pressed up against his body. Even through both of our jackets, I swear I can feel the heat pulsing between us.

"Yes?" I ask breathlessly, but it's cut off when his lips meet mine.

Oh my god. My body melts against his, and my eyes close of their own accord. His hand runs through my hair, and it sends some sort of feeling racing through me. I press closer, but then a wet snowflake lands on my cheek and snaps me back to reality.

I pull back, gasping, body still leaning against Jace for support, because I'm not sure I can entirely trust my legs right now.

He's breathing heavily too. "Wow," he gets out, and I just watch him for a moment, before I lose my senses again and reach for his lips. We kiss for another timeless moment, and I can't imagine how I ever felt cold before. This time he's the one who breaks it off, a battle playing across his face as he stares at me. I can't say what my face is replying. I don't think many thoughts are going through my head right now. I see his gaze return to my lips, and I lick them unconsciously. He blinks hard, then steps back.

"Let's go on that walk now," he offers, holding out his hand. I take it, but the contact feels too little now. I push those feelings down, attempting to focus instead on our surroundings.

Luckily Jace does know this area, and he leads us to the nearest intersection. From there, there are plenty of things to look at. The night is quiet, and although the snow lightly falling doesn't stick, it does lend the atmosphere a romantic element. We return to our earlier conversation, and move on from there to talk of our families, pets, close friends; everyone and everything important to us.

Eventually the cold does both of us in, and we begin to circle back to the restaurant and our parked cars. Once we've reached my car, I reluctantly drop Jace's hand and turn to face him.

"I had a really good time tonight," I tell him honestly.

"Does that mean you'll accept my offer of a second date?" he asks, lips twitching.

I smirk. "I think that can be arranged." Then I unlock my car and reach for my door handle. Before I can, however, Jace grabs my hand, stopping the motion. I look at him questioningly.

"I want to do something properly," he says softly. I can see his breath puff out in the frozen air between us. Then he leans in and kisses me quickly and gently, lips closed. It's simple, and very sweet. He pulls away before I can really register what's just happened, whispers, "Good night, Naya," and walks away. It takes a moment before I remember that I'm still cold and that my car is right beside me, offering me shelter. I turn back around and open the door, climbing inside. I take a few seconds to bring my mind back to the task at hand – distracted driving kills, kids – then get home quickly. The roads are much quieter this time of night. I leave my daydreams for when I get home and crawl into bed, snuggling under the sheets and smiling blissfully.

Chapter Twelve

The next day, I don't wake up until noon. Damn, I really must've needed to catch up on sleep if I managed almost a full twelve hours last night. I'm supposed to meet Addie in an hour, so I have to rush. I pull myself out of bed reluctantly, just wanting to stretch and luxuriate. Instead, I get dressed and apply my usual school-day makeup look, grab a granola bar, and give my mom a spontaneous hug goodbye on my way out.

"Where is she going?" I hear Connor mutter to my mother before I close the door. I snort and shut it firmly behind me, nearly skipping to my car. I'm in very good spirits today.

I text Adeline when I've reached the mall, and we meet up outside of a clothing store.

"Hi, Nay!" she squeals when she sees me, pulling me in for a big hug.

"Hi," I mumble into her hair, which is now on my face. Jeez.

I guess distance really does make the heart grow fonder. She finally pulls back, a few dark blonde strands sticking to my lip gloss before she retreats a step, taking them with her.

"How *are* you?" she asks, grinning hugely, showing off her pearly whites.

"Um, hungry, actually," I admit. "I woke up late. Can we go to the food court?"

She nods complacently. "Absolutely. How was your date last night?" she asks as we begin walking.

I look at her, surprised that she remembered. But then I recall how she had gossiped throughout high school, and decide to keep my answers simple so she has nothing juicy to tell. "It was great," I say with a smile. "We watched that movie – have you seen the trailer for it? – *Tell Me You Love Me (Or I Might Have to Kill You)*." She nods but doesn't speak, so I continue. "And then we went to Età Dorata." I raise my eyebrows mischievously, acknowledging the price. "And he paid for my meal."

"Um, girl, that sounds awesome!" We reach the court and I spot a frozen yogurt stand. I'm in the mood for some sugar, so I point it out and we head toward it. "Sounds way better than any of your dates with Asher."

I nod. Addie has heard about many a disastrous night with Asher throughout our grade twelve year. I study the menu quickly then decide, "I'll have a medium banana coconut special." I turn to Addie. "What're you getting?"

She frowns. "Nothing. I'm on a strict no-dessert diet." She eyes me up and down. "How are you looking so good?" she asks enviously.

I grin. "Regular workouts." She humphs, then moves onto

telling me about her latest date. She's a serial dater, and it sounds like still no one has managed to nag her heart. We take my froyo to go, and hit up a few trendy clothing stores. I buy a few pieces of clothing, although the prices of the name brands prevent me from splurging too much. I also buy myself a new pushup bra, blushing profusely when Addie teasingly asks me what I'll be needing that for.

After we ring up our purchases, I spot a book store a few spots down and realize that I should probably stock up on some novels for the summer. Addie reluctantly agrees to accompany me in, although she takes out her phone and begins studying it instead of the books as I peruse the shelves.

Fifteen minutes later, I've collected several novels that I'm planning to purchase. I'm surprised that Addie hasn't started asking if we can leave yet, but she still seems immersed with her phone. Her eyes are flicking rapidly across the screen, over and over again, and I wonder if she, too, is reading. I smirk. That would be a first. I pick up another book that looks interesting and flip it over to check out the summary, when abruptly, Adeline starts shrieking, causing me to fumble and nearly drop the paperback.

"Oh. My. *God*!" she nearly screams, as I watch her in alarm. "You went on a date with Jace fucking *Morrow*?!"

"I – *what*?"

She shoves her phone in my face and I automatically grab it with one hand, balancing my books in the other. It appears that Addie had been reading a celebrity gossip website. My eyes bounce over the words, settling instead on the pictures. They're of Jace and me, from last night. *What the hell?* They're slightly blurry and underexposed, but both of us are definitely recognizable. Beneath them are two pictures of me with Aviva, one from the second red carpet event, and one from Aviva's Snapchat story. I try to swallow, but my throat is dry and I can't complete the motion. Why is my throat so dry? Shakily I sit down, dropping my books carelessly next to me on the floor.

I scan back up to the top of the page and finally read the title: **Who is Naya?** *They know my name.* How do they know my name? Ugh. Stupid question. Aviva put it on her Snapchat. Skimming through the rest of the article, it looks like my first name is all they have, thankfully. My last name is not mentioned anywhere that I can see. I take a deep breath and slowly start reading from the beginning of the article.

I know everyone else was just as shocked as us here at Pop Plus when Burning Embers, *the first movie based on the hit trilogy by Della Carlos, cast Jace Morrow to play Dante, the hero of the story. Although Jace resembles the Dante described in the books, with his green eyes and brown hair (and, you know, overall smoking hotness!), Jace is still a relatively unknown actor, with only minor parts credited on his IMDb page. Fans of the books were hoping for their fave actors to snag the part, but we figure that Jace must have acted his butt off in the audition in order to beat them out! Although the movie hasn't even started filming yet, Jace's fame is already skyrocketing!*

Which leads us to these intriguing photos, taken just last night! Jace appears to be on a date, at a fancy Italian restaurant in Toronto. And who is the lucky lady? None other than Aviva Jersey's good friend Naya! Could Naya be Jace's girlfriend? Here are some interesting facts about Naya that we dug up:

1. *Naya is nineteen years old and attends the University of Toronto.*
2. *She and Aviva follow each other on Twitter and Instagram, but she and Jace don't!*
3. *She has attended two movie premieres with Aviva in Toronto (that we know of!)*
4. *Her favorite color is green.*
   ...What the *fuck*? How do they know that? I shiver and duck my head back down to continue reading.
5. *And most exciting for us (although maybe less so for fans of Jace!), Naya and Jace were spotted kissing outside of the restaurant last night!*

Not much comes up when all you can Google is a first name (Naya doesn't list her last name on her social media), so we hope you appreciate the work we put into finding these facts! Now it's your turn, social media stalkers – *cough cough* – whoops, social media mavens. Find out more about Naya. Where does she come from? How does she know Aviva and Jace? Is she also an actor? What's her full name? Who is Naya???

My hands are shaking, making it difficult for me to finish the article. I feel vaguely nauseous. Mutely, I hand Adeline's phone back to her. I think she's talking to me, but there's a weird ringing sound in my ears and I can't concentrate on her words. Phrases from the article keep bouncing around in my head.

I don't know what to do. I don't know what to think. Why didn't I know that Jace is an actor? Hell, not even Aviva knew. I think back on our conversations last night. I knew that he was very interested in movies, and I knew that he was working, but he never said he was an *actor*. A surge of rage runs through my body, and I take a deep breath to settle it. I don't think the anger is directed at Jace for not telling me, or Aviva for not knowing, or me for not putting two and two together (come on, Naya! You met him at a movie premiere!), or even at the magazine's creepy invasiveness, but rather the entire situation. It's just all too much.

I need to talk to Jace. I need to get away from Addie. With a *whoosh*, all the sound comes rushing back, and I can hear Adeline still babbling on in my ear.

"What?" I interrupt, perhaps rudely, but Addie doesn't seem to notice or care.

"I *said*, I knew you were tight with Aviva Jersey, but you're dating *Jace Morrow* too? Damn, Naya! What the hell happened to you since high school? How did you start hanging out with famous people?"

"You... you already knew that Aviva and I are friends?"

"Um, *yeah*! Girl, I love Aviva Jersey, and when those paparazzi photos showed up with *you* in them? Ah! I *screamed*! I knew I had to see you again!"

My heart is beginning to race, and my breathing is shallow. I need to get out of here. Slowly I stand, picking up my books and taking them to the cash register. On autopilot I hand the girl behind the register my credit card, then take the bag of books when she holds it up for me. Addie is still blathering on, but I'm not listening anymore. The rage bubbles up within me again, but this time I know exactly who it is directed at: Adeline. Aviva was right about her, after all.

I speed walk out of the book store, Addie trotting along behind me like an obedient dog. I spot signs for a washroom and beeline for it, dragging Addie along by her arm when she starts to slow. The washroom appears to be empty, after a quick search of the stalls, so I drag her to the back before finally letting go.

She brushes off her arm, looking kind of irritated. "Jeez, Naya, words! Just *tell* me when you have to pee!"

"Why did you contact me again?" I hiss at her.

She abruptly stops rubbing her arm, and walks to the mirrors instead. Staring at her reflection and smoothing down her hair, she replies, "Because I missed you, silly."

"Damn it, Adeline, tell me the truth!" I shout. She stiffens. I never call her by her full first name aloud. Slowly she takes her eyes away from the mirror and cuts them over to where I stand, in between the rows of empty stalls. She turns to face me, a mischievous grin taking over her face.

"Okay," she singsongs, "I saw you in that mag with Aviva Jersey."

"What *mag*?" I ask desperately, hating her slang.

"I don't remember," she says exasperatedly. "I think there were more than one. Like, just candid pics. One of you at her apartment or something?" She shrugs. "And so I figured I should get in touch with you again." She digs a lipstick out of her pocket and turns back to the mirror to apply it.

"Why?" I croak out. She looks over at me with raised eyebrows. I can tell she doesn't want to say the words out loud, but I need her to. I *need* to hear them. "*Why?*" I yell at her.

Her hand jumps, creating a red smudge at the side of her mouth, and it brings me some small amount of satisfaction to see a crack in her perfect face. "Ugh. Naya!" she complains. "Fine!

All I'm saying is, you don't have to be a fame hog! Do you even want to be famous? No!" she answers for me. "So share it. Just hang out with me, let the paps take some photos..." she wiggles her eyebrows suggestively.

My nausea has increased. Aviva was spot on. As usual. And I'd gotten mad at her for trying to look out for me. This whole mess could have been avoided if not for my stubborn belief that Addie actually liked me. *Missed* me. Wow. What a concept.

"I mean," Adeline continues, "You're pretty good at seeking out publicity. Like, you're BFFs with Aviva Jersey? And *dating* Jace Morrow? How'd you pull that off?"

I swallow. "I didn't know that either of them were famous when I met them," I mutter miserably.

Addie snorts. "*Right.*" Then, in an undertone, "Fame hog."

I'm done. I'm so far past done with this girl. "You know the only thing worse than a fame hog, Adeline? A fame *whore.*" I bump her shoulder on my way out the washroom, sending her off balance, causing another lipstick smudge. Her infuriated shriek is the last thing I hear before I'm back into the crush of the crowd.

I find my car through eyes blurred by tears. Once inside my car, I check to make sure all my doors and windows are closed tight, and then I scream loud enough to make my throat raw. Then I sit in silence for several moments, not looking at anything in particular, not thinking anything in particular; just existing. When I come back to myself, I take out my phone, block Adeline's phone number, delete her contact, then open up the texts between Aviva and me. I pause, then type out one sentence.

You were right.

Then I move over to Jace's number and without pause, not allowing myself to overthink it, ask if he's free to meet up. There's no response from Aviva yet, but Jace answers quickly.

So eager to see me again already? ;)

I swallow, then bring up my browser and type in *Jace Morrow Naya date* and find the site that Addie had shown me. I copy the URL and send it to Jace. I tap my fingers against the wheel as I wait for his reaction. There's a longer pause this time, I assume because he's reading the article. He gets back to me just as the tension is beginning to overwhelm me again. I take a deep breath and feel the pressure recede.

Damn, they sure invade people's privacy quickly... I'm sorry Naya.

I frown. I was expecting a bigger reaction. *So can we meet up? I really want to talk about this.*

Yes, of course. I'm at my apartment right now. Do you want to meet me here?

I agree and he sends me his address. I punch it into my GPS and put my car into drive. It doesn't take long to get there, and I am long past my crying stage at this point. Now I'm just angry, although it's not as strong as the rage I felt earlier. It's more of a helpless frustration.

Jace buzzes me up as soon as I press the bell. Once I reach his door, I attempt to school my features into something more presentable, but I'm not sure how successful I am. I rap three times on his door, and hear his footsteps approaching. A flutter of butterflies fill my stomach, the sensation hitting me abruptly. I'd been too focused on my anger to really think about the fact that I'm seeing Jace again. He opens the door, face slightly wary, but it transforms to concern when he takes a good look at my expression, whatever it may be. "Come in," he says quietly, moving to the side so I can pass through.

I take a look around. It's a nice apartment, although smaller than Aviva's. The couch is dark leather and there's a colourful abstract painting hanging on the wall behind it, with a large TV screen on the wall across from it. A sturdy wooden coffee table sits across from the couch, and my eyes wander to a door in the corner. I figure it must lead to his bedroom and bathroom, and although I'd normally want to see more, I'm not in the mood right now. Jace is silent behind me, and when I turn back to look at him, he just meets my eyes. I can't read what he's thinking. I exhale and sit on the couch, and he follows me, settling on the coffee table directly across from me.

"What's going on?" he asks softly, leaning toward me.

I freeze, momentarily distracted by a strand of hair falling onto his forehead. I divert my eyes, swallow, then spill everything, from Addie first contacting me, to Aviva's warning, to the disaster of a shopping trip today. He listens patiently, placing his hand on my knee in encouragement to continue when I falter before describing Adeline's betrayal.

"She never really wanted to be friends again," I bite out. "She just wanted to be famous." Jace begins to stroke his finger over my knee, and I feel the anger begin to disperse. I sigh. "This is kind of awkward, but... uh, well, I never actually knew you're an actor."

His finger freezes on my leg, and I bite my lip. "Are you sure? I swear I..." He looks off to the side, and I can see that he's mentally scanning our conversations the same way that I did, reviewing our conversations about his life and work. He shakes his head briefly before looking back at me.

"I didn't mean to keep it a secret," he says, one side of his mouth twitching up. I nod. I had never thought that it had been intentionally hidden.

"I can't believe that I never asked what your job was when we were discussing your work," I mutter, and he chuckles.

"Well, Naya, I suppose I have something to tell you," he says conversationally, leaning in towards me and steepling his hands between us thoughtfully.

I shuffle forward until my knees are touching his, playing into the covert atmosphere. "Oh? A secret?" I ask.

"Very secret," he agrees. "The truth is... I'm an actor." He shakes his head at himself reproachfully.

I gasp. "An... *actor*?"

He nods, trying hard not to smirk. "I'm so sorry." I grin, but his face darkens, and returning to seriousness, he whispers, "I really am sorry that you were blindsided by this."

I look down and shrug. "Not your fault." He gently tilts my chin back up so he can read the truth in my face. In this position, his face so close to mine, I flash back to the comment he'd made last night, before he kissed me the second time. "Can I ask you something?" I ask.

He nods and says, "Of course," almost automatically.

"After our date," I whisper, "before you kissed me good night..." His eyes dart to my lips and back up again, probably unintentionally. "You said that you wanted to do something *properly*. What did you mean by that?"

"Oh," he murmurs. He studies something behind me as he answers, not meeting my eyes. Is he embarrassed? "Well, when you pulled away from our first kiss, I just thought that maybe we were taking things too quickly."

I blink. "But I kissed you again after I pulled away."

He half smiles. "But you did pull away."

I take a slow breath in as I try to formulate my explanation. "It's not really that we were going too fast. Or, well, maybe it is..."

"Naya, it's okay, we–"

"No, listen," I say, and he stops. "My last relationship... everything was just so fast. The physical, the emotional attachment... I ended up losing a lot of friendships because I spent all my time with him. And when it ended, I just felt... lost. Does that make sense?" I look up at him.

"Yes."

"I just don't want to rush into this. I don't want to make the same mistakes." I lean forward again, trying to recapture the closeness. "Trust me, it's not that I didn't want to kiss you," I tell him humorously.

His eyebrow quirks up, and he leans forward again too. "You sure?"

I lean into him. One second we're apart and the next our mouths are moving in unison, no thought in between. My hands explore his arms before settling behind his neck, as his hands move from my knees to my thighs, then skip up to my waist. For several long moments I just revel in the union, before I recall that I had been trying to make a point. I pull away, breathing ragged. Jace leans his forehead against mine.

"See?" I mutter. "Nothing against kissing. Just against repeating mistakes." He chuckles. "But I know you're not my ex. And I think I know what to avoid doing now."

He leans back, placing his hands on the table behind him. "New relationship, new standards?" he suggests.

My breathing hitches. "Is that what this is? A relationship?"

I see a tick in his eyebrow, and I smile in encouragement. "All I know is that I really like you, Naya," he tells me.

"Likewise," I whisper, hoping not to interrupt him.

"And I don't want to go out with anyone else. And I don't want you to, either. So uh, yeah, I guess. I do want a relationship."

My smile is threatening to split my cheeks. "Okay."

"Okay?"

I snort. "*Okay*. Does this mean we can follow each other on social media now?" I ask, referencing the article that had initiated this meeting in the first place.

He laughs. "Of course. Gotta make it Instagram official, right?" He moves next to me on the couch and we both pull out our phones. I lean against him as we exchange information, and, once done, turn on the television across from the sofa. We watch a couple of episodes of whatever is currently on; I'm not paying attention. I turn my head into his chest slightly. He smells really good.

As the second episode ends, I realize that it's almost dinnertime. I rise, stretching. "I should get home."

He stands and walks me to the door and gives me a hug before opening it.

"You know, we really should plan our next date," he calls after me as I head for the elevator.

"Text me!" I yell back, and I can hear him chuckling as he shuts the door behind him. I can't stop a huge grin from spreading over my face.

I'm half-heartedly practising Latin verb conjugations the next day when my phone buzzes, immediately drawing my attention away from my homework. It's a message from Jace.

I'm texting you.

I grin, recalling my last comment before I left yesterday. I reply, *For any reason in particular? ;)*

His response comes in before my screen falls back asleep. *Nah, just checking to make sure my phone still works.*

I laugh aloud. *Oh, awkward, and here I was, about to propose a date idea...*

I mean, I'm open to the idea, if you still want to share.

I bite my lip. *Idk... I might have to share my second-best idea now, with that lack of interest.*

Sigh I guess I deserve that. What's your second-best idea?

I pause for a second. I hadn't actually had anything in mind. I'd just been playing with him. Looking back at my unfinished homework sitting on my desk, I type slowly, *Oh, it's so bad you'll never want to see me again. It's a... wait for it... study date.*

He answers much more quickly than I'd expected, and with a much different response than I'd expected. *Oh, the torture. Sure, let's do it.*

I shake my head bemusedly. What is it with actors *wanting* to do homework? *When are you free?* I ask.

I have nothing on tomorrow.

Looking around at my room, I'm acutely aware of its small size, and the fact that it's in my parents' house. Oh god. My parents. I am not ready for Jace to meet my mom yet. I just know she'd put him through an examination extensive enough to rival the Spanish inquisition.

You want to join me on my lunch break then?

Sure. Where should I meet you?

I give him the location of my last class before lunch and the time it ends, and then we text a while longer about nothing in particular. I can feel my Latin work staring at me accusingly, but I ignore it, figuring I'll make up for this time tomorrow at lunch. Homework has never seemed so appealing.

Monday morning passes much more easily than usual, and I know it's because I'll be seeing Jace as soon as lunch comes. I jump up as soon as my professor dismisses my Latin class, rushing to the door and scanning the hall outside. I see Jace almost immediately. I'm a bit caught off-guard, because I'd been expecting him to be wearing his hat disguise again, and he's not. I guess he's not worried about paparazzi here. I grin widely and walk up to him slowly, before stopping right in front of him and saying, "Hi."

"Hi," he returns. He gives me a quick peck on the cheek, then takes my hand and swings it a bit, leading me towards the exit. "Where to?" he asks as we leave the building.

I bask in the air, which has finally begun to warm up, and I hear my stomach rumble. I shrug. "I'm starving. Do you know anywhere good to eat around here?"

"How much time do you have for your break?"

"Two hours," I reply with satisfaction. "And then just one more class until I'm done for the day. Except for newspaper editing."

He stares at the ground for a moment as he considers. "There was this place my family used to get Chinese from when I was a kid. It's not too far from here. You down for Chinese food?"

"Yeah, sure," I say, and we agree to take Jace's car, since it's roomier (and newer) than mine, and since he knows exactly how to get to the restaurant.

The outside of the restaurant looks just like every other shop on the strip, but the inside is not what I'd been expecting. It's tiny and old-fashioned, and I hear phrases in Mandarin floating around between the staff. There are only a few tables inside, and I suspect more people get takeout than actually eat inside. The food appears soon after we order, and Jace and I carry it to one of the little tables meant for four people. I dig in immediately, the aroma making my mouth water.

"So you have one more class today?" he asks. "What is it?"

"Science." I shrug. "I'm not in a Science program, so it's not specialized. Just a broad overview, going over stuff we didn't cover in high school."

His eyebrows raise incrementally. "That sounds interesting. Is that what you have to study today?" He indicates my backpack, reminding me of what I really should be doing now.

I cringe. "Yeah. That and some Latin. I'll start once I finish eating."

He laughs but doesn't push it further. Instead we start talking about his acting job that I'd read about in that magazine.

"So it's based on a book series?" I ask him.

"Yeah. It's interesting to compare the script to the book. See what was taken out, what was added. We want it to be as close to the book as possible to keep the book fans happy, but at the same time, not everything can fit into the 2 hours we have for the movie. And not everything in the book would look cinematically interesting, so some things are altered."

"You haven't started filming yet, have you?" I inquire.

He shakes his head. "We start soon, though. My first day on set is next week." His lips quirk up automatically at the thought.

"This obviously isn't your first project," I state, and he nods in agreement. "What else have you been in?"

He rattles off a few titles, none of which I've seen, but when I ask him to tell me more about them, he looks at my empty plate sternly and asks jokingly, "Now, you wouldn't be trying to procrastinate, would you Naya?"

I blink. I really hadn't been. I'd just been caught up in his words and had forgotten all about the work I have to do. I make a face and sigh dramatically, but get up and throw away my waste before digging my laptop out of my backpack and setting it on the empty space next to me. Jace trades sides so he's sitting beside me and can see the laptop screen too. I adjust it so that it's between us equally.

He scans the screen, eyes flicking back and forth across my Science notes. I watch him, warmth flooding my stomach as I take in his profile. His biceps flex as he leans forward on his arms. My tongue flicks across my lips automatically. After a moment, he looks back over at me, and I blush.

"I think I'm doing more work than you are right now." He smiles.

I cough. "Yeah." I dig my unfinished Latin work out of my backpack and place it in front of me as Jace scrolls down a page on my laptop.

"This is interesting," he murmurs, and I turn back to him again. "This is something I might like to study whenever I end up in university."

"You could come to my class," I suggest. "Tons of people skip, especially this close to the end of the year. There are always open seats. And I doubt many people will be surprised by an unfamiliar face in a class of 300."

He pauses for a moment, then nods. "Yeah. Why not? Should be interesting. I'd better keep studying this then, if I want to have any idea what your professor is talking about."

I giggle. "Okay, you do that until I finish this Latin stuff. Then I need to skip to the end of my Science notes and study that."

He shakes his head disappointedly. "Wow, spoilers. Maybe I can read *really* fast and make it to the end in time."

He doesn't, of course. My notes are thirty pages long. He's only on page seven by the time I finish my Latin exercises and have to move onto Science. He complains jokingly as I scroll all the way down to page twenty-nine.

My Latin exercises had been easy enough to finish beside Jace, because they required active writing, and Jace's silent focus next to me hadn't been distracting. But now, staring at the screen, closer to Jace, I can feel his heat beside me and smell that cologne that is so intoxicating, and when he leans back and begins playing with the ends of my hair, my mind just stops working. I stare at the screen blankly as my entire focus is pulled to the body next to me. I blink once, twice, and a third time before I can shakily bring myself to concentrate on my notes. I slowly begin to comprehend the words in front of me, although my mind starts to wander away again... *no*. Thank goodness I don't have a test coming up, or I'd be screwed. All I really need to do is review, not memorize, so as long as I can focus enough to understand *what*, exactly, I'm reading, I'll be fine.

It takes me twice as long as it usually does to go through the two pages, and when I finish, I only have twenty minutes left before my next class. It's only a ten minute drive back to campus, so I wonder if I should skim through my notes again, but when Jace begins to braid my hair, I give up and snap my laptop shut.

"You know how to braid?" I murmur.

He chuckles. "You learn a lot on set. Do you have a hair band?"

"There's one in my bag."

He leans down, one hand still wrapped around my hair, and pulls it out of my backpack. He brings together a few more strands of hair, then ties the braid. He runs a finger from the top of my head to the bottom of my hair, and I realize that not only is it a braid, but it's a *French* braid. Apparently Jace is better at styling my hair than I am.

I sigh. "Time to go." I pack up my laptop and Jace throws out the remainder of his meal, then we return to his car. He drives back to school, and I direct him to the closest parking lot to my Science class. We're five minutes early, and people are still filing inside as I find two seats next to each other near the back of the classroom and sit down. I see a few girls turned towards up, whispering to each other, and I move closer to Jace possessively.

"It's too bad you didn't bring your hat today," I mutter, but he just shrugs nonchalantly.

"It looked better on you anyway," he replies absently, looking around and taking in the lecture hall.

A few more people rush through the doors, and then the professor begins speaking. I lean forward intently, taking precise notes. This is one class that I need to listen to very carefully. I may get away with being distracted in English, but I can't half-ass my Science class. Thankfully, Jace seems equally immersed when I take a quick peek over at him halfway through the lecture, so I don't have to worry about him being bored or otherwise distracting me.

At the end of the lecture, I take a deep breath of relief and snap my laptop shut again, turning to Jace. "So?" I ask. "How'd you like it?"

He looks towards me contemplatively, but I can tell he's not really seeing me. He focuses again after a few seconds and says, "It wasn't what I was expecting. But I didn't dislike it."

I laugh. "Well, you have time to decide if it's something you'd ever want to take." I shove my laptop into my bag and stand up. He does the same, and I look up at him, once again reminded of our height difference, which had been temporarily diminished while we were sitting side by side. He clasps my hand and leads me back out of the room and towards the exit again.

"Where to now?" he asks, cocking his head. "You have newspaper editing, right?"

"Right," I grin. "It's on the other side of campus. I usually walk there, but we can drive, if you want."

He shrugs. "I don't mind the walk. It's nice out."

"Okay," I agree easily. We start off in the direction of the editing building, which is about a ten-minute walk away. For the first few minutes, I'm too distracted by Jace and our conversation to notice my surroundings beyond a vague idea of keeping on the right track, but about halfway there, I realize that there are even more eyes on me than usual. Well, I guess they're only on me by default, since Jace is obviously the one attracting the extra attention. I squeeze Jace's hand tighter unconsciously as my eyes dart around, and he pauses mid-sentence to look down at me.

"What's wrong?"

"Hm?" I look back at him. "Nothing. I mean, just..." I indicate the people around us with overt eye movements.

He looks around, and a few people look away, giggling or blushing, but some stare right back at him unabashedly. "Ah," he says, sounding slightly uncomfortable. He shrugs. "Sorry."

"No, don't apologize," I rush to say. "It's just weird for me."

"You're not used to it? Because of Aviva, I mean?"

"Aviva and I don't really go out in public beyond premieres," I explain.

He pauses, then tugs me toward a tree off of the footpath. We stop there, and he studies my face as he asks, "Are you okay with us being out in public?"

"Yes," I insist. "It's not you. I just don't really like that much attention. But I'll get used to it, I'm sure. I want us to be public."

Jace smiles, but it looks slightly strained, and I can tell he's not entirely convinced. So I place my hands against his chest and back him up a few steps until he's leaning against the tree, then I stand on my tip toes and press my lips to his. It's just supposed to be a reassuring gesture, but after the first kiss I just can't resist another. I press my lips to his again, and this time I don't have the restraint I did before. My body sways toward his, and my arms reach around his torso until they reach the tree behind him. He responds, sliding his hand into my hair, mussing the braid that had been so perfect. I begin to slide my hands under his jacket, but although the weather has been warming up, my hands are still cold when they reach his stomach, and he hisses a bit at the contact. It jolts some awareness back into my brain, and I pull back, leaning my head against his shoulder.

"Sorry," I laugh, and he laughs too. This time there's no strain in his face.

"We should keep walking," he says, and I recall where we'd been headed. Right. Newspaper. That reminds me...

"Um, so you know how I mentioned my ex before? How everything moved so fast with him?"

He frowns incrementally, and I realize he probably thinks I'm about to say we shouldn't kiss in public or something. That's not my problem at all.

"He's at newspaper editing," I rush on, before he can come to any conclusions. "I see him every school day. We don't really talk, but..." I shrug. "Just thought you should know. To be prepared, or... whatever."

He nods, looking thoughtful. "I would like to know. Thank you." We move back onto the path, and I notice a group of girls gaping at us. My cheeks burn as I think of what they must have just witnessed. I'm not totally embarrassed, though. I feel a sense of pride, too, deep and feral, at claiming what is mine.

When we arrive at the editing building, Jace comes inside with me. We stop outside the room for a moment as I discreetly point Asher out through the window. I guess I'm a little bit late today, after the impromptu makeout session on the way here.

"Do you want to come in for a minute?" I ask Jace, as I apply some lip gloss to my now-dry lips. "I can show you what I'm working on."

Jace's eyes track the lip gloss brush as it swipes across my mouth, before he replies. "Sure. That would be nice."

My lips part in response to his gaze, but I really am going to be late to newspaper, so I divert my eyes and return the lip gloss to my bag before pushing in the door and leading Jace into the room and to my desk.

"Take a seat," I offer, and he does, before pulling me down onto his lap. I squeak with surprise, and he chuckles.

"Let's see what you're working on," he murmurs, turning me so we're both facing the computer screen. I can feel his breath against the back of my neck, and it takes me a moment to recall my username and password to log into the university network. I pull up the paper I'm currently editing, and show him some of the changes I've made.

"And then they end up like that," I tell him, pointing back towards the entrance, where the supply of finished newspapers sits. I catch Savannah's eye and realize she's staring at me on Jace's lap with wide eyes. I blush and stand up. "I really do have to work now," I tell him, pouting.

He stands too and stretches, and a slice of abs peeks out from beneath his shirt before he adjusts it again. "I should go anyway," he tells me, then his eyes catch on something behind me. Before I can turn to see what, he leans down and recaptures my lips, and I totally forget to care about anything else. My hand warm enough this time, I reach the tips of my fingers under his shirt and trace the ridges of his lower abs. He pulls back first this time, breathing harder than usual, and I blink to refocus. "I'll see you later," he tells me, and I agree, dazed. Then he turns and leaves, closing the door behind him. I take a shaky breath and sit back down. Do my legs usually feel this weak? I hear some movement to my right, and I recall that Jace had been staring at something before he kissed me. I turn towards the sound and see Asher staring at me sullenly. I turn back to my computer screen quickly. Asher had obviously seen the kiss. I abruptly wonder if that had been Jace's intention. I grin.

"Naya?" I hear from my left. I turn and see Savannah is talking to me.

"Uh, yeah?" I ask uncomfortably. Savannah doesn't usually make conversation with me.

"Was that *Jace Morrow*?" she asks incredulously, and I realize that I'm going to have to face more questions than anticipated.

"Yeah," I reply, trying to sound unaffected, although I'm starting to feel a little embarrassed. I turn back to my work, but only a few more seconds pass before I hear another chair scrape up beside me. I cringe, hoping against hope that it won't be who I think it is. I turn reluctantly to see – yup – Asher. I stare at him, waiting for him to explain his presence, but after several awkward moments of silence, I decide to speak first.

"Is there something you wanted to say, Asher?"

His expression turns stormy, and I clench my jaw. "Really, Naya? You're over us that quickly, huh?"

I blink rapidly. "What? Isn't that exactly what you wanted? *You* broke up with *me*," I remind him acidly.

"Well, maybe that was a mistake," he shoots back, and I take a deep breath, suddenly aware of everyone else watching us.

"Can we talk later? Privately?" I hint.

He looks around the room, meeting each pair of eyes. "No, here is just fine," he says loudly, clearly aware of our audience.

I huff. "Okay, fine then. No, I don't think our breakup was a mistake, *obviously*, seeing as how I have moved on."

Asher's eyes grow cold. "So he's your new boyfriend?"

My insides ignite with flames. Does he really have no idea the damage he'd done to me, cheating on me and breaking up with me, leaving me single and friendless? How difficult it had been to move on from him, onto healthier relationships? It had not happened overnight. Hell, it's been over half a year! I refuse to let Asher see how much he's affecting me though, so instead I match his coldness and respond icily, "Yes. He is."

Asher smirks. "Wow, Naya, you've changed. I never thought you'd be one to date a guy just because he's famous, but I guess I was wrong."

My face heats again, but this time with anger. I'm not embarrassed anymore, but I am acutely aware of everyone still watching, and keeping the words I want to throw at Asher inside my mind instead is giving me a headache. I take a deep breath before continuing. "Believe it or not, I didn't know Jace was famous when I met him. I like him for a lot more than his job.

And we may not have been dating long, but he's already a better boyfriend than you ever were," I can't resist adding.

Asher's eyes flash. "So you've already been slutting around with him?" he asks callously, and now I'm not just angry, but I'm hurt. This is not the guy I used to know. The one I thought I loved. I won't let my pain show, though. I control my tone carefully as I respond, "No, Asher, some guys are actually led by their brains rather than their dicks. Although I know that may be difficult for you to understand."

"Oh, and I suppose you didn't know Aviva Jersey was famous either, when you became besties with her?"

"No, I didn't, because she was in disguise!" I blurt out, finally too fed up to filter my words. I abruptly shut up when I realize what I've said.

"What kind of disguise?" Asher asks, suddenly curious, but I just laugh harshly.

"Forget it." I stand up. I don't want to give Asher the satisfaction of driving me away from newspaper, but I also know I won't be able to do my work properly today, so I gather my stuff back up and stride towards the door, muttering apologies to a couple of people I pass on the way out. To Savannah, I simply say, "I'll be back tomorrow." I slam the door behind me.

Chapter Thirteen

I swear I'm getting even more stares than yesterday, when I had Jace, an actual celebrity, with me. *What is going on?* Why am *I* the one caught up in so much gossip? I nearly persuade myself to ignore everyone, until a particularly ostentatious group of girls catch my attention. Then, entirely without forethought, I approach them and blurt out, "What's going on?"

They seem surprised at being confronted, and two drop their eyes, but the third girl, unabashed, simply shrugs and holds out her phone to me. I take it and look down at the screen. It's another gossip site, this time one I've actually heard of before, and there appears to be a video to play. I tap the screen and the clip begins immediately, obviously preloaded.

Although I can't hear the words being said, I immediately recognize the setting. It's the newspaper room from yesterday. Someone from newspaper was filming my fight with Asher! My stomach drops. I know everyone who was in that room, and I would never have previously thought that any one of them would invade my privacy like this, not even just recording it in the first place, but then selling it to the tabloids! Why anyone would pay for it I have no clue, but here it is. The video continues to play, and I realize that it's been transcribed, so that now even the deaf can get the play by play of my ex-boyfriend drama. My eyes prick with tears, so I quickly hand the girl her phone back, ignoring the stupid smirk on her face as she receives it, and walk quickly away.

I attend my classes, trying to immerse myself in the learning process, trying to forget everything else, but it's impossible. My mind continuously jumps back to the fight with Asher, trying to determine who in that room could have filmed it, and *why*. I feel violated. I consider dropping newspaper editing, but I've put so much effort into it this year, and it's so close to the final issue, that I know I can't.

At lunch I compose a text to Jace. *So this happened yesterday... I didn't know I was being filmed.*

I find the link to the video and copy it, then paste it into the message to Jace before hitting send. I chew my sandwich, not really tasting it, as I wait for a reply. It comes ten minutes later.

Shit. Are you okay?

I sigh. *Yeah. Kinda. Mostly.*

Do you want me to hire a hitman?

I snort. *For who? Asher or whoever filmed it?*

Either. Both?

Now I'm grinning. *I'm gonna have to refuse. But thanks.*

Oh well. There's always next time ;)

I shake my head in amusement. *I'm going to skip newspaper today.*

Probably a good idea.

I'm about to respond when another text from him comes in.

Sorry, I have to go. Meeting. Talk later?

My fingers pause, then type out, *Of course.* Then I pocket my phone and finish my sandwich.

That night, I arrive to the gym a few minutes early. I look over at the treadmills, and am contemplating running tonight instead of using the elliptical trainer, when Aviva enters.

"Want to use the treadmills tonight?" I ask her, still mentally debating the matter. After an oddly long pause, I look over at her.

"Uh, no, that's okay," she finally answers.

I recall the last time I used the treadmills, how she didn't want to run on them then either. "Why don't you like treadmills?" I ask teasingly, but her face doesn't lighten.

"What do you mean?" she asks, heading towards the ellipticals.

"The treadmills. You never want to run?"

She merely shrugs, starting up the elliptical trainer. "How was your day?" she asks as her legs begin moving.

I know this isn't honesty. I know she's hiding something. And although I'm sick of secrets, I'm not in the mood to confront her right now. So I drop the subject and join Aviva on the elliptical trainers, spilling today's events as we warm up and getting her take on everything. I can tell she's still not entirely herself, so I fall silent after a while.

Abruptly, Aviva asks, "Do you want to do something tomorrow?"

I grimace. "I need to do homework tomorrow. It's only halfway through the school week."

"Okay. That's fine. We can do another study date. Your place?"

I'm surprised that she wants to study more, but figure she just really needs to talk and a study date is better than not getting together at all.

"Uh yeah, sure. How about five?"

She nods resolutely. "Great." Then she laughs, somewhat shakily, although that could be just as easily caused by her rapid movement. But after that she finally starts to return to herself, telling me about a new project she's been signed onto with a popular director. "It's a remake," she says, "which can turn out great or terribly. Obviously we're hoping for great." She grins over at me.

"You work a lot," I comment neutrally.

She sighs blissfully as her machine slows, allowing her to cool down. "Yeah. It's everything I ever could have dreamed of."

I make sure I'm prepared for school, by digging out an old tennis cap of my dad's from the back of the closet. I'm pretty sure it hasn't been touched since the '80s, but I'm not working with many options. I brush my hair back into a tight bun resting at the base of my neck and stick the hat overtop. There. Not *quite* as recognizable. Maybe I should ask Aviva where she bought her Brynn wig from. I smirk. I don't think I'm at that stage of desperation yet.

My mini disguise works to a point. I get fewer stares while walking on campus, but more in class, probably because I refuse to take the cap off. Whatever.

I reluctantly head to newspaper editing and take a deep, calming breath before walking swiftly through the door, not making eye contact with anyone. The volume of the room drops swiftly, but no one tries to talk to me, so I do my best to just ignore everyone. After ten minutes or so, the atmosphere of the room is approaching normal again, allowing me to focus slightly more on my editing work. I stay for exactly as long as required, not a minute more, despite not yet being caught up on my work. Oh well. I exit exactly the way I'd entered, with a steady gait and focused gaze.

When I get home I have about half an hour before Aviva is expected, so I head up to my room and kill some time with the books I'd bought on that disastrous shopping trip with Adeline. Caught up in a novel, I barely register the doorbell ringing. Then my mind clicks back into reality, several seconds too late; I can already hear Connor's steps thudding towards the front door. I jump up and race down, but he opens the door before I can stop him. His reaction is almost comical. I can only see him from the back, but his entire body just freezes, and his normally racing lips are for once not making a peep.

"Hey," Aviva says, spotting me approaching. I smile at her and push Connor out of the way so she can enter. She does so, stepping around Connor carefully. He mutely closes the door behind her.

"C'mon," I tell her, nodding my head towards the staircase. She starts up and I follow behind, yelling to my mom that we'll be studying in my room. Connor glares up at me from below, obviously pissed that I didn't let him talk with Aviva. I roll my eyes at him. Like I'm going to intentionally expose Aviva to his toxicity. I hear my mom's acknowledgement just before I close my bedroom door behind us.

Aviva sits down on my bed, running her hands over the bedspread. I sit at my desk and pull out my textbooks. "Today is a *fun* day," I tell Aviva sarcastically. I look up, waiting for a response, but she's still running her fingers absentmindedly over my blanket. "*Why, Naya?*" I ask, mimicking the expected response. "Well," I respond to myself, "because today we are studying for exams." For my efforts, I receive a half-hearted smile.

Aviva does her part. Although her energy isn't at the expected level, she does help me to review, and I think that with that damn actor memory of hers, she might even manage to memorize more than I do. After almost an hour, when she's asking questions and I get at least three quarters of the answers right, we take a break.

"Hey, Naya?"

I think I hear a bump outside my door and my head whips toward the noise, but then I'm called back by Aviva clearing her throat. "Yeah, sorry?"

"Can we... talk?"

I focus my full attention on her. "Yes, of course." This is the first time Aviva has asked for a full sit-down serious talk. Considering the gravity of our last one, when I found out that Brynn was actually Aviva Jersey, I'm curious and mildly concerned at what this one will be about. "So... what's going on?"

She's silent for several moments, and I begin to feel uncomfortable. "You know that you can trust me," I remind her.

She nods slowly. "I think I finally realize that." She takes a deep, shuddering breath, and I think I see a tremor go through her. What the hell kind of secret has she been keeping that would provoke such a visceral reaction to just talking about it?

"Do you remember Ivy?"

I nod, recalling my nickname for her. *Poison Ivy*. The girl who sold Aviva's secret relationship with Callan to the tabloids for no apparent reason. The girl who'd had that inexplicable, unshakeable hold over Aviva.

"When I was fifteen... that's when Ivy was my best friend. That's also when..." The pause seems to stretch out forever, my mind racing as I try to anticipate her next words. Whatever she's about to say, I can feel just how deep the scars it left on her still are.

"I was anorexic," she finally whispers.

I freeze, momentarily taken aback, my mind racing back over every thought I'd ever had about Aviva's body. I'd always been envious of her figure and her toned muscles, and although she's slim, I never thought she could be considered overly skinny. But as I think back to watching her in *Death by Pom-Poms*, I can recognize that she had been quite thin. At that age, though, when you see a skinny girl, you don't automatically assume something is wrong. *Maybe she just hasn't started puberty yet. Maybe she's going through a growth spurt. Maybe...* Maybe she has an eating disorder.

"How long?"

"Two years." She looks very pale, and almost afraid. "From fifteen to sixteen. I'm lucky, I guess. That it didn't last longer. A lot of people... it's not so short for them."

"But you're fine now?"

"Yeah. For the most part."

"The most part?" I can hear a touch of panic in my voice, but I hope she doesn't. I want her to feel comfortable, or at least as comfortable as she can, and I don't want my wildly shifting emotions to affect her.

"I still have *issues*, I guess. I just don't act on them anymore."

"What does Ivy have to do with this?" I ask, suddenly recalling Aviva's intro to this tale.

She smiles sadly. "I'd like to put all the blame on her. Say that my anorexia was her fault, but I can't. No one really knows what *causes* an eating disorder. But there are plenty of factors. And she definitely didn't help. She was always on me about my body. Not even in any really obvious way, but like – *oh no, Vive, don't wear that, it makes your thighs look huge.* Or, *no, Aviva, you know you look preggers when you wear tight dresses.* Or, *you better wear six-inch heels with that outfit or your legs will look fat.* Trash like that."

I can feel my face heating up with anger at this Ivy, more poisonous than I'd ever believed. "And you just took it?" I ask incredulously.

Aviva's mouth opens and closes before she speaks. "You don't understand. She was my friend. She–"

"Friend, my ass," I interject.

"She wasn't usually like that. She could be really sweet too. I don't know for sure if she knew what she was driving me to do, but when I'd refuse dessert or just ask for a salad without dressing, or just water out for lunch, she'd look really happy, and I'd just – I'd feel good about it. There was a lot of pressure on me. I was already acting, which I loved, but it comes with a lot of people watching your every move off-screen too. And in all honesty, this was before the big social media craze. I had Facebook, but I wasn't really using it anymore, and I didn't have Twitter or Instagram yet. All the pressure about my weight wasn't coming from external sources. It was all from Ivy, and from myself."

"But you didn't really think you were fat, did you?"

Her eyes are shiny, and I scooch closer to her on my bed. She leans over and rests her head on my shoulder. "No. I knew I was skinny. But the anorexia... even if you know that, it doesn't stop you from wanting to lose weight. I just felt like I had a lot of fat on me, and I *hated* it. I didn't think I was fat, but I could feel all the extra skin, and..." She takes a deep breath and sits up straight again. "I restricted, and I ran on the treadmill *all the time*. Every extra minute I had. I *hated* it, I hated it so much, but anorexia snaps her fingers and you have to do what she says."

"That's why you don't like the treadmills," I realize, and she nods in agreement.

"So when you say you're *mostly* over it...?"

"I don't starve myself. I have a dietician who gives me meal plans and stuff so I eat what I should. I only work out an appropriate amount, with you," she says, swinging a small smile my way. "But I think I still have a skewed view of myself. And sometimes I still hear that dumb hoe's voice in my head, telling me that I shouldn't eat dessert, or to go do a hundred jumping jacks. Sometimes I can't look in the mirror unless my whole body is covered up. But it gets easier. I'm much better than I was at the beginning of my recovery."

"Good," I sigh with relief. Then, inquisitively, "That dumb hoe?"

"The anorexia." Aviva looks over at me. "Oh, you thought I meant Ivy? Well yeah, her too I guess. Although she's more of a dumb bitch." She laughs a little, and I join in cautiously.

"Why'd you tell me this now?" I ask carefully.

She shrugs. "I just feel like it's been weighing down on me for so long. The thing is, I never got specialized treatment. Callan was pretty much my whole support system. He helped me to try and fix my thinking. He convinced me to push Ivy out of my life. He's the only other person who knows that I was anorexic."

"Your parents don't–" She shakes her head in the negative. "Oh. Wow. Thank you."

"I'm just glad to get it off my chest. To feel like I actually have a friend that I can trust. And I know you've told me a lot of personal stuff too, and I felt bad for holding back. I have a lot of secrets that I can't tell anyone. It feels really good to be close enough to someone that I don't *have* to hold everything back."

I hug her. I'm not a big hugger, and I don't think she is either, but I feel like we both need it in this moment. I want to comfort her, but I also need to fill something in myself. I feel so bad for her, but I know she didn't tell me because she wants pity.

"I won't tell anyone," I vow, and she nods.

"I know." Her voice lightens. "Now, how about we get back to studying? This has been kind of depressing."

"And studying *isn't* depressing?" I joke, relieved to see her laugh. Then I bring my books over and we review side by side on my bed.

That night, Aviva's confession resonates through my head.

Fans think they know everything about Aviva, but there's so much more to her than her public persona. So much more that they'll never know. People go through a lot of bad stuff, and so few people ever find out. The difference with celebrities is that everyone thinks their lives are great. And sure, Aviva has a nice apartment and gorgeous clothes, but that didn't buy her happiness. If anything, her fame drove her to an eating disorder. I'm vaguely sickened when I think of my former mindset regarding celebrities. I hadn't even really thought of them as real people, but just characters onscreen, or the instruments behind a song on the radio. I just wish it hadn't taken me until I met Aviva to realize that just because a person is famous, that doesn't make them less of a real person.

14

Chapter Fourteen

The next day at school, the weirdest thing that happens is that I realize I'm getting used to all the stares. I just meet the eyes of the onlookers until they look away, each pair of eyes that drops sending a little thrill of victory down my spine.

At the gym that night, Aviva is loud and boisterous, which is just as much not her as the silence. To an observer, she may seem confident, but to me, it just seems like another mask. I ignore it, hoping that she'll drop her defences if I treat her like normal. Gradually her over-the-top enthusiasm melts away, the elliptical trainer probably also stealing her energy, and she begins to act more like herself. At the end of the gym session, after she takes a swig of water, she mentions that she's returning to Los Angeles in a couple of weeks.

"Oh." My face drops, already anticipating the loneliness.

"*But–*" she interjects before my cynicism advances too far, "I was wondering if you wanted to join me for a bit. There's a party two weeks tomorrow, at one of my friends' places. You'll be done exams by then, right?"

I stare at her gleefully for a moment before yelling, "Yes! Oh my god Aviva!"

She laughs at my reaction. "Don't get *too* excited. It's not that big of a deal. Parties are parties, you know? No matter where they happen."

It's not even the party that I'm really looking forward to, but the chance to see Aviva's regular life, and meet some of her other friends. For a moment dread overwhelms me at the thought of them judging me, but I take a breath and make the conscious decision to push that thought away. If I'm good enough for Aviva, then I'm good enough for the others. After all, I'm the one Aviva turns to in her time of need, who she shares all her secrets with. I smile again. I've never had a friend who I clicked with so easily, who I could read so well, and who I became close with so quickly. I feel like I can say that she's my best friend and have the title returned without any doubt, which is something I've never had before. It feels really good.

The next day is Friday, which already makes me happy, but it's also the end of the second-to-last week of classes, which makes it even better. When I finish working and shut down the computer after newspaper, I shove my chair in with a startlingly loud screech, then walk out with my head held high and a smile on my lips, just thinking about being in L.A.

That night I reach the gym before Aviva, which isn't unusual, but her extended absence after I arrive is. I text her to ask if she's on her way and receive a quick reply.

Sorry, my manager called me in to talk about some PR thing. I'll come right after! Shouldn't be tooooo long :/

I reply with an assurance that I'll still be here, then decide to start on my workout, since I'm just standing here otherwise. Ten minutes in, my phone rings. I look down to see that it's Aviva. Damn. I hope she's not cancelling.

"Hey, you still coming?" I ask, slightly out of breath.

"Are you fucking *kidding* me, Naya?" Aviva furiously shrieks from the other end. I freeze, completely taken off-guard. Aviva doesn't pause for one second, though. "You know, I thought, I really fucking *believed*, that you were different. You were a different kind of person. That you –"

"Aviva, what the hell are you talking about?" I finally cut in after my brain starts functioning again.

"You know what, I'm not doing this over the phone. I want to see your face. Come to my apartment."

"I – I'm in the middle of a workout!"

All I can make out from her end is snarling and some more swearing, which in all honesty kind of scares me. I have never heard Aviva swear like this before and I have no idea what would incite this kind of fury in her. But I obviously need to find out.

"Okay! Okay, I'll drive there right now."

The call ends abruptly, and I'm left staring at my phone screen in shock. My feet stopped moving sometime during the call, without my mind making the conscious decision to. I stumble off the elliptical trainer and walk towards the door, my pace gradually quickening until I'm nearly running to my car.

I don't remember the drive to Aviva's apartment, but all of a sudden, I'm here, staring up at the intimidating building. It's dark out. I step out of my car and shiver, wrapping my arms around myself. Inside, I nod at the man behind the reception desk and he nods back. I ride up to the thirtieth floor with a pit in my stomach, each floor that passes bringing me closer to a conversation that I'm not sure I'm ready to have. I don't know what to prepare myself for. I have no idea why Aviva is angry with me.

The elevator stops and the doors *whoosh* open much too quickly. I pause for too long and the doors start to close again, jolting me into action. I stop them and step out, take a deep breath, then knock on Aviva's door. It opens immediately, almost before my knuckles leave the wood, and I'm facing angelic wrath incarnate. Somehow her beauty makes the effect even more terrifying.

Aviva isn't yelling anymore, but this is no better. She grips my arm gently, but I flinch nonetheless. She pulls me inside; I don't resist. The door slams behind me and I flinch, but Aviva doesn't react. She walks away from me very deliberately, and I swallow. I try to wait her out but each additional second that passes makes me feel smaller and smaller. *No.* This isn't okay. I haven't even done anything wrong!

"Aviva," I say, trying to sound confident, but my voice cracks.

She whirls on me so quickly that I reflexively take a step back.

"I'm going to ask you a question, Naya, and I want the truth," she says in a dead voice. Her face appears calm but I can see the storm raging within her eyes. This is nowhere near the anger I experienced after the news of her new movies were leaked. This is so much worse. I nod, but she keeps staring at me, so I choke out, "Yes. Of course."

Slowly, each word calculated, she asks, "Did you tell the press that I was anorexic?"

I stare at her in shock. "Of *course* not!" She continues to stare at me, no emotion crossing her face. "Aviva, I would never! You *know* that!"

"You were the only person who knew, aside from Callan, and he would never tell. So I'll give you one more chance. *Did. You. Tell?*"

I feel something warm on my cheek, and swipe at it to find my hand wet. Awesome. As if this situation wasn't bad enough, now I get to humiliate myself by crying in front of Aviva in the face of her anger. Aviva sounds calm as she delivers the next couple of words: "Get out."

My head jerks up. "What?" I ask in shock.

"Get. Out."

"I didn't tell. It wasn't me, I swear. I didn't even *know* –"

"Naya, I swear to God, get out of my apartment! *Now!*" And the ice princess starts to crack. I see the mask fall, revealing only vulnerability beneath, and although she's currently furious with me, I feel for her. So I nod slowly and turn to leave. This is clearly not the best time to have a productive conversation. I back up, with one final, "Aviva, I swear it wasn't me," before she shuts the door in my face. I blink dumbly, trying to figure out what just happened. I make my way into the elevator and press the button for the ground floor. At least no one else is here to witness the mess I'm sure I appear to be now, with my sweaty gym clothes and tear-streaked face. I rush to my car as soon as the doors open again, not wanting anyone in the lobby to look at me.

As soon as I get into the driver's seat I break down, screaming and pounding the steering wheel, cursing my life and my naïveté. Of course my luck would end. Of course my life would go back to being crappy. Everything was just too perfect! A best friend, a boyfriend, finishing my first year of university, and a trip to L.A. all coinciding? Never! Not for Naya! Good things come at a cost. Good things must be balanced out. Find something new, something else must be taken away. My thoughts become less coherent as my gasping sobs start to make me feel dizzy.

I find my phone and dial Jace. He picks up after the first ring. "Hey, you, what's up?"

"Are you home? Can I come over?"

Immediately his cheerful tone drops. "Of course. What's wrong?"

"I'll be there in ten."

He pauses. "Okay."

I just breathe for several seconds, not speaking. He doesn't either. Finally I say, "Thank you," and hang up. Shakily I start my car, forcing my hands to stop trembling before I shift into drive and leave the parking lot.

I'm slightly more composed by the time I arrive at Jace's place. He still sits beside me solemnly and waits for me to explain what's going on. Without getting into too much detail, and never actually breaching the topic of Aviva's eating disorder, I explain tonight's events. Even if the news are apparently out, I still won't be the one to tell them.

"I swear I wasn't the one to leak it," I whisper to Jace, and he lays a hand on my leg reassuringly.

"I believe you," he says, and I exhale shakily. At least I have one person on my side. One person who actually believes me when I'm telling the truth. I look at my watch and stare at it for a moment uncomprehendingly. 10 p.m. How did it already get so late?

"I should go," I murmur, but I don't move.

Jace looks at me for a second, then says softly, "You don't have to." I look back up at him, trying to understand his meaning. "Totally PG," he assures me. "Even G, if you want. I can take the sofa." After a pause, he asks, "Is it too soon? Is this weird?"

"No," I assure him. "I really don't want to go home right now. Thank you." After another pause, he tells me to give him a minute, while he disappears into his room, presumably to clean it up. I go to the kitchen and get myself a glass of water, sipping it slowly. I'm drained now. I'm not even nervous about staying over at Jace's, which I normally certainly would be. I remember to call my mom and tell her I won't be coming home tonight.

"Brynn invited me to sleep over, since I haven't seen her in a while," I tell her. My voice doesn't even break.

"Okay, but you're missing Family Game Night." She sounds unworried. "See you in the morning!"

"Good night," I tell her. "I love you."

There's a slight pause, then she warmly returns, "I love you too, Naya." I hang up.

Jace comes out of his room again then, gripping a couple of pillows under his arms and heading for the couch. "It's okay," I tell him. I smile awkwardly. "We can share the bed. PG is fine."

He smiles back. "But nothing R-rated?"

I shake my head. "Not tonight." He nods and returns to his room with the pillows. I follow him. "Sorry, I'm not exactly prepared. Do you have anything I could sleep in?" I look down at my gym clothes. "These probably stink."

He shakes his head. "They're fine. But sure." He opens a drawer and pulls out an oversized T-shirt. "Will this work?"

I grin, finally feeling some semblance of a positive emotion. "Yes." I take it from him and go to the bathroom to change. When I return, he's not in his room anymore, so I take my time crawling into his bed. I drop off nearly immediately. I barely notice when he comes back in and curls up behind me, but it still provides me with some comfort. I sleep surprisingly well.

The next morning, I wake up to the smell and sounds of eggs frying. I grin and roll out of bed. I find the washroom before greeting Jace, hoping I don't look like *too* much of a mess. I sigh when I see my reflection. I splash my face with cold water, hoping to liven up my skin a little. I still have dark circles under my eyes, despite my dreamless sleep, and mascara flecks decorate my eyes and cheeks. I pick them off, wishing I had some makeup remover. I pull my hair into a high ponytail and stare into the mirror for several more seconds, recognizing that this is as good as it's going to get. I shrug and find Jace in his kitchenette.

"Hey, you," I say, leaning in and hugging him. He's hovering over the stovetop, flipping the eggs. He smiles down at me and kisses the top of my head.

"How are you feeling?" he asks, and I shrug.

"Much better than last night. Um..." He looks down at me again at my pause. "So I realized that every time I've come over I've been an emotional mess. So, I thought I should apologize for that."

He chuckles. "Don't feel bad. I'm glad you feel like you can turn to me. Toast?"

I nod. "It doesn't have to be just one-way, though. You can turn to me too. I don't always have to be the mess in this relationship."

He grins at me while he places two pieces of bread in the toaster. "Thank you. I'll keep that in mind."

We eat and talk about the upcoming week. Of course it's just my luck that Jace is leaving tomorrow to begin shooting *Burning Embers*, which means my final week of classes will be entirely all work and no play. Hopefully I'll be too busy to focus on his absence. He kisses me good-bye at the door, and it's sweet. Somehow it makes my knees shake ten times more effectively than our makeout sessions.

After breakfast I head home. My mom greets me at the door. "Hey honey! How was your sleepover?"

I really don't want to lie to her. "It was good. But I should go study. Exams coming up soon."

She smiles. "Okay. Work hard."

I retreat to my room, and I really do study. If I place all my focus on my schoolwork, I don't have to think about Aviva's accusations and her anger at me.

15

Chapter Fifteen

I try to focus the next few days. I really try. But it's not like we're actually learning anything new in the last week of classes. I text Jace at least once a day, but the timing is sporadic, now that he's at work on *Burning Embers*.

On Monday, I actually return to newspaper editing. After all, I have nothing to hide, right? But it's awkward as hell, and I don't want to go back. Everyone stares, and I can't get any work done.

I see in a few magazines at the drugstore when I go to pick up some ibuprofen on a break, that Aviva hasn't denied the anorexia scandal. I actually end up purchasing one of the magazines, and learn that Aviva publicly commented on it, and is in the process of setting up an eating disorder recovery group. I'm so impressed at how she took something that is still so difficult for her to open up about, and shared her experience with the world. But then, that's Aviva. She's always been impressive.

On Tuesday, the size of my Anthropology class just serves to reinforce my loneliness. I'm surrounded by people, and yet I have no one here to talk to. I decide, screw class and screw newspaper. I don't need to attend either. So Tuesday at lunch, I leave campus. I tell my mom I'm not feeling well and spend the rest of my day in my room at home.

Wednesday, I don't even go to classes. My mom knows that I have nothing due today, so she allows me another day to study from home.

It isn't until Thursday around five p.m., after studying from home all day again, that I recall I have to add on some citations to a paper due tomorrow in class. I take out my laptop and peer at the battery level – 100%. This is necessary, since the charger hasn't been working as effectively or as routinely lately.

I find all the sources and cite them in MLA format for my English course. But *just* as I'm about to save, my laptop dies on me, despite being plugged in. *Crap!* There go all my citations!

"Mom!" I wail from my bedroom.

"What?" she calls up to me from downstairs. She approaches the bottom of the staircase.

"My laptop died and I need to finish my essay! It needs to be done and printed today!"

"Well, Dad's on the computer."

Neither of my parents have laptops. That only leaves– "Please, Mom. I want to finish it as soon as possible."

She nods. "Okay." She raises her voice. "Connor?"

A muffled "What?" emerges from his room.

Mom projects her voice so there's no way he can't hear. "Naya needs to borrow your laptop for a school project. You're not using it, are you?"

"No, but Mom–"

"Connor, I won't take more than an hour, I swear." I grimace. Another hour spent on something that I already finished. I really need a new laptop.

Connor grumbles some more but allows me to take his laptop from his room and bring it to my room to continue working. I find the rough draft of the essay in my email again, and tiredly try to find the same sources I'd used as citations before my computer died. I copy the final URL I needed, close the browser, and press paste into my bibliography – but nothing pastes. Ugh. I must not have pressed Ctrl + C hard enough. I bring up the internet browser again and run over to History. Connor uses the family computer more than his laptop – we all do – so there shouldn't be much in the browser.

I don't see the link I'm looking for at first, because my eyes are immediately drawn to lettering in all caps a little further down. SUBMIT HERE - $$$! I freeze, before my hand is drawn towards the link without any conscious thought, and I click on the button. The page loads, and even though I'd been semi-expecting it – even though the title page had been a big enough hint – bile still rises in my throat when I see that the Submit page is just one page of many on the Star Magazine website. I bring up more of the browser's history and see several other celebrity magazine webpages listed, several times with a similar page requesting celebrity dirt for money. Oh, this is bad.

Connor has been the only other person using this laptop. I know that for certain. But just because he was looking at submitting to celebrity sites, that doesn't mean the information was necessarily about Aviva, right?

I can't kid myself. It's not like he knows any other celebrities. I need to confront him. But I need to think first.

I take a picture of the history on my phone before shakily finding the link I'd needed to cite, and completing my paper. I save it on Connor's laptop and e-mail the final version back to myself. It's been forty-five minutes; not quite the hour I'd asked for, but I don't want to wait any longer.

I want to talk to Aviva. She would know how to act in this situation. But she's still screening my calls. And Jace isn't here to back me, either. I need to do this myself. And I need evidence.

Slowly, I walk into Connor's room. He ignores me, playing video games as I place his laptop back on his bed. I almost chicken out. I'm almost on my way back out the door before I pause, take my phone out of my pocket, start recording the conversation, then slip it back into my jeans.

"Connor," I say loudly, and he jerks in his seat.

"What the hell? You just made me lose the game!"

"I want to ask you something."

He looks at me with irritation. "So ask."

I take a deep breath in to settle myself. "I saw something. On your laptop."

He side-eyes me. "What? If it was porn, I don't know what you were expecting–"

"No!" I blush. "Did you..." I giggle slightly out of discomfort. "I mean, I don't think... that is, did you sell Aviva's anorexia story to the press?" I finally blurt out.

Connor stares at me. He pauses for a second, then asks,

"What?" entirely unconvincingly. I continue watching him. "No," he amends a second later, but the denial holds no more weight than the question.

"You did," I slowly realize.

His face reddens, and he throws his game console aside. "Yes, okay? Yes, I did it. I sold her story."

"Do you know the amount of *damage* you've done?!" I demand. "How did you even know?"

"I... overheard," he says, and I recall how he'd been standing right outside my room another day when I'd had Aviva over. He'd been eavesdropping.

"Why?" I ask, trying to remain calm.

"I wanted to go out with her, alright?"

His confession stuns me so much that I actually take a step backwards. I feel shaky. I don't know what kind of answer I'd been expecting, but it wasn't this.

"Why would leaking her story... cause her to want to go out with you?" I ask carefully.

"Well, I figured she would eventually see that you were innocent, and blame her boyfriend, instead. Callan?" Connor sneers. "What a stupid name."

"Okay, but–"

"Then she'd be around here more often, and I could win her over while she needs someone to talk to. Before she's officially back on the dating market. It would give me an edge." His eyes are frantic, and I'm frightened by what I'm seeing.

"Why would she *ever* blame Callan over me? She's been dating Callan for three years! And known him even longer!"

Connor is silent for a moment. "Well, then she deserved her

story being leaked, for not being willing to give me a chance," he finally answers moodily.

I don't feel well. I have to get out of this room and away from Connor. I stumble to the bathroom and heave a few times into the toilet, but nothing comes out. Only belatedly do I remember my phone recording everything. I stop it and edit the last couple of minutes out, so the confession ends when I leave Connor's room.

I want Aviva to know, but I don't think I could hear her anger against Connor at this point. After all, even if he did do something wrong – *very, very* wrong – he's still my brother. I need to digest everything before I talk to her. Besides, she probably still wouldn't answer a call from me. So instead, I set up an email. I title it "PLEASE READ – IMPORTANT PROOF" and attach both the picture I'd taken of the browser history, as well as the recording of Connor's confession. I don't type anything else, but send it off to Aviva, taking a sigh of relief when it's out of my hands again. Now I can only wait.

I can't focus on any more schoolwork the rest of the day. Thank god I finished citing my paper earlier. I do still have to print it out, which I manage from my parents' computer, when Dad is done with it. I contemplate telling my parents everything, but the situation is complicated, and I'd rather see what Aviva thinks needs to be done before discussing her business with my whole family.

I can't sleep. I toss and turn. Finally, I decide to take a sleeping pill. I retrieve one from the cupboard and set my alarm on extra-loud, hoping its piercing ring will be enough to rouse me in the morning.

16

Chapter Sixteen

Not a big surprise: I sleep past my first alarm due to the sleeping pill. Thankfully, my emergency second alarm wakes me, and I groan as I drag myself out of bed. I have to go to class today, to hand in my English essay if nothing else. I'm going to be an hour late, because there is no way I'm leaving this house without a shower, something to eat, and a little bit of makeup. I'm going to look good on my last day of first year.

When I arrive on campus, I have officially missed the first hour of my English lecture. But, since the essay isn't due until our tutorial this afternoon anyway, I'm not particularly worried. I still haven't heard from Aviva. I checked my texts and emails this morning, and there's been no response. Maybe she just hasn't seen it yet?

I sit through the second hour of my class, not even caring

to be embarrassed about showing up halfway through. At least I came today.

But the time passes slowly. Or maybe my mind is just racing.

I think I have to tell my parents about what Connor did. After all, he's still a minor and legally under their control. And his *reasoning* – it was so convoluted, it makes me worry about him.

I check my email again, under the desk. Still nothing from Aviva. I check my spam box too, but her name is most definitely not there. I sigh and put my phone away. At least Jace is flying home tonight. Maybe he can talk to Aviva and get her to see reason.

Class finally ends, and I walk quickly towards the parking lot I left my car in. Just as I arrive, though, another car zooms into the lot – a black car with dark windows. Tinted windows? Who the hell has tinted windows at U of T? We're smart kids, not heirs and heiresses.

The car stops uncomfortably close to me, and I take a half-step backwards. Then Aviva steps out.

Oh. I guess that's who would have a car like that. But why is she here?

A few more cars reach the lot after her. She ignores them, and strides up to me without apprehension and engulfs me in a hug. I freeze. I guess that means she's seen my email.

Then she starts crying and apologizing, and I melt and wrap my arms around her. Suddenly I notice flashing, and see men (and a woman) climbing out of the new cars and taking photos of us. They must have been following Aviva.

"Let's go somewhere else," I encourage her, and we both get into her car for its tinted windows, leaving mine in the lot for now. She drives aimlessly but carefully. I think the paparazzi are still on our tail, but she just ignores them. She wipes the tear tracks off of her cheeks and flashes an apologetic grin at me at a red light.

"I know he's your brother, but I could really *kill* Connor," she says.

I nod. "I don't blame you."

She's silent for a moment, and I don't say anything either.

"Are we... okay?" Aviva finally asks, and that's when I recognize the burning sensation in the pit of my stomach: anger. I'm *angry* with Aviva, for blaming me and not taking my word, and then for just popping back up and acting like we could carry on like nothing's happened. But something has happened. Something big. I just didn't see the anger before; it was disguised by how bad I felt for Aviva, and how much I missed her. But I see it now.

"Honestly, Aviva, I'm upset," I say calmly. "I can do my best to forgive you, but I can't ever go through something like this again. So you need to decide whether you can trust me or not. Final decision."

Aviva nods slowly. "Well, I think we've established that I'm the screw-up in this relationship." How ironic. She's the one with her whole life together.

She nods again, decisively this time. "I trust you. I promise." I suppose that's all I can ask for.

She tells me about the eating disorder recovery network she's been setting up, called ANRED – Aviva's Network for Recovery from Eating Disorders. I tell her how impressed I was to hear about it.

She half-smiles. "Well, as long as my past was in the open for everyone to see, I figured I might as well do something about it. And it may have been my publicist's idea, but I really want to help people, I swear."

I nod. "I know you do."

After some more meandering around town, during which time we grab some burgers from a fast-food joint, Aviva drops me back off on campus for my English tutorial.

She rolls the window down as I get out of the car. "I'll see you soon, right?"

I smile. "Gym tomorrow?"

She grins at me, teeth blindingly white in the daylight. "Yeah, okay." Then, "Bye!" And she drives away.

I successfully hand in my English essay to my T.A. in the tutorial. We're allowed to leave early since the essay was our version of an exam. I head to newspaper editing. I'm determined to have my last day here be positive.

I'm the first to arrive in the editing room. Unsurprising, since there's still half an hour left before we usually convene. I see a few people pause at the door when they come in, surprised to see me after the video incident and my absence over the last few days. I smile and meet each one, eye-to-eye. They look away quickly.

The only one who doesn't meet my gaze is Asher. And honestly, I'm fine with that. If we can't be friends, I'd rather he just ignore me.

I finish my editing for the final issue of the year early. This issue will be available for all the students returning for exams. I stand and stretch, then gather my things and yell a "bye!" to the room at large. I get a few mumbled replies.

I text Jace on my way out of the room.

Are you almost home?

His response is almost immediate.

Two hours away!

I grin widely. Can I meet you at the airport?

He sends a smiling emoji, then, *I'd like that.*

We talk for a while longer, but not about anything important. I'm mostly trying to put off the conversation I have to have with my parents about Connor. But when I mention it, Jace immediately encourages me to go home and just get it over with.

...Do I have to?

Yes. Good bye. He tacks on a blowing a kiss emoji, to make the abrupt ending of the conversation not quite so harsh.

I smirk. He's right. So I put my phone away and insert the keys into my car, dread building in my stomach as I shift into drive. I get home around 4 p.m. and smell something cooking already when I get inside. Dad is home too. He usually gets home around the same time as me. I take a centring breath. I don't know if Connor is home.

"Mom?" I call as I approach the kitchen.

"Hey, hon." She smiles, wearing a white apron and oven mitts, apparently just having checked on whatever's in the oven.

"I have to talk to you about something. And Dad. Is Connor here?"

"No, he's on a date. Why, do you need to talk to him too?"

I pause. "Um, no. It's about him."

My mom and dad sit at the kitchen table, facing me on the

other side. I watch the timer on the oven count down from thirty-seven minutes.

"Naya?" my dad prompts. "What did you want to talk to us about?"

I start by telling them about Aviva's eating disorder, and how she has now recovered.

"That's great that she's better now," Mom interjects, "but how is this related to Connor?"

I clear my throat. "Um, Aviva is... Aviva Jersey, the actress?"

My father looks amused. "We know, Naya. Connor has informed us of that."

"Okay. Well, Connor sold out her anorexia secret to the press after eavesdropping on her telling me. In private."

My parents are taken aback, I can tell. My father no longer looks so amused.

"How do you know?" my mom asks quietly, and I show them the same picture and recording that I'd emailed to Aviva.

"When were these taken?" Dad asks.

I sigh. "Yesterday." I pause, before adding, "Um... I'm going to the airport later. To pick up my boyfriend, Jace. And I'll be having dinner with him too."

Mom raises her eyebrows. "Boyfriend?"

My dad cuts in, "Airport?"

"Yeah. We can talk about this tomorrow, all right?"

They begin to argue with me, but cut themselves off before they begin. They know I'm right. And maybe that was a sneaky way to get my news out. But Connor needs to be their first priority at the moment, leaving me and my boy drama on the back burner.

I waste some time in my room as I hear my parents trying to get ahold of Connor on the phone. I try to study some more for my Anthropology exam, but I can't focus. I'm too excited to see Jace again.

It takes me thirty minutes to drive to the airport and find parking. It's expensive, but I don't particularly care at the moment. Jace and I text and he tells me which terminal to find him at.

I search the face of everyone I see as I pass them, but I don't see him in the terminal. I'm about to text him when I hear a murmur arise from the crowd and some photographers crowd at the bottom of the escalator, yelling, "Jace! Jace!"

I turn towards the escalator and sure enough, there he is. I watch him as he scans the crowd, face neutral and extremely handsome under his dark sunglasses. I know the moment he sees me because he puts the sunglasses on top of his head and grins at me. We maintain eye contact his whole trip down the escalator.

"Is he looking at *me*?" a twenty-something girl in front of me shrieks, and I giggle imperceptibly. I begin to walk past them, but there's a crowd beginning to form around Jace, and I can't reach the front of it. That is, until Jace spots me again and pushes people out of the way to drag me into his circle.

My hand tingles in his. I didn't really realize just how badly I'd missed him until he was back again. I don't even mind when he leans down to kiss me in front of the screaming crowd surrounding us. Although I do limit the kiss to five seconds. Okay fine, maybe ten. But that's it.

"We have a lot to talk about tonight," I tell him as I break away from his lips. My words come out a bit shakily.

One of the paparazzi behind Jace snaps a photo of my face and I blink dazedly, white sparks flashing behind my eyelids. I guess that's why Jace was wearing sunglasses. "Naya, right?" the paparazzo asks, and I blink again, frowning.

"Yes." Jace answers for me.

"Are you two dating?" the paparazzo asks. Why is he wearing a baseball cap inside of an airport? There's no sun in here.

Jace looks at me, a smile dancing on his lips. I take the question.

"Yes, we are." I smile and wave at the girl who had been standing in front of me before and thought Jace was looking at her.

Jace turns back to the pap and claps him on the shoulder. "Sorry man, gotta go. Date night, you know?" He indicates me with a hooked thumb over his shoulder, although his other hand is still clasped in mine.

"Lucky man," the pap returns, snapping one last photo before backing off a bit.

Hey, if that's the worst I get out of my fifteen minutes of fame, I'm happy.

Jace has to take selfies with a lot of fans, some attracted by the paparazzi, some here even before the paps showed up. I stay away from the photos, but a few people request I be in their second photos alongside Jace, so I oblige with a shy smile. It feels weird to have strangers want me in their selfies. Jace doesn't let the whole process take more than twenty minutes. His assistant Andy has gotten his luggage in the meantime, and drags it to a large black van awaiting us.

"Oh, I can't leave my car here," I tell him.

Jace eyes the paparazzi carefully. A few are still lingering around us.

"Let's drive to your car. Then you and I can take off from there and meet up with Andy back at my place."

I agree, and we do just that. We lose the paparazzi after we take off in the black van. I catch Jace up on everything that's unfolded since we last talked after we switch cars, while I drive us back to his apartment; namely, Aviva's return and tearful apologies. We discuss that for a while, before Jace updates me on the filming he's been doing the past week for *Burning Embers*.

We pick up some take-out on our way home. We've both had enough public exposure for today.

"So, since you've made up with Aviva now, does that mean you'll be heading out to that party in L.A. that you mentioned before?"

I turn to him and grin. "You know, I haven't confirmed since our fight, but I'd say it's back on the table, yes."

"Well, why don't you stay for longer than a weekend? Stay a week and come watch me on set. It'll be fun."

I nearly choke on my spaghetti and meatballs. "Yes! That sounds amazing!"

He grins at me, then pulls me in for a messy kiss which jolts me into spilling some tomato sauce on my outfit. I squeal, but I'm soon more distracted by Jace.

Good things are coming. But I can also appreciate the good things that have happened. I've gained a new relationship with a caring guy. I've strengthened my relationship with my best friend. I've created more communication within my family – necessary communication. This past week may have been one of the worst in my life, but it also led to *right now*. And right now, I'm happy.

Alexandra was first published in grade eight, and has continued writing ever since! She started writing Identity at age 19, and finished at 23. She majored in English at the University of Toronto. She also loves to act, sing and song-write, and model. Her favourite person happens to be her cat, Winter.